Literacy Assessment

for Today's Schools

Monograph
of
The College Reading Association
1996

Editors

Martha D. Collins
East Tennessee State University

Barbara G. Moss
The University of Akron

ISBN 1-883604-25-7

iii

CONTENTS

**Developing and Assessing Emergent Literacy
Through Children's Literature**

Preface

Assessment is one of the most important issues in the field of literacy learning and teaching in the 1990's. As teachers at all levels work to create constructivist classrooms, we seek assessments that are authentic, meaningful, and process-oriented. This College Reading Association monograph entitled "Literacy Assessment for Today's Schools" provides a blueprint for teachers who want increasingly sophisticated methods for monitoring student growth and as a resource for in-service educators to provide new ideas as literacy instruction changes. The monograph is divided into two sections. Section One, entitled "Assessment in the Classroom and Beyond for Tomorrow's Schools," examines literacy assessment as it pertains to school age children. The chapters in this section address a wide range of assessments including retellings, attitude scales, and checklists.

Section Two, entitled "Literacy Assessment through Portfolios," illustrates how portfolios can be used in a variety of different settings from the classroom through higher education. The chapters in this section explore ideas for using portfolios with preservice and inservice teachers as well as developmental and adult learners.

We hope that you will find the monograph useful and informative as our thinking about literacy assessment moves through transitions from testing to assessment.

Martha Collins

Barbara Moss

Section One

Assessment in the Classroom and Beyond for Today's Schools

Assessment Criteria in First Grade: What Do Teachers Want To Know About Students' Reading and Writing?

Elizabeth Pryor

Summit County Educational Service Center

This study focused on the criteria seleted by three first grade teachers in their literacy assessment and the impact of those criteria on the assessment process. The study questions are a) What criteria did teachers use? b) Why did they select those criteria? c) How is the assessment process affected by the criteria? Results of the study indicated assessment criteria varied according to teachers' beliefs about how students learn and about the reading/writing process. Further, the assessment criteria largely determined how teachers gathered and documented assessment data.

Reading and writing in elementary and secondary schools of the United States are increasingly assessed and evaluated by standardized tests that are perceived by many as providing a useful measure of accountability (Heald-Taylor, 1989; Wiggins, 1993). Many states are in the process of reforming their existing testing programs to make them more appropriate and usable (Roeber & Dutcher, 1989; Valencia, Pearson, Peters, & Wixson, 1989). Recent research, however, suggests that teachers continue to rely more heavily on their own informal assessments than on standardized test results because their own observations and judgments in the classroom context provide a more descriptive and functional tool for diagnostic teaching of reading and writing processes, setting purposes for instruction, and suggesting pedagogical changes in individualizing instruction (Antonacci, 1990; Linek, 1991; Harste & Bintz, 1991; Pryor, 1990, 1991; VanLeirsburg, 1990). Standardized tests have a negative effect on teaching and learning (Kirst, 1991; Perrone, 1991) because test results cannot aid teachers in gathering the immediate data needed for effective instruction and quality learning (Shepard, 1989).

The problem is that we know little about how and what teachers assess to get this immediate data (Antonacci, 1990; Hutchinson, Raines, & Hiebert, 1989), particularly at the beginning of first grade when such assessments often shape students' self-concept as literacy learners (Shavelson, 1983) and often results in their being semi-permanently labeled as belonging to a certain ability group or track (Allington, 1983).

Purpose of the Study

The purpose of the larger research from which this study was drawn was to provide a thick, rich description of literacy assessment and evaluation in first grade to add to the small, but growing body of knowledge about teachers' assessment processes by developing case studies of three first grade teachers' assessment processes. The purpose of the piece reported herein was to examine and describe the criteria that the three teachers used in their assessment of literacy.

The research questions for this piece of the larger study were as follows: 1) What criteria do teachers assess? 2) Why do they select those criteria? and 3) How is the assessment process affected by the criteria?

Description

Three first grade teachers were selected by non probability, purposive sampling. The criteria for their selection were a) a minimum of 4 years of teaching at the first grade level and b) recommendations as exemplary first grade teachers with a holistic orientation toward literacy instruction.

The setting of this study was a K-6 elementary school in a small, midwestern town. The school had 410 students, 43% of whom were from low-income families, and was beginning its first year as a pilot site for Classrooms of the Future, a school reform project. Because two of the Classrooms of the Future goals were "team teaching" and "instruction tailored to individual needs," the three teachers devised a classroom organization plan that grouped all the first grade students into twelve ability groups for reading, with a maximum of six students in each color-coded group. Each teacher had four groups at a time in her room on a rotating basis because, as one teacher (Kelley) said, "Each of us has different strengths so the child has a better chance of understanding what they're trying to learn with three teachers."

The data were collected during the first report period of the school year (eight weeks, late August - mid October). Data were collected through interviews, observations, and documents such as questionnaires, copies of lesson plans, assessment artifacts, field notes, and transcripts of think-alouds obtained during collaborative lesson planning and determination of progress reports. ETHNOGRAPH (Seidel, Kjolseth, & Seymour, 1985) was used to store and sort the data, and triangulation (Denzin, 1970) and the constant-comparative methods (Glaser & Strauss, 1967) were used to analyze the data.

Each case was written; then a cross-case analysis was conducted to build a theoretical model of teachers' literacy assessment process.

Findings

Significant variation occurred between and among teachers in the criteria they chose to assess. Although the three teachers assessed widely differing criteria, each teacher seeking to explore different aspects of students' literacy development, they also assessed some common criteria as well.

Kelley

Kelley (pseudonym), said her assessment process was to construct a "mosaic" picture of each child's strengths and strategies, then to search for signs of progress and growth in reading and writing by observing, listening, and questioning, and, finally, to store the information principally by remembering critical incidents. This process was ongoing and integrated with instruction so that Kelley was constantly looking for progress and making revisions in the "mosaic" as she taught.

Kelley assessed four domains of criteria: a) letters/ sounds/words (greatest emphasis), b) metacognition and prior knowledge, c) ability to read and write strategically, and d) desire to read and write. (See Table 1 for definitions and examples of these criteria.) Metacognition (students' ability to verbalize their thinking and reasoning) and prior knowledge were the criteria most unique to Kelley. When queried about the abundant "how" and "why" questions Kelley asked about students' reading and writing, she explained that she had three purposes: to explore students' thinking processes, to get them to think about their own mental processes, and for them to model for each others different ways of thinking and reasoning. She stated:

> I want to get inside their thinking processes to find out what method [strategy] they're using, but I also want them to think about what method they're using so they can apply it the next time.... Sometimes, too, when they say it out loud ... they're teaching somebody else.

Although Kelley believed the latter three criteria to be most important, she said that the external constraints of the report card and the basal reading materials necessitated that she primarily assess student knowledge of letters/ sounds/ words.

6

Table 1
Kelley's Criteria for Assessment and Evaluation of Literacy

Domain	Definition	Examples
1. Letters/ Sounds/Words	Students demonstrate their knowledge of letters, sounds, and words, and understanding of concepts and conventions of print.	Invented spelling, letters, sounds, sight words, handwriting
2. Metacognition and prior knowledge	Students demonstrate their ability to verbalize their own thinking and reasoning processes and their prior knowledge.	"I want to get inside their thinking processes." "What do you know about __?"
3. Ability to read and write strategically	Students demonstrate their ability to read and application of strategies.	"Really" reading, self-correction, book-handling.
4. Desire to read and write	Students demonstrate risk-taking behaviors and motivation to read and write.	Confidence, participation, affective responses

    In her think-aloud that was audiotaped while doing progress reports, however, Kelley (unlike the other two teachers) considered many more literacy criteria than those identified on the progress reports (see Table 2) because she believed these criteria were important in literacy learning. She was occasionally able to use this additional data to add weight in determining students' grades on the progress reports, but she was unable to use much of the data because of the limitations of the items on the progress reports to be evaluated.

Table 2
Kelley's Additional Criteria Mentioned During Progress Report Preparation

Criteria	Student 1	Student 2	Student 3
Reading (or attempts)	X	X	X
Self-confidence	X	X	X
Letter/sound correspondence	X	X	
Self-correction		X	X
Literacy at home	X	X	
Book knowledge	X		
Print conveys meaning			X
Uses resourcesfor help	X		
Drawings	X		
Fluency		X	
Desire to read			X
Other literacy activities			X

Barbara

In the beginning of this study, Barbara (pseudonym) was unaware of much of her assessment criteria, and she focused her assessments on routines, procedures, and groups for about three weeks. As she participated in the study, however, she said she became more aware of her process and the amount of information she knew about her students. Barbara also began to pay more attention to the content of assessment.

Relying largely on grades taken from students' paperwork and on instructional interactions, Barbara's goal in her assessment of literacy became to uncover what students did not know. Barbara's own description of this process was, "At this time of year, literacy assessment is making sure everything's in place so that they can read and understand. It's me finding out what is missing and plugging in the holes so that they can get the point."

Barbara's five domains of criteria were: a) letters/ sounds/words (most predominant), b) ability to do paperwork and projects correctly, c) ability to read, and d) oral language skills. Table 3 details Barbara's definitions and examples.

Table 3
Barbara's Criteria for Assessment and Evaluation of Literacy

Domain	Definition	Examples
1. Letters/ sounds/ words	Students demonstrate knowledge of letters, sounds, sight words, and understanding of speech to print "connection."	"What is this letter?" "What sound does this letter make?" Spelling Handwriting
2. Ability to read	Students demonstrate their ability to read with fluency and comprehension and to use prior knowledge to aid comprehension.	"What was the puppy doing?" "Has anybody helped their mom bake a cake?"
3. Ability to do paperwork and projects	Students demonstrate their knowledge and abilities by doing papers and projects correctly and following directions.	"I look for right answers. Whether or not they know. Do they make careless mistakes, follow directions."
4. Oral language skills	Students demonstrate their ability to speak appropriately.	"Can they tell stories?" Sentence structure Focused or rambling?
5. Desire to read and write	Students demonstrate that they want to learn to read and write.	Effort, attention, participation, confidence, enjoyment "I watch for who's paying attention . . . and who's having a good time."

Barbara's assessment criteria were largely focused on students' lack of knowledge of letters, sounds, and sight words so she could teach them what she believed they needed to know in order to learn to read. Her other two major

Table 4
Sally's Criteria for Assessment and Evaluation of Literacy

Domain	Definition	Examples
1. Letters/ sounds/ words	Students demonstrate knowledge of letters, sounds, and words, left to right progression, and phonemic segmentation.	"Can you break the words into letters? What would 'cat' sound like? /ku/ /a/ /tu/" "I want to make sure that you know the words we're reading."
2. Ability to read and write	Students demonstrate their ability to read with fluency and expression, can acknowledge literacy at home	Spelling Sequence, "knows what a sentence is,"
3. Ability to do paperwork and projects	Students demonstrate their knowledge and abilities by doing paperwork and projects completely, correctly, neatly, and according to directions.	"Go back and check to make sure you've done them right, make sure you've done them all. "What do I want you to put on on your paper first . . . next. . . last?" Handwriting
4. Attention/ listening	Students demonstrate their ability to pay attention and listen.	"You need to listen all the time and be ready." "Either they didn't know or they weren't listening."

criteria were students' ability to read fluently and comprehend and the ability to do assigned paperwork and projects correctly, following directions. Her most unique criterion was students' oral language development.

Sally

Concern for children's self-esteem and sense of achievement were the hallmarks of Sally's (pseudonym) views about assessment and evaluation of literacy. She wanted to learn about her students' knowledge and abilities, but she also wanted to simultaneously support and preserve their confidence in themselves as capable learners. She thought literacy assessment was "basically just being aware, knowing each child in your class."

The data Sally sought about her students' literacy development fell into four domains: a) letters/ sounds/words, b) ability to read and write, c) ability to do paperwork and projects completely and accurately, and d) attention/ listening. Definitions and examples of these criteria are displayed in Table 4.Attention/listening was the criterion unique to Sally. She strongly believed that she could tell if students were learning by observing their attention/ listening. Sally believed attention and listening equated comprehension and knowing, and she frequently reminded students how important it was for them to pay attention and listen during instructional periods.

Cross Case Analysis

The three cases in this study were analyzed for similarities and differences which revealed patterns, relationships, and categories. The cross-case analysis data were synthesized to produce a theoretical model of teachers' literacy assessment process.

Table 5 displays the ways the three teachers emphasized certain criteria in their assessment of literacy as revealed in the cross-case analysis. All emphasized letters/sounds/ words as their major criterion; this was the only one assessed in common by all three teachers. However, although they all assessed letters/sounds/words, each teacher defined the criterion in qualitatively unique ways (see Tables 1-4). Kelley's domain of letters/sounds/words for example included students' understanding of concepts and conventions of print which she defined as encompassing print's conveying meaning, directionality, and book conventions (e.g., author, illustrator, title page). Barbara's domain incorporated students' understanding of the connection between speech and print, and Sally's domain also comprised left-to-right progression and phonemic segmentation.

Table 5
Teachers' Emphasis and Reliance in Assessment Criteria

	Teachers		
Criteria	Kelley	Barbara	Sally
Letters/Sounds/			
Words	High	High	High
Ability to read	High	Low	High
Ability to write	High	-	Medium
Ability to do			
papers	-	High	High
Desire to read			
and write	Medium	Low	-
Metacognition	High	-	-
Oral language/			
dictation	-	Low	Low
Attention	-	-	High

The teachers' selection of criteria for assessment of literacy was influenced by a wide variety of factors. Table 6 reveals these influences and their strengths. Teachers' beliefs and prior experiences, the constraints of the progress report card, and the expectations of administrators and parents were the three chief influences on the criteria the three teachers selected for literacy assessment. Of these, beliefs stood out as the major influence impacting every teacher's literacy criteria. In particular, their beliefs about reading and writing, about children as learners, and about what children need to know in order to learn to read and write largely determined the assessment criteria. Kelley's assessment process reflected her beliefs that reading and writing are meaning-construction processes, that children learn to read and write by reading and writing, and that children come to first grade with much knowledge about language. She believed that her job was to discover and build on that knowledge. The assessment processes used by Barbara and Sally mirrored their beliefs that reading is more word- and performance-oriented, that children must have letter and sound knowledge in order to learn to read, and that their job as teachers was to discover and teach what the children did not know (as Barbara phrased it, "plug up the holes"). All three teachers reported considerable dissonance with the constraints of the progress report card, although they said they thought administrators and parents liked the reports and would be displeased if they were changed.

Table 6
Strength of Influences on Criteria Selection

Influences	Kelley	Barbara	Sally
Beliefs	High	High	High
Prior experiences	High	High	High
Administrators/ parents	High	High	High
Classroom organizational scheme	Low	Low	Low
Time	Medium	Low	-
Progress report card	High	High	High
Instructional activities/ materials	High	-	-
Concern for students' self-esteem	Medium	Low	Low
Other two teachers	Medium	Medium	Medium

Findings

The literacy assessment criteria used by the three teachers in this study had certain characteristics: a) each teacher had at least one criterion unique to her, b) although all the teachers identified a common criterion, each teacher defined it differently, c) many assessment criteria were unrelated to literacy, d) the criteria reflected the teachers' beliefs and values, e) the criteria included externally-imposed criteria, and f) the teachers said they did not alter their literacy criteria during the year, but expectations of and standards for student performance changed.

The literacy assessment process revealed in this study was profoundly complex and was driven by the assessment criteria used by the teachers. The assessment procedures and documentation teachers employed depended upon the criterion being assessed, and the whole assessment process was impacted by a variety of influences (see Figure 1).

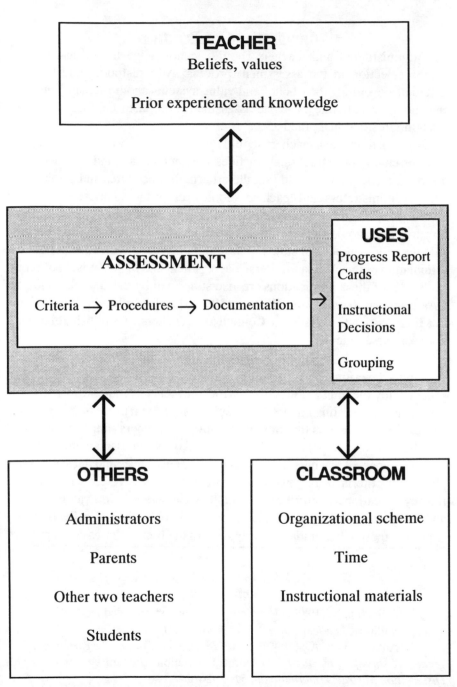

Figure 1. Factors Influencing Teachers' Literacy Assessment

Implications for Practice

Administrators and teachers should acknowledge the critical role of criteria selection in the assessment process. Administrators and teachers should also examine their belief and value systems about literacy education and should collaborate to revise assessment criteria to be congruent with changing instructional practices.

Administrators and teachers should formulate literacy assessment criteria based on changing instructional practices, curricular goals, and current recommended practices and should link the criteria to procedures and documentation. Administrators and teachers should, furthermore, revise report card criteria for congruency with curricular goals and changing instructional practices and should explore alternative methods to report student progress. Additionally, parents and students should be involved with educators in the formulation of the criteria for literacy assessment and in the revision of report cards. All of these implications are also supported by the *Standards for the Assessment of Reading and Writing* (1994) developed by the International Reading Association/National Council of Teachers of English Joint Task Force on Assessment.

Implications for Research

Given the critical and rapidly changing nature of assessment, researchers should study the interaction of the various influences on literacy assessment criteria and the ensuing impact on the entire assessment process. They should also explore the factors that inhibit and support teachers' implementation of their beliefs since they play such an influential role in assessment.

The impact of teachers' beliefs on assessment criteria and the leading role played by criteria in the assessment process are vitally critical factors in literacy education. ... so critical, in fact, that teachers, administrators, parents, and researchers should focus their energies on publicly and collaboratively exploring these vital, fundamental aspects of the literacy assessment process.

References

Allington, R. (1983). The reading instruction provided readers of different ability. *The Elementary School Journal, 83,* 548-559.

Antonacci, N. A. (1990). *Reading assessment in kindergarten and first-grade: A survey of teachers.* (Doctoral dissertation, Harvard University, 1990). *Dissertation Abstracts International, 51.* 3026A.

Denzin, N. K. (1970). *The research act: A theoretical introduction to sociological methods.* Chicago: Aldine.

Glaser, B. G., & Strauss, A. L. (1967). *The discovery of grounded theory.* Chicago: Aldine.

Harste, J., & Bintz, W. (1991). A vision for the future of assessment in whole language classrooms. In B. Harp (Ed.), *Assessment and evaluation in whole language programs* (pp. 219-242). Norwood, MA: Christopher-Gordon Publishers, Inc.

Heald-Taylor, G. (1989). *The administrator's guide to whole language.* Katoneh, NY: Owen.

Hutchinson, T. A., Raines, P. A., & Hiebert, E. H. (1989, December). *Alternative assessments of literacy: Teachers' actions and parents' reactions.* Paper presented at the meeting of the National Reading Conference, Miami, FL.

International Reading Association/National Council of Teachers of English Joint Task Force on Assessment. (1994). *Standards for the assessment of reading and writing.* Newark, DE: International Reading Association and Urbanna, IL: National Council of Teachers of English.

Kirst, M. (1991). Interview on assessment issues with Lorrie Shepard. *Educational Researcher, 20*, 21-23, 27.

Linek, W. M. (1991). Grading and evaluation techniques for whole language teachers. *Language Arts, 68*, 125-132.

Perrone, V. (Ed.). (1991). *Expanding student assessment.* Alexandria, VA: Association for Supervision and Curriculum Development.

Pryor, E. (1990, November). *Assessment and Evaluation of Reading and Writing in Whole Language Classrooms.* Paper presented at the meeting of the National Reading Conference, Miami, FL.

Pryor, E. (1991, December). *A case study of an experienced whole language first grade teacher's assessment and evaluation of reading and writing.* Paper presented at the meeting of the National Reading Conference, Palm Springs, CA.

Roeber, E., & Dutcher, P. (1989). Michigan's innovative assessment of reading. *Educational Leadership, 46* (7), 64-69.

Seidel, J. V., Kjolseth, R., & Seymour, E. (1985). *THE ETHNOGRAPH* (Version 3.0). Corvallis, OR: Qualis Research Associates.

Shepard, L. A. (1989). Why we need better assessment. *Educational Leadership, 46* (7), 4-9.

Valencia, S. W., Pearson, P. D., Peters, C. W., & Wixson, K. K. (1989). Theory and practice in statewide reading assessment: Closing the gap. *Educational Leadership, 46* (7), 57-63.

VanLeirsburg, P. (1990). The evaluation of whole language learning in the elementary classroom. *Journal of Language Experience, 10*, 21-27.

Wiggins, G. (1993). Assessment: Authenticity, context, and Validity. *Phi Delta Kappan, 75*, 200-214.

Learning About Literacy Through Retelling

Gail G. Smith
Lehigh University

Diane Keister
Southern Lehigh School District
Center Valley, Pennsylvania

Retelling is the process of recalling a text after hearing or reading it. This article reviews current published research about retelling as an assessment tool embedded in instruction. However, the focus of the article is on retelling as an assessment technique. Since directions for retelling can vary, differences in directions are reviewed before the focus on retelling as an assessment technique begins. The relationship between retelling and comprehension, the information provided by retelling, rubrics for retelling, the developmental nature of language and retelling, and the recognition of retelling as a presentation task are included. The article concludes with a discussion of unanswered questions raised by the review of research and suggestions for needed research.

Most of us, at one time or another, have shared a personal story with a friend. Telling stories is part of everyday conversation, a way that children and adults communicate. It seems natural that telling or retelling a story would be part of language learning and assessment. Retelling, in a variety of forms, is widely used, but what does the research teach us about it and what questions are yet unanswered? This article reviews the definition of retelling and its use as an assessment technique embedded within instruction. This exploration leads to discussion of the relationship between retelling and reading comprehension and the definition of comprehension itself. The questions raised through the research review lead to areas for further research.

Background

Retelling or free recall is the process of recalling a text after hearing or reading it. A listener or a reader may retell a story or narrative text orally or in written form. If the retelling is done orally, the experience is often taped for further study. There are many variations of the task which may be performed individually or in a small group. Sometimes students retell a story immediately after reading or hearing it. Other times, students read the text several times before the retelling.

Many writers believe that retelling is congruent with the current body of knowledge about reading. Within the definition of reading as "transaction with texts" (Botel & Lytle, 1988, p. 22), a process where the reader brings a background of knowledge to construct meaning from the text, retelling may offer the potential for readers to demonstrate how they engage in that process. As they retell a story, readers share the meaning they have constructed often revealing both the background they employ and the connections they have made. Morrow maintains that retelling "allows the reader or listener to structure a response according to personal and individual interpretations of the text" (1988a, p. 128). In the process of retelling the story, the reader builds meaning which fits into his or her own schemata (Tierney, Bridge, & Cera, 1978-1979).

Overview

Retelling may function as a means to assess student growth, through either quantitative or qualitative processes. When quantitative interpretations are used, the assessor logs the recall of text based story elements or main ideas. A score is derived from the number of elements that the reader is able to recall. In qualitative analysis, the observer notes the story elements but also analyzes the retelling for generalizations and interpretations drawn from the text as well as the comprehensibility of the whole (Morrow, 1988a).

Further, retelling demonstrates the various elements of ideal assessment as described by some analysts. For example, Bembridge (1992) professes that an ideal assessment instrument should include the following: be congruent with classroom materials and methods; be observational and interactive providing data for comparison and reporting; be easy to administer; and be diagnostic, illustrating a student's strengths and weaknesses. Retelling meets these criteria. The retelling reflects the themes and genres of the classroom settings, demonstrates the interaction of students and the text, reflects the strategies that students use and do not use, and provides diagnostic information. Unlike many measures, a retelling requires a production task. Rather than recognizing an answer from a variety of choices, the reader must produce his or her own answer. This process demands recall of information, organization of the recalled parts, and verbal proficiency, all without the cues which may be conveyed by the questions or syntax in a multiple choice or cloze assessment (Feldman, 1989; Marr & Gromley, 1982). Furthermore, according to Valencia, McGinley and Pearson (1990), retelling seems to be one measure which might be included in a portfolio containing continuous, multidimensional, collaborative, knowledge-based and authentic materials.

Experts such as Brown and Cambourne (1987) embed the use of retelling as an assessment tool in instruction. In their model, students write a retelling and later "share and compare" (Brown & Cambourne, 1987, p. 33-34). They learn the components of what constitutes a good retelling and assess their work against the criteria they have established.

Directions for Retelling

The student directions for retelling vary depending on the age of the reteller, the form of the retelling, and the purpose of the retelling. For example, young students may be told, "A little while ago I read a story (Name *[of]* the story). Would you retell the story as if you were telling it to a friend who has never heard it before?"(Morrow, 1986, p. 141). If the student stops, prompts may be given. Morrow (1988a) employs prompts like these: "Once there was a ..." or "How did the story end?" (p. 141). Clark (1982) asks the student to "tell everything that he or she can remember." When the students stops, the examiner probes, "What else can you remember?" (p. 436). Alternative directions offered by Brown and Cambourne are, "Just read it [*the story*] for enjoyment and then retell it. You can express the meanings in your own words if you want to. I'm more interested in how you interpret it than in the amount you remember" (1987, p. 4). Brown and Cambourne, in their Share and Compare component, have partners work together to reflect upon the retelling. The following summarizes questions they ask of each other:

"What did I include/omit that is different to what you included/omit-
ted?"
"Do you think that I muddled-up, changed, or omitted anything that
alters meaning?"
"Did you use any words/phrases that are different from the story that
still mean the same thing?"
"If I could borrow a bit of my retelling and include it in yours, which
bit would you take? Why?" (pp. 33-34).

Brown and Cambourne assess students' linguistic growth and encourage students' self assessment in the process of reading, writing, listening, and talking. Others use the process as a teaching process. For example, Koskinen, Gambrell, Kapinus, and Heathington (1988) instruct, "We can become good storytellers if we practice" (p. 894). Teachers model retelling, provide for guided practice, and then pair up students for retelling. One partner plays the role of the "storyteller" and the other is the "listener." Students take turns with each role. The listener uses prompts to encourage the storyteller and a reaction sheet which reports one piece of the retelling that the storyteller did well.

Retelling as an Assessment Technique

The different instructions for retelling elicit different information about how the student recalls, organizes, and reflects on the text. Therefore, the instructor needs to consider the objectives of the task and must carefully formulate the directions accordingly. In considering the objectives, the researcher or instructor reflects his or her theory of the relationship between retelling and comprehension.

The Relationship between Retelling and Comprehension

As has been described, story retelling has been widely used as a research tool and an instructional practice. In many of those research situations, free recall is designated as the measure of reading comprehension. For example, Cullinan, Harwood and Galda (1983) state that they used recall data to assess reader comprehension "since story recall is one of the best ways to check on comprehension" (p.34). Yet, perusal of research and articles reveal an assortment of assumptions and rubrics which reflect some different definitions of reading comprehension.

The following review of assumptions and practices raises a variety of issues. One such question is, "Does retelling, in fact, measure comprehension?" Goodman, Watson and Burke (1987) employ miscue analysis and retelling procedures to describe the reading profile of a child. Yet, they believe that, "as revealing as retelling a story can be, however, it can *never* represent a reader's total understanding of a text" (p. 45). Goodman (1982) suggests two parts to the process. Comprehending is the "process of trying to make sense of text," while comprehension is "what readers understood" in the text (p. 302). Gambrell, Pfeiffer and Wilson (1985) report that retelling indicates something about reader's assimilation and reconstruction of text information; therefore, it reflects comprehension. Morrow (1988a) argues "because retelling can indicate a reader's or listener's assimilation and reconstruction of text information, it can reflect comprehension" (p. 128). Pickert and Chase (1978) contend that "this technique [*retelling*] assesses a student's ability to comprehend, organize, and express connected speech" (p. 528). Cullinan et al. (1983), Gambrell and Jawitz (1993), Morrow (1985, 1986, 1988b), and Page (1977) represent a sample of researchers who have used retelling to assess comprehension in a variety of experimental settings.

In the midst of the assumption that retelling is comprehension, Cullinan et al. (1983) raise one important question about the direct relationship between the two. These researchers suggest that the quality of the retelling may be affected by the student's distaste for the plot line or by peer pressure. If, indeed, the reader is less able to retell a story that he or she did not like or less able to retell a story that his or her peers did not like, then isn't the reliability of the method in question? Or, is differential comprehension as a result of "liking or disliking" a particular text or peer pressure implicit as part of the definition of reading as "transaction with text"? Further, does the influence of "taste" interfere with other measures of comprehension such as a standardized test which employs paragraphs with multiple choice answers? Other considerations include the native language of the child and the child's gender. Garcia (1994) cautions against using retellings in a non-native language to assess a second language learners actual comprehension. Moreover the influence of gender appears to affect performance on retelling in terms of production, creativity, and judgmental statements about the story (Olson & Davies, 1989).

Rubrics for Retelling

While researchers and authors employ retellings as a reflection of comprehension, their scoring rubrics for measuring student behaviors vary significantly. One would expect that if retelling and comprehension were synonymous, then the elements described for measuring them would be synonymous. However, retelling rubrics appear to reflect their authors' differing constructs of comprehension. Some researchers, for example, organize rubrics on the basis of the story events. Goodman et al. (1987) consider character analysis, events of the story, plot, and theme. Gambrell et al.(1985) suggest a scoring system based on the quantity and type of story information retold. Marshall (1983) recommends a checklist where the elements of the story grammar are scored with a plus if the item is mentioned, a check if the item is mentioned after a probe, and a minus if the item is not mentioned. Other rubrics use a story structure basis and add other items. King (1977) suggests using retelling to evaluate readiness, comprehension and language growth by recording the amount of the story retold, its logic, and the quality and complexity of the language employed. Clark's process (1982) breaks the text into "pausal units by placing a slash wherever a good reader would normally pause during reading" (p. 437). The retelling score is based on the total number of units recalled, the sequence and the mean importance level of the units recalled. Morrow (1988b) defines a coding system focused on story structure, meaning, print and illustrations. After transcribing tapes of student retellings, responses are categorized and quantified.

Kalmback (1980) argues that analysis of retellings needs to take "into account both the reader's contribution and the contribution of the original text" (p.22). Therefore, merely counting events against the original story falls short because it reflects only the contribution of the text. "The real evidence of reading comprehension in a retelling lies not so much in what is recalled but how it is recalled" (p. 23). When reading is defined as a constructive process and "the meaning constructed from the same text can vary greatly among people because of differences in the knowledge they possess," (Anderson, Hiebert, Scott and Wilkinson, 1985, p. 9), then, consideration of a reader's background is important. In their informal technique, Pickert and Chase (1978) and later Seltzer (1989) use an informal retelling rubric that shows comprehension, organization, and expression. In Seltzer's terms, comprehension refers to "understanding of grammatical forms and vocabulary words"; organization refers to the "ability to integrate visual and auditory information to recall sequence of events"; and expression refers to "expressing the story in fluent, connected sentences using correct grammatical forms" (p. 37). The Tasmanian Education Department (1989) defines the evaluation of the written or oral retelling in these terms: (a) *meaning* defined as "ideas, clarity, relevance to form/purpose" in the written form and "ideas, clarity, originality" for the oral form; (b) *structure* defined as "organization of writing, unity between parts and whole and sequence" in the written form and as "sequence of ideas, events, and repetitions/self corrections" in oral form; (c) *conventions* defined as "spelling, usage, punctuation, appropriate vocabulary" for the written form and "conventions appropriate for questions, conversation, clarity, diction in the oral form;" and last, (d) *cognitive abilities* defined as "ability to predict, infer, hypothesize, generalize" in the written form and "tense, plurals, word complexity, appropriate to form" in the oral form (p.42). Hernadez-Miller (1991), Morrow (1988a), and Valencia et al. (1990) cited the Retelling Profile developed by Irwin and Mitchell (1983) which includes items reflecting text-based comprehension information, reader's response and reaction to text, and reader's language use.

Assessment of retellings is not confined to fiction. Brown and Cambourne (1987) recommend the following criteria which apply to both fiction and nonfiction material: meaning (clearness of main points, appropriateness to the form of text); structure (unity and sequence); conventions; and cognitive abilities (accurate predictions, inferencing, hypothesizing, generalizing). Anthony, Johnson, Mickelson, and Preece (1991) define specific criteria to be applied to the retelling of expository text. They consider clearness and completeness of ideas, effectiveness of supporting detail, accurateness of the sequence of procedures, and the logic of arguments. Stiggins (1991) presents a holistic rubric which focuses upon the student's ability to generalize the coherence, completeness, and comprehensibility; the connection to background knowledge; and the richness of the piece. Goodman et al. (1987) recommend creation of a scoring key for each expository passage. The guide provides the basis for monitoring during the retelling and is organized around specific information, generalizations, and major concepts.

In every example, the items that the authors include and do not include in their rubrics reflect their constructs concerning reading comprehension. When the rubric is based entirely on story structure or specific nonfictional characteristics, the author communicates that he or she values the recall of explicit text items. When an author creates a rubric that includes a reader's reaction to the text, the author reflects a definition of reading which includes prior knowledge and integration of the written text to the reader's experience.

Further study of the various rubrics may be needed in order to construct an easy-to-use, meaningful measure. Without some consistency, instructors raise questions as to which method to use and how to interpret the results of information they have gathered.

Other issues arise in the development of an appropriate rubric. How does oral language facility relate to the ability to retell? Does the product of written language differ from that of oral language? Is the preference of the reader reflected in the results? Should the rubric for an expository retelling differ from the rubric for a narrative retelling? Is probing from the assessor during a child's retelling appropriate? If so, what kinds of probes or prompts are appropriate and should scoring reflect the probing assistance?

Information Provided by Retelling

Reflecting her interest in the thinking processes and strategies that students employ when approaching various forms of comprehension assessment, Powell (1988) compared retellings, multiple choice tests, and cloze procedures. Her results indicate that when writing a retelling, subjects report using these strategies: considering prior knowledge, rereading the text, paraphrasing, judging the importance of a portion of text, and attending to text structure. Subjects consider different strategies when approaching a multiple choice task: eliminating, guessing, reading ahead, judging the importance, and considering the organization. Although the lists of strategies used exhibit differences, student descriptions of their thinking during both the retelling and the multiple choice tasks reflect similar metacognitive processes to those which were described in a reading situation when students were not being assessed. So, within the limits of her study, Powell theorizes that the products of retelling and multiple choice reflect the same process as the products of reading when it was not being assessed. Therefore, she concludes that they possess construct validity. However, these conclusions lead to several questions. Does the formal process of evaluating recalling compartmentalize or minimalize a complex process? In fact, is the complex process actually reflected in the product?

Tierney et al. (1978-1979) studied the information offered by students during retellings. Their findings reveal that in the free retelling, students recall textually explicit and textually inferred information. However, during probed recalls, the information differs in content. Students relate more inferred items and fewer explicit items. Goodman (1982) theorizes that "with supportive probing during retelling, readers continue to organize and think through what they have read" (p. 306). This theory, supported by these findings, may reveal that free recall and probing, together, may provide more information about student comprehension than a situation demanding recall without probing.

The examination of the rubrics, themselves, provide another aspect of the information provided by retellings. Many of the researchers or writers include language as a focus for assessment. King (1977), for example, notes language complexity and quality as factors while Seltzer (1989) recognizes the expressive quality of the language and the grammatical correctness used in the language. Rubrics for written retellings may be different than rubrics for oral retellings (e. g. the Tasmanian Education Department, 1989). Is this distinction appropriate? Does the production of written language differ from that of oral language? If so, should rubrics be designated as appropriate for only one language form? This leads to questions about the developmental nature of language and its effects on retellings.

The Developmental Nature of Language and Retellings

Reflection on the scoring process of retellings leads to consideration of the developmental acquisition of language and of story structure. Applebee (1977) reports that as children progress in age, the stories they create grow longer and more complex, beginning with a string of unrelated events and growing to highly structured explications. Cullinan et al. (1983) add to the study of the developmental nature of children's comprehension of literature by noting that the form and the content of the reader's recall progresses with age. Thus, their findings support the notion that children's comprehension of literature is developmental and progresses through several levels. Besides the age factor, cultural background may affect the expectations of text structure that a student brings to a text. These factors may need to be considered in the use and evaluation of student retellings, although, thus far, most rubrics and analyses have not included these factors.

Moreover, some researchers maintain that language development is an important factor in the analysis of story recall. Morrow (1988a) points out that "knowledge and use of language is crucial to a child's development of literacy" (p. 134). Therefore, in her studies (1986, 1988b), she employed two measures of language development, the Hunt "t-unit," a strategy which identifies an independent clause including all of its subordinate clauses, and the Botel, Dawkins and Granowsky (1972) Formula of Syntactic Complexity which assigns a weight to syntactic elements. In story analysis, King (1977) considers "the quantity of language used (length of story), the complexity of the language (number of words per main clause and subordinate clauses), and vocabulary diversity" (p. 413). Samples taken over time intervals document student oral language growth. Lehr (1991) suggests that the ability to identify the theme of the story during the retelling improves with the age of the child. Montague, Maddux, and Dereshiwsky (1990) note that differences in the amount and type of information retold varies through high school. Based on these studies, language development as related to understanding of story structure may be another consideration in evaluating retellings especially in young students.

Young children who practice retelling stories appear to improve their ability to recall more story elements and to increase their language complexity (Morrow, 1985, 1986, 1988b). However, Morrow, Sisco, and Smith (1992) report that in the case of children who have learning disabilities, language complexity may not significantly improve although ability to include more story elements does improve. The authors caution that their intervention did not focus on language development, per se. Other researchers support the use of retelling in teaching oral proficiency for second language learners and encourage its use to support student growth in composition (Hurley, 1986; Stewig, 1985). Authorities, however, do not agree that language development is an appropriate focus for retellings. Yet, many researchers and authors include language components as part of their criteria for assessment. Language production difficulties, however, are not considered in the scoring process.

Retelling as a Presentation Task

Goodman et al. (1987) suggest that, in the process of comprehending, students need time to think about and reflect on their reading. Presenting, sharing with one's self or others what they have discovered and reflected upon and by relating those discoveries to past experiences, enhances students' comprehension, providing for "a way of confirming new knowledge and of testing it against an audience" (p. 44). Goodman et al. believe that responding to a story through the use of illustration or drama and dance or discussion or other presentation methods "provide powerful opportunities for readers to relive, rehearse, modify, and integrate their interpretations of the author's messages into their own reality—in other words, the opportunity to enhance the construction of meaning" (p. 44). Retelling is one of these presentation forms and several researchers have explored the use of retelling as a method of presentation.

Linden and Wittrock's research (1981) supports a "generative model" of learning which postulates that a reader's comprehension is built on relationships between the background knowledge of the reader and the text. In this study, the subjects' comprehension was enhanced when they generated images, illustrations, metaphors or summary sentences. Other researchers explore the use of presentation strategies to enhance comprehension. After studying the drawing, oral language and composing behaviors of first graders of limited English proficiency, Bartelo (1984) points to relationships among the behaviors. Through her observation, she notes that drawing may provide a "thinking out-loud," a "rehearsal for processing ideas" (p. 28). Students who referred to illustrations they had drawn which included many details produced more language in their retellings than students who referred to illustrations they had created which included fewer details. Bartelo concluded that the detailed drawings aided the retelling process. Gambrell and Jawitz's (1993) study of reading performance supports the theory that comprehension is enhanced when students are instructed to attend to the illustrations and form mental images for the stories. In an earlier study employing a comprehension task, Gambrell et al. (1985) show that a treatment group who were asked to retell a story outperformed a treatment group who illustrated a story on a measure of comprehension. Wagner (1988) advocates using drama in the language arts curriculum. She maintains that "in reading and writing, children engage in a form of conscious symbolization; they assign meaning to arbitrary forms (letters) just as they do to objects in drama" (p.49). Testing this theory, Henderson and Shanker (1978) asked children to answer comprehension questions reflecting recognition and recall of details, sequencing events, and identifying the main idea. They compared a group of children who completed workbook pages and a group who engaged in interpretive dramatics. In each measure of comprehension, the results favor the group who engaged in the drama activities. Moreover, the students preferred the drama activities. The research appears to support the theory that various presentation forms such as drawing, drama, and retelling provide a format where students analyze, construct and share their meaning construction, thereby improving comprehension.

Unanswered Questions

Reflection and analysis of the research and practice of retelling leads the reader to a number of questions. The ability to retell does appear to be related to comprehension; however, the nature of the relationship remains undefined. Does retelling measure the product of comprehension but not the process? If the assessor probes beyond the story structure, requesting that the student provide and explain his/her process in determining a theme, a connection to another text or experiences, or if that assessor requires that the subject compare and reflect on his/her retelling against a model or rubric, then some evidence about process is demonstrated. However, some rubrics require this evidence and some do not.

Further investigation into the common factors of existing retelling criteria provide a basis for construction of a common rubric. However, that investigation and simplification requires caution so that the process measured represents more than the mere "basalization" of a complex dynamic process.

Although retelling appears to have face validity, another question remains — does retelling possess construct validity? Powell's (1988) research confirms some congruence between the processes used in retelling and the multiple choice measures. Other researchers have employed retelling techniques considering the validity intuitively obvious. Further, inter reliability remains a question. Or should reliability become a major issue? Tierney concludes that "many things that can be measured 'reliably' aren't worth reporting anyway" (1993). A firm basis for demonstrating reliability and validity remain a matter for study.

But the questions don't end there. Most retelling structures reflect story grammar. Yet, knowledge of story grammar appears to be developmental. Does retelling practice provide the framework for faster development of this knowledge? Morrow's work (1985, 1986, 1988b) appears to provide some evidence that it may. If so, how does it relate to the development of other text structures? McGee and Richgels (1985) point out that like narrative text, expository texts possess various structures. Williams and Taylor (1984) conclude that performance of tasks which reflected a knowledge of expository text structure improved with age. Can retelling of expository text enhance students' understanding of its structure?

Considering these issues brings the reader to a clearer picture of the questions which remain. These questions lead to further research which is necessary to clarify the relationship between retelling and comprehension.

Needed Research

Throughout this exploration, retelling is consistently reported as a valuable technique which can integrate instruction and assessment. Yet, it is difficult to develop a complete understanding of its nature or to determine one rubric for its analysis. Further research may reveal insights into these issues. Teachers share stories from big books and later students choral read the same stories. In reading workshop, students read and respond to books that they choose. And in writing workshop, students write about topics of their choice. They share their pieces with other writers checking for clarity and understanding. All of these practices involve students as thinkers and communicators. Retelling, as an instructional practice and an assessment procedure, appears to reflect these same language processes. For example, Morrow's (1985) research suggests that a common factor was responsible for gains in the comprehension measure and retelling. Further research is needed to clarify these relationships and identify these common factors.

Study of the metacognitive processes that readers use when involved in retelling tasks is needed as well. Further study would provide data to refine the construct of reading comprehension. Powell's research (1988) explores this topic in terms of what strategies students employ when engaging in certain assessment tasks. Other research is needed to investigate the common factors reflected in retelling as compared to other reading and writing tasks.

Although it would be helpful to determine a consistent scoring rubric, the studies of Applebee (1977) and Cullinan et al. (1983) support the developmental nature of the acquisition of story structure. Therefore, age-appropriateness and one's ability to produce language needs to be considered in the research and development of common rubrics. At this time, little research has been conducted to explore the nature and workings of expository retellings. Research in this area is needed to enhance the knowledge base about the developmental nature of text structure and the relationship between story and expository text.

With further study researchers may explore the nature of comprehension itself. Some would argue that retelling provides a means of assessing comprehension within the instructional setting, i.e. it may have the potential to be a relatively pure form of assessment. Others would wrestle with the question of whether retellings provide insights into the process as well as the products of comprehension. Through further study, information can be gathered to enhance the understanding of retelling and its role as a means of assessment. In the process, we will increase our knowledge of the interaction between readers and the texts they read.

References

Anthony, R. J., Johnson, T. D., Mickelson, N. I., & Preece, A. (1991). *Evaluating literarcy: A perspective for change.* Portsmouth, NH: Heinemann.

Anderson, R. C. , Heibert, E. H., Scott, J. A., & Wilkinson, I. A. G. (1985). *Becoming a nation of readers: The report of the commission on reading.* Washington, C. D.: National Institute of Education.

Applebee, A. N. (1977). Sense of story. *Theory Into Practice, 16,* 342-347.

Bartelo, D. M. (1984). *Getting the picture of reading and writing: A look at the drawings, composing, and oral language of limited English proficiency children.* Plymouth, NY: Plymouth College. (ERIC Reproduction Service No. ED 245 533).

Bembridge, T. (1992). A MAP for reading assessment. *Educational Leadership, 49,* (8), 46-48.

Botel, M., Dawkins, J., & Granowsky, A. (1972). *Syntactic complexity: Analyzing it and measuring it.* Philadelphia: University of Pennsylvania.

Botel, M., & Lytle, S. (1988). *PCRP II reading, writing and talking across the curriculum.* Harrisburg, PA: Pennsylvania Department of Education.

Brown, H., & Cambourne, B. (1987). *Read and retell.* Portsmouth, NH: Heinemann.

Clark, C. H. (1982). Assessing free recall. *The Reading Teacher, 35,* 434-439.

Cullinan, B. E., Harwood, K. T., & Galda, L. (1983). The reader and the story: Comprehension and response. *Journal of Research and Development in Education, 16* (3), 29-38.

Feldman, D. (1989, November). *Before and beyond questioning: The rationale and process of retelling.* Paper presented to the Annual New York State Reading Conference, Kiamesha Lake, NY.

Gambrell, L. B., Pfeiffer, W., & Wilson, R. (1985). The effects of retelling upon reading comprehension and recall of text information. *Journal of Educational Research, 78,* 216-220.

Gambrell, L. B., & Jawitz, P. B. (1993). Mental imagery, text illustration, and children's story comprehension and recall. *Reading Research Quarterly, 28,* 265-276.

Garcia, G. E. (1994). Assessing the literacy development of second-language students: A focus on authentic assessment. In K. Spangenberg-Urbschat & R. Pritchard (Eds.), *Kids Come in All Languages: Reading Instruction for ESL Students.* (pp. 180-205). Newark, DE: International Reading Association.

Goodman, Y. M. (1982). Retellings of literature and the comprehension process. *Theory Into Practice, 21,* 301-307.

Goodman, Y. M., Watson, D. J., & Burke, C. L. (1987). *Reading miscue inventory alternative procedures.* New York: Richard C. Owen.

Henderson, L. C., & Shanker, J. L. (1978). The use of interpretive dramatics versus basal reader workbooks for developing comprehension skills. *Reading World, 17,* 239-243.

Hernandez-Miller, M. E. (1991). *Effects of reading workshop on students' retellings.* Palm Springs, CA: Paper presented to Annual Meeting of the National Reading Conference. (ERIC Document Reproduction Service No. ED 343 102)

Hurley, J. (1986). *Classroom techniques for teaching oral proficiency.* Youngstown, OH: Youngstown University. (ERIC Document Reproduction Service No. ED 280 303)

Irwin, P.A., & Mitchell, J.N. (1983). A procedure for assessing the richness of retellings. *Journal of Reading, 26,* 391-396.

Kalmback, J. (1980). *The structure of narrative retellings.* Houghton, MI: Research prepared at Michigan State University. (ERIC Reproduction Service No. ED 216 317).

Koskinen, P. S., Gambrell, L. B., Kapinus, B. A., & Heathington, B. S. (1988). Retelling: a strategy for enhancing students' reading comprehension. *The Reading Teacher, 41,* 892-896.

King, M. (1977). Evaluating reading. *Theory to Practice, 16,* 407-417.

Lehr, S. S. (1991). *The child's developing sense of theme: Responses to literature.* New York: Teachers College Press.

Linden, M., & Wittrock, M. C. (1981). The teaching of reading comprehension according to the model of generative learning. *Reading Research Quarterly, 17,* 44-57.

Marr, M. B., & Gromley, K. (1982). Children's recall of familiar and unfamiliar text. *Reading Research Quarterly, 18,* 89-104.

Marshall, N. (1983). Using story grammar to assess reading comprehension. *The Reading Teacher, 36,* 616-620.

McGee, L. M., & Richgels, D. (1985). Teaching expository text structure to elementary students. *The Reading Teacher, 38,* 739-748.

Montague, M., Maddux, C. D., & Dereshiwsky, M. I. (1990). Story grammar and comprehension and production of narrative prose by students with learning disabilities. *Journal of Learning Disabilities, 23,* 190-197.

Morrow, L. M. (1985). Retelling stories: a strategy for improving young children's comprehension, concept of story structure, and oral language complexity. *The Elementary School Journal, 85,* 646-661.

30

Morrow, L. M. (1986). Effects of structural guidance in story retelling on children's dictation of original stories. Journal of Reading, 18, 135-151.

Morrow, L. M. (1988a). Retelling stories as a diagnostic tool. In Glazer, S. M., Searfoss, L. W., & Gentile, L. M. (Eds.), Reexamining Reading Diagnosis. (pp. 128-149). Newark, Delaware: International Reading Association.

Morrow, L. M. (1988b). Young children's responses to one-to-one story reading in school settings. Reading Research Quarterly, 23, 89-107.

Morrow, L. M., Sisco, L. J., & Smith, J. K. (1992). The effects of mediated story retelling on listening comprehension, story structure, and oral language development in children with learning disabilities. In C. K. Kinzer & D. J. Leu (Eds.), Literacy Research Theory and Practice: Views from Many Perspectives. Forty-first Yearbook of the National Reading Conference (pp. 435-443). Rochester, NY: National Reading Conference.

Olson, A., & Davies, A. (1989, April). The influence of gender differences on story retellings. Reading, 23, 32-38.

Page, W. D. (1977). Comprehending and cloze performance. Reading World, 17 (1), 17-21.

Pickert, S. M., & Chase, M. L. (1978). Story retelling: An informal technique for evaluation children's language. The Reading Teacher, 31, 528-531.

Powell, J. L. (1988). An examination of comprehension processes used by readers as they engage in different forms of assessment. Indiana University: Ed. D. Dissertation. (ERIC Document Reproduction Service No. ED 298 449)

Seltzer, D. A. (1989). Assessment and early childhood education. Overland Park: KS: Research and Training Associates, Inc. (ERIC Document Reproduction Service No. ED 330 446)

Stewig, J. W. (1985). Children's literature: An impetus to composition. Houston, TX: Paper presented at Annual Meeting of the Texas Joint Council of Teachers of English. (ERIC Document Reproduction Service No. ED 255 917)

Stiggins, R. (Speaker). (1991). Assessing reading proficiency (Video Recording). Portland, OR: Northwest Regional Educational Laboratory.

Tasmanian Education Department. (1989). Retelling: An effective teaching practice—a powerful evaluation strategy. North Hobart: Tasmania, Australia, Department of Education. (ERIC Document Reproduction Service No. ED 326 899)

Tierney, R. (1993, October). Negotiating learner-based literacy assessments: Some guiding principles. Presentation at the Keystone State Reading Association Conference, Lake Harmony, PA.

Tierney, R., Bridge, C., & Cera, M. J. (1978-1979). The discourse processing operations of children. Reading Research Quarterly, 14, 539-569.

Valencia, S., McGinley, W., & Pearson, P. D. (1990). Assessing reading and writing: Building a more complete picture for middle school assessment. Champaign, Illinois: University of Illinois. (ERIC Document Reproduction Service No. ED 320 121)

Wagner, B. J. (1988). Research currents: Does classroom drama affect the arts of language? *Language Arts, 65* (1), 46-55.

Williams, J. P., & Taylor, M. B. (1984). Constructing macrostructure for expository text. *Journal of Education Psychology, 76,* 1065-1075.

Profiling Students' Achievement in Language and Literacy: Merging Perspectives

Gerry Shiel and Patrick Forde
St. Patrick's College

In this chapter, recent advances in the development of performance-based assessments in language and literacy are discussed in the context of emerging systems for profiling student achievement. After identifying the main characteristics of student profiling systems, five criteria for evaluating such systems are specified. The criteria relate to function, structure, curriculum-relatedness, technical adequacy and manageability. These criteria are then applied to two profiling systems - one developed in Victoria, Australia, the other in England and Wales. The paper concludes with a discussion on general difficulties relating to the development and uses of profiling systems, and looks at how such systems may develop in the future. Throughout the paper, a distinction is made between profiling systems that are primarily designed for use at the classroom level, and those that are more useful for reporting on large-scale performance-based assessments.

In recent years, the assessment of language and literacy has been closely scrutinized by researchers and practitioners in education. The validity of using standardized tests to measure the outcomes of instruction has been questioned repeatedly (Shepard, 1990; Hiebert, Valencia & Afflerbach, 1994). Now, as instructional practices are beginning to come into line with current theories of literacy acquisition and cognitive development, many educators have called for improved methods of literacy assessment, at the classroom level and at the school, district and state levels (see Calfee & Hiebert, 1991; Hiebert & Calfee, 1992).

While ideas such as authentic assessment (Valencia, Hiebert & Afflerbach, 1994) and portfolio assessment (Tierney, Carter & Desai, 1991; Glazer & Brown, 1993) have been embraced and implemented by many educators in the United States, there is widespread recognition that much remains to be learned about these new approaches (Valencia, Hiebert & Afflerbach, 1994). Although performance-based assessments may be particularly suited to informing instructional practice at the classroom level, their validity and reliability, their manageability, and their effects on instruction and learning at the school, district and state levels have been questioned, and hence they have not, as yet, gained complete acceptance among the broader educational community including policy makers (Haertel, 1992; Linn, Baker & Dunbar, 1991). Indeed, while several states have recently embarked on large-scale performance-based assessment programs (e.g., Abruscato, 1993; Guskey, 1994; Weiss, 1994), it is clear that many of these programs are experimental in nature, and that changes can be anticipated in the years ahead as more research on performance-based assessment becomes available (Afflerbach, 1994).

Educators in countries outside the United States have also expressed concern about the effects of traditional assessment programs on instruction and learning, and have begun to look at how the outcomes of performance-based assessments can be used to meet the informational needs of administrators, parents, teachers and pupils.

This chapter focuses on student profiling - a method for interpreting, recording and reporting performance-based assessment information. First, student profiling is defined in the context of assessment and reporting in language and literacy. Then five criteria which incorporate performance-based assessments are set out. Following this, two approaches to profiling the literacy achievements of students are described. One, the *Victoria English Profiles* (Victoria Department of School Education, 1991) was developed in Australia and has been in use for some years. The second, the student profiling system based on *National Curriculum Assessment* in England and Wales (e.g., School Examinations and Assessment Council, 1993a, 1993b, 1993c), is still undergoing change. In the concluding section of the chapter, general difficulties relating to the development of student profiling systems for the assessment and recording of achievement in language and literacy are summarized, and future trends in the development of these systems are discussed.

What are Language and Literacy Profiles?

Educators have profiled student achievement in language and literacy for many years, particularly in the case of students with possible reading or learning problems. Well known reading profiles such as the *Reading Miscue Inventory* (Goodman, Watson & Burke, 1987) and the *Durrell Analysis of Reading Difficulty* (Durrell & Catterson, 1980) provide information on students' achievements across several dimensions of language and literacy, often on a series of comparable scales, so that the strengths and needs of students across the different dimensions are apparent.

Student profiling, as outlined in this chapter, represents a method of interpreting, recording and reporting on the achievement of students with reference to their performance on literacy tasks in typical classroom settings. Profiling provides a means of synthesizing the results of observations of student outcomes in such dimensions as oral language (speaking and listening), reading comprehension, writing, metacognitive strategies, and attitude/motivation. In some instances, teachers may be encouraged or required to administer specific tests or tasks to provide a basis on which to make judgements about student achievement. In other instances, greater reliance may be placed on teachers' own holistic judgements of student achievement. Finally, the products of performance-based assessments such as portfolios or writing samples may be externally evaluated.

In general, pupil profiles in language and literacy have the following properties:

1. They are holistic. They reflect as wide a range of achievement as possible so that a rounded picture of the individual's achievements in language and literacy emerges.

2. They reflect a qualitative approach to assessment in language and literacy, describing achievement rather than assigning scores or grades. However, quantitative components are not excluded when they contribute to the overall understanding of student achievement (Broadfoot, 1987).

3. They are capable of serving both formative and summative functions (Department of Education and Science, 1988; Hitchcock, 1993). The process of compiling a profile can be useful in a formative sense in that it may facilitate instructional planning; the product can serve summative requirements by providing overall indices of a student's achievement.

4. They are criterion-referenced or self-referenced rather than norm-referenced (Gipps & Stobart, 1993; Griffin & Nix, 1991). They describe what the student can do rather than how the student compares with other students.

5. They are capable of demonstrating progression, giving continuity to a pupil's assessment at different stages (Shorrocks, Frobisher, Nelson, Turner & Waterson, 1993).

Profiling systems in language and literacy generally consist of ordered sets of *indicators* based on the content and process objectives of a curriculum. The indicators describe what pupils should be able to do as a result of instruction and learning, and are often linked to curriculum objectives. *Bands or levels* are formed when indicators are grouped together to provide a more meaningful description of achievement. Teachers may be asked to synthesize a student's achievement across all the indicators within a band in order to rate student achievement at that band (or level) with reference to students' performances in classroom assessment contexts, or the situations in which teachers gather evidence about a student's achievement.

There are several examples of profiling systems in addition to those discussed in detail here. The *KEEP Literacy Assessment System* (Paris, Calfee, Filby, Hiebert, Pearson, Valencia, Wolf & Hansen, 1992) was used to evaluate the effectiveness of a whole-literacy program for native Hawaiian students in Grades K-3. *The Primary Learning Record* (Hester, Ellis & Barrs, 1993) has been used in both the United States and the United Kingdom to document progress in talking/listening, reading and writing. The *Australian National English Profile* (Australian Education Council, 1994) interprets and documents progress in speaking/listening, reading/viewing and writing across 8 levels of achievement.

Evaluating Profiling Systems

Pupil profiling systems may be examined along several different dimensions. The five dimensions discussed here are function, structure, curriculum relatedness, technical adequacy, and manageability. These dimensions are not mutually exclusive and are discussed in the order below for convenience only.

Function

The function of a profiling system may be classified according to four categories of information: formative, diagnostic, summative and evaluative (Department of Education and Science, 1988). *Formative* assessment information, which is gathered by teachers during ongoing instruction and assessment activities, recognizes the positive achievements of students and helps to identify future learning needs. Because formative information provides feedback and helps students to establish personal goals, it may be as useful to students as it is to teachers (Pole, 1993). *Diagnostic* assessment information facilitates the identification of learning difficulties; it generally involves an in-depth assessment of an individual, either by a classroom teacher or by a resource teacher. *Summative* assessment information allows for the recording of a student's overall achievement on different aspects of language and literacy at the completion of a program of study. Some form of aggregation across dimensions of language and literacy may be involved. *Evaluative* assessment information, which is derived from summative data, facilitates the evaluation of the work of individual schools or larger administrative units.

This classification system may be subsumed under two broader categories: formative/diagnostic and summative/evaluative.

Problems of interpretation and status may arise when a student profiling system designed to provide formative/diagnostic information is used to generate summative/evaluative information, or when summative/evaluative information is used for formative/diagnostic purposes. In some cases in which summative information is used for accountability purposes, the value of any associated formative assessment may be greatly diminished (see Gipps & Stobart, 1993).

Structure

The structure of a profiling system in language and literacy can be described in terms of the range of areas covered by the system, and the depth and complexity of the assessments and allied reporting schemes within and across those areas. Some profiling systems are comprehensive to the extent that they cover many aspects of language and literacy and their interrelatedness, while others may cover one broad aspect of literacy (e.g., reading or writing) in considerable depth.

An issue related to the range of levels within a system concerns the degree to which the levels are cumulative. In cumulative profiling systems, each level (or band) builds on the previous level as its indicators describe progressively more complex literacy behaviours. The levels may be interpreted either as stages through which students pass, or performance standards (benchmarks) which they must achieve in order to make further progress. Cumulative systems seem to be particularly well suited to describing the achievement of the most-able and least-able students over time.

In non-cumulative profiling systems, students may be assessed on independent sets of indicators at successive grade levels. In the *Work Sampling System* (Meisels, Dichtelmiller, Dorfman, Jablon & Marsden, 1993), for example, the clock is reset as the student begins each grade level, and the student achievement is evaluated with reference to new (though sometimes overlapping) sets of indicators each year. Using such systems, it may be more difficult to see progress over time, particularly in the case of lower-achieving students.

Curriculum Relatedness

The performance-based assessments that underpin profiling systems contribute to the development of stronger links between curriculum, instructional strategies, learning and assessment (Calfee & Hiebert, 1991; Valencia & Place, 1994). Curriculum relatedness is supported in those cases in which the indicators and levels in a profiling system reflect a theoretically-based existing curriculum. When performance-based classroom-level assessments are used with the profiling system, the link between curriculum and assessment is further supported when pupils are judged on how well they perform activities derived from ongoing instruction. In large-scale assessments, the strength of the links between curriculum and assessment may depend on the degree to which the assessment tasks found within the profiling system are typical of those carried out by students in the course of instruction and learning.

An important dimension of curriculum relatedness concerns the manner in which a profiling system is developed. Some systems are developed by groups of curriculum and measurement experts with little direct input from teachers, while others rely on various levels of teacher input. If teachers are involved in various stages of the system's development (see, for example, Valencia & Place, 1994), then the components of the profiling system - the indicators, the levels, the assessment contexts, etc. - are likely to reflect the existing curriculum. On the other hand, if the profiling system is developed primarily by experts, it may encourage teachers to embrace new ideas about assessment. An ideal model may be one in which both experts and experienced teachers make major contributions to the development of the profiling system.

Technical Adequacy

Reliability and validity are key factors in evaluating the technical adequacy of a profile. According to Haertel (1992), "the same issues of reliability and validity arise for the interpretation of performance-based assessments as for other kinds of assessments. However, the relative emphasis on different aspects of reliability and validity may differ, and evidence of reliability and validity may take somewhat different forms" (p. 986).

On classroom-level performance-based systems reliability and validity are established by means of judgements rather than correlations (Calfee & Hiebert, 1991). A classroom-level performance-based assessment is reliable and valid to the extent that multiple sources of evidence converge to support a particular conclusion.

Where externally-imposed performance-based assessments are concerned, the traditional criterion of reliability is subsumed by considerations of transfer and generalizability (Linn et al., 1991). The results of an assessment are deemed to be generalizable if performance on the assessment task can be generalized to other related tasks. Generalizability theory (see Cronbach, Gleser, Nanda & Rajaratnam, 1972) appears to be well suited to appraising this aspect of performance-based assessment. Using generalizability theory, the error due to raters and to the sampling of assessment tasks can be estimated, and these estimates can be used to determine the generalizability of the performance-based assessment.

When assessing the validity of large-scale performance-based assessments, consideration should be given to the quality and comprehensiveness of the content covered, the fairness of assessments (whether or not the content and processes had been taught), the meaningfulness of the tasks for teachers and students, and the intended and unintended consequences of the assessments (Linn et al., 1991). Up to now, few performance-based assessments have been evaluated in relation to all of these different aspects of validity.

In evaluating the reliability of a profiling system, consideration also must be given to how consistently raters (judges) synthesize the achievement of a student across indicators to arrive at an evaluation of the student's achievement. It is often possible to address this issue by looking at the effects of moderating procedures in promoting consistency across raters. The validity of a profiling system should be considered independently of the validity of the measures upon which the system is based.

Comparability across components of a profiling system may be a concern of some educators. If a profiling system purports to summarize achievement on different aspects of language and literacy such as reading and writing, then evidence should be provided to demonstrate that the reading and writing scales are linked. The evidence might, for example, point to shared indicators across these related language processes.

Manageability

A fifth general issue that should be considered in evaluating profiling systems is their manageability. The performance-based assessments that underlie some profiling systems are considered more challenging and more time-consuming than traditional assessments (Marzano, 1994). The preparation and administration of assessment tasks, the interpretation and recording of performance, the development and evaluation of portfolios, and the communication of results to parents and others all take time. The need to assess and record achievement in a specific way during ongoing instruction may be difficult, particularly in the early stages of using a new profiling system. When the demands on teachers are excessive, either due to the sheer volume of assessment and recording, or to a lack of adequate training and support, a profiling system, learning and assessment may be regarded as unmanageable. Profiling systems, therefore, should be manageable.

From Theory to Practice: Two Profiling Systems

In this section, two recently developed profiling systems are discussed in terms of the five criteria outlined above.

The Victoria English Profiles

In the late 1980s, the Victoria (Australia) State Department of Education developed comprehensive systems for profiling student achievement in English and mathematics. The *Victoria English Profiles* provide a system of assessment and recording based on teacher judgements of their students in three areas: spoken language, reading and writing.

Function. The *English Profiles* generate information on the language and literacy achievement of students useful for formative, summative or evaluative purposes. The *Profiles* can provide formative assessment information that documents individual or groups of students' performance on specific indicators. Summative information is available in the form of overall indices of individual student achievement in spoken language, reading, and writing. The extent to which there is conflict arising from the multiple assessment functions of the *English Profiles* is unclear in the absence of published research on the matter. However, given that the *Profiles* were originally developed for classroom use (Dwyer, 1992), and that the *1992 Victorian Achievement Studies* involved profiling representative samples of students at selected grade levels rather than all students in that state, it is unlikely that the formative and summative functions of the *Profiles* would have been greatly undermined.

Structure. The *Reading Profile* is a sequential series of 9 bands, each of which consists of a set of indicators. A band is defined as "a broad description of a range of reading behaviors rather than a definition of a discrete point in development" (Griffin, 1990b). The reading bands are not tied to specific grade levels. They range from Band A, which consists of indicators of emergent reading behaviors and attitudes, to Band I, which consists of indicators of advanced (high-school) reading skills. In general, pupils move through one band for every two years of schooling.

Band C, for example, contains 13 different indicators classified as reading strategies, responses to reading, or interests and attitudes. Among the indicators are "finding where another reader is up to in reading a passage" (reading strategy), "writing and doing art work that reflects understanding of text" (response to reading), and "seeking recommendations for books to read" (attitudes and interests). As teachers rate students across the indicators in a band, simultaneous consideration is given to strategies, responses to reading, and attitudes and interests.

The *Reading Profile* is cumulative to the extent that the indicators (and hence the bands) represent a continuum of achievement in reading (Griffin, 1990a). In the development of the *Profile*, several hundred teachers rated their students on a great many reading indicators, determining whether the behaviors or attitudes represented by each indicator were emerging, developing or established. The application of statistical techniques based on item response theory (IRT) (see Masters, 1988), enabled the profile developers to map the indicators onto an underlying scale of achievement. The bands were subsequently formed by clustering groups of adjacent indicators. Some indicators, which did not possess the mathematical properties demanded by the IRT partial-credit scoring model, were excluded from the bands. Teachers using the final form of the *Profile* rate students on each band or group of related indicators. Hence, their judgements are holistic in nature. Though there is no requirement to administer specific tests to inform those judgements, several assessment contexts are suggested for each band. For example, it is suggested that teachers base their judgements on some or all of the following assessment contexts when deciding if students have developed the behaviors and attitudes in Band C: shared reading, reading conferences, uninterrupted sustained silent reading, story retellings, running records, cloze activities, parent observations, Reader's Theatre, and creative drama. At higher bands, assessment contexts include standardized tests of reading comprehension. Significantly, no specific criteria are offered for linking performance in the assessment contexts to ratings on the bands, though it would be possible to do so.

Curriculum relatedness. The *English Profiles* may be considered criterion-referenced because teachers place students on a progression of development defined by tasks (represented by the indicators) rather than by the positions of other students (Griffin, 1990a). Moreover, the terms "instructional level" has been used to describe those bands at which students are developing behaviors and attitudes at the time when rating occurs. However, unlike some traditional criterion-referenced assessments, the *Profiles* do not consist of exhaustive lists of skills, each of which must be assessed and interpreted separately. Rather, the emphasis is on holisitc evaluation based on actual classroom performance. While the performance of students on particular indicators or bands may suggest some general directions for instruction, the *Profiles* are not intended to be prescriptive as any set of indicators is only a sample of the total possible pool of indicators.

At the time when the *English Profiles* were developed, there was no mandated curriculum in English in the state of Victoria. While the *Profiles* do not relate to a specific curriculum, it is clear that their content (the indicators and many of the assessment contexts) generally reflect recent research in holistic approaches to teaching oral language, reading and writing.

Technical adequacy. The reliability and validity of the *English Profiles* have been investigated using techniques more often associated with the evaluation of these constructs in the development of standardized tests.

Both the *Reading* and *Writing Profiles* were studied as part of the *Victorian 100 Schools Study* (Griffin & Rowe, 1988). Over 5,000 students in Grades 1, 3, 5, 7 and 9 were rated using the *Profiles*. Alpha reliability coefficients for the *Reading Profile* ranged from .72 to .89 suggesting internal reliability. Equivalent coefficients for the *Writing Profile* ranged from .64 to .85. Test-retest reliability coefficients for the *Reading Profile* ranging from .89 (Grade 1) to .93 (Grade 9) were obtained, as were inter-rater reliabilities ranging from .85 (Grade 5) to .89 (Grade 3).

A measure of the concurrent validity of the *Reading Profile* was generated by correlating ratings on the *Reading Profile* with students' overall scores on the standardized *Test of Reading Comprehension* (TORCH) (Mossensen, Hill & Masters, 1987). The correlations ranged from .55 (Grade 3) to .72 (Grade 7). An overall correlation of .62 was obtained.

While no data are provided on the reliability and validity of many of the assessment tasks that teachers consider in rating students, the *Profiles* themselves appear reliable to the extent that their reliability indices compare favorably with those of other standardized rating scales and standardised tests. Hence, the aggregation of the performance of individuals and groups seems justified. However, few of the validity issues raised in an earlier part of this chapter have been addressed, although the fact that the various assessment contexts represent typical classroom-based activities provides evidence of content validity.

Manageability. The *English Profiles* appear to be relatively easy to use and do not make extensive time demands on teachers. While specific assessment contexts are suggested, many of these reflect performance-based activities that teachers already use. A change in emphasis occurs, however, to the extent that teachers must adopt a reflective stance as they look at student performance in these contexts. The degree to which teachers can do this efficiently and effectively is related to their knowledge of the *Profiles*, their familiarity with the instructional contexts, and the ease with which they can establish links between these contexts and the indicators. Unfortunately, the research base on how teachers use the *Profiles* is not extensive. For example, relatively little is known about how much inservice education teachers require in order to use the *Profiles*, how much moderation is desirable to ensure that teachers within schools develop a shared understanding of the *Profiles*, or how much on-going support is desirable.

Conclusions. The *English Profiles* appear to be appropriate for interpreting, recording and reporting student progress in language and literacy. The formative and summative functions of the *Profiles* combine effectively, allowing teachers to glean some information on students' learning needs, while providing parents and administrators with useful summative information. Significantly, credit is given for partial mastery of the content and attitudes represented by the bands. The *Profiles* are cumulative in that the bands and indicators are located along continua of achievement and represent a criterion-referenced view of assessment since students are rated with regard to bands and indicators along the continua rather than in relation to each other. The content of the bands and assessment contexts appears to be compatible with a holistic perspective on curriculum and assessment. Although little has been done in regard to evaluating the reliability of the recommended assessment tasks, the *Profiles* themselves have been shown to be reliable and valid. In general, the *Profiles* appear to be easy to use.

Assessment of the National Curriculum in England and Wales

As a result of the 1988 Education Reform Act, a National Curriculum for England and Wales was introduced for the first time, and all public schools were obliged to provide their students with access to the curriculum during the period of compulsory education (ages 5-16). *National Curriculum Assessment* (NCA) involves two components: the assessment of students by their teachers in the core subjects (currently English and mathematics) using external tests, including performance-based assessments and paper-and-pencil tests at ages 7, 11, 14 and 16; and the ongoing assessment of students by their teachers across all National Curriculum subjects including the core subjects. Both the externally-developed assessments (known as standard tasks) and the teacher assessments are relevant to this chapter because performance on these assessments is reported with reference to an age-independent hierarchical ten-level scale underlying all National Curriculum subjects and their components. Hence, the assessments yield profiles of achievement. Profiles are generated for five components of English: oral language (teacher assessment only), reading, writing, spelling and handwriting/presentation.

Function. The functions of *NCA* are to provide teachers with formative information to assist them in determining students' instructional needs, to provide parents with summative information on their children's achievement, and to provide the public with (evaluative) information on the performance of schools and local education authorities (LEAs) (see Department of Education and Science, 1988). In general, formative assessment information is generated through teacher-made assessments while summative (and hence evaluative) information is generated by administering and scoring standard tasks. The conflict between the competing functions of *NCA* has been apparent since its inception. In the case of English, for example, performance on the standard tasks is of much greater interest to the media and the public, and hence it enjoys a higher status than do teacher assessments which generate formative information. While the process of administering standard tasks may provide teachers with some formative information, the requirement to report achievement in terms of aggregate scores (summative data) means that such formative information may be lost.

Structure. The structure of the profiling system based on *NCA* is generally similar across subjects and subject area components. Here, the structure of the English reading component of *NCA* at the end of Key Stage 1 (age 7) is described.

Six benchmarks or statements of attainment have been specified for English reading at Level 2 (the level achieved by the average 7 year old). These include: "reads accurately and understands straightforward signs, labels and notices" (2a), "demonstrates knowledge of the alphabet in using word books and simple dictionaries" (2b), "describes what has happened in a story and predicts what will happen next" (2d) and "reads a range of material with some independence, fluency, accuracy and understanding" (2f) (SEAC, 1993a).

To begin assessment on the standard tasks, the teacher must estimate the level at which the student is likely to succeed. For English reading at Level 2, three performance-based assessment tasks are administered. First, the student is asked to read classroom signs (see 2a above). Then the student is asked to find a word in a dictionary using alphabetical order (2b). Finally, the student is asked to read aloud a designated passage from a book selected by the teacher from an approved list. The teacher maintains a running record of the student's reading (2f). Specific criteria have been specified for each task. In order to demonstrate attainment on 2d, for example, the student must identify at least 2 main ideas and make a valid prediction. On 2f, the student must read with meaningful phrasing and intonation, and must not have received help on more than 8 words. It has been claimed that criterion performances such as this have been selected with reference to the percentage of students likely to succeed or fail at a particular level (James & Conner, 1993; Shorrocks, Daniels, Frobisher, Nelson, Waterson & Bell, 1991). To achieve Level 2, a student must reach the criterion level of performance on each of five statement of attainment that are assessed with standard tasks (School Examinations and Assessment Council, 1993a). A student who fail to do so must rated at a lower level since partial credit is not available.

Few guidelines are available to teachers to assist them in conducting their own classroom-based assessments in English although some LEAs provide inservice education and appoint moderators to assist teachers in this effort (see Dearing, 1994). Currently, any discrepancies between a student's performance on the standard tasks and the teacher assessments are resolved in favor of the standard tasks. Now, however, it appears that greater weight will be attached to teacher assessments in resolving such discrepancies (Dearing, 1994), though how this will be done remains unclear.

Curriculum relatedness. There is a link between the National Curriculum and its assessment to the extent that the ten-level hierarchical scale spans both. The curriculum and the statements of attainment that underlie the assessment system were formulated by committees of experts. The assessments are "criterion-referenced" to the extent that students may be assessed on the statements of attainment at the next highest level if they can demonstrate mastery of the knowledge and skills specified for a given level. It has been argued, however, that the statements of attainment found in *NCA* do not satisfy the stringent requirements for criterion-referenced tests laid down by Popham (1980) since such qualifiers as "simply", "regularly", and "common" allow a variety of interpretations (Wiliam, 1993a).

At face value, the strong links between the National Curriculum and its assessment might appear to represent an ideal situation. However, the fact that the statements of attainment generally represent discrete skills or processes means that teachers must assess these skills individually, except, perhaps, in the area of writing, where several statements can be assessed in relation to one piece of written text. The fragmentation of the curriculum into discrete units in order to support the assessment process is disturbing, particularly in language and literacy, where students typically integrate subskills as they engage in meaningful interactions with texts.

Technical adequacy. Much has been written about reliability and validity of *NCA*. The following points, which are particularly relevant for the assessment of language and literacy, have emerged:

1. There is a lack of standardization in the administration of the standard tasks and problems in making judgements about students' performance (Madaus & Kellaghan, 1993; James and Conner, 1993).
2. Different statements of attainment have been interpreted in different ways by different teachers (Shorrocks, Daniels, Frobisher, Nelson, Waterson & Bell, 1991; James & Conner, 1993).
3. Moderators in English, who are employed to ensure that there is

consistency in interpretation of statements of attainment across schools and LEAs are inconsistent in terms of the advice they offer, and the documentation provided by teachers to moderators is often insufficient to allow them to appraise the validity of teacher assessments (James & Conner, 1993).

4. There are significant reservations among teachers about the validity of standard assessment tasks (Shorrocks, Daniels, Stainton & Ring, 1993) and many teachers believe that the outcomes of teacher assessments are fairer reflections of student ability than scores on standard tasks (Shorrocks et al., 1993).

5. Researchers have repeatedly expressed concerns about the reliability and validity of the standard assessment tasks and have argued that these constructs should be operationalized in new ways to suit NCA (Hutchison & Schagen, 1994).

The research clearly indicates that there are serious problems with the technical adequacy of *NCA*. Some of these are due to the political nature of the assessment program and to the hasty manner in which it was introduced (Hutchison & Schagen, 1994).

Manageability. Since their introduction in the late 1980s, there have been problems with the management of standard tasks in classrooms (see Shorrocks et al., 1991; National Union of Teachers/School of Education, Leeds University, 1993; Madaus & Kellaghan, 1993). Among the problems that have been identified are: (a) the disruption of the routine of the school as school personnel were reassigned to assist with testing; (b) the excessive amount of time required to administer the standard tasks; and (c) the increased stress on the teachers involved in testing.

In relation to teacher assessments, which are statutory for the core subjects, teachers spend considerable time completing checklists of statements of attainment for each subject area component and maintaining extensive portfolios of students' work in order to generate data on which to base their own assessments. However, the greatest negative impact on the manageability of national curriculum assessment may be that teachers in general do not appear to be convinced of its validity.

Conclusions. The experiences with *NCA* highlight the difficulty of attempting to generate both formative and summative assessment information in the context of high-stakes assessment. The requirement to generate summative information in the form of aggregated scores means that the valuable formative information may be lost. The structure of *NCA* is often unwieldly. There are too many statements of attainment for some aspects of language and literacy, and most must be assessed individually in the course of administering standard tasks or making teacher assessments. Questions have also been raised regarding the value of the hierarchical ten-level scale for describing achievement in language and literacy. The extent to which *NCA* is criterion-referenced has also been questioned. Indeed, it has been claimed that the specification of criteria for success or failure on some statements of attainment (e.g., oral reading) reflects a norm-referenced perspective on assessment.

There are several problems with the technical adequacy of both the standard tasks and teacher assessments of the *NCA*. Finally, teachers appear to find the administration and scoring of standard tasks to be difficult and to interfere with their regular teaching. Taken together, these problems raise serious questions about the usefulness of *NCA* as a profiling system.

While some of the problems with *NCA* are currently being addressed (see SCAA, 1994), it remains to be seen whether proposed changes will go far enough to regain the confidence and cooperation of teachers. The proposals include the use of level descriptions (brief, paragraph descriptions) rather than lengthy lists of statements and the development of less time-demanding standard tasks. Unfortunately, the proposals do not specifically address how teacher assessments might be developed in such a way that it would be possible to eventually dispense with standard tasks.

Merging Perspectives

The descriptions of the *Victoria English Profiles* and *National Curriculum Assessment* presented in the preceding sections clearly demonstrate the difficulty associated with developing and using profiling systems underpinned by performance-based assessments. It is clear that, in considering such systems, great care must be taken to establish the purposes of assessment and to make specific provisions to generate the types of assessment information required. The Victoria *English Profiles* have been used in survey research rather than in high-stakes assessment. Therefore, they appear to retain their usefulness as a classroom-based profiling system that provides some formative information. Since *NCA* profiling involves high-stakes assessment, and since the administration of standard tasks is mandatory, the formative aspects of *NCA* have received relatively little attention.

The structure of *Victoria English Profiles* is quite different from that of the *NCA* profiling system. Assessment using the *Victoria English Profiles* is based on teachers' holistic judgements of student achievement and attitude on bands consisting of indicators. In contrast, *NCA* requires teachers to consider each of its statements of attainment separately, to administer mandatory standard tasks, and to use a complex series of aggregation rules to arrive at summative indices of student achievement. Clearly, the *Victoria English Profiles* are more in line with the on-going instructional and assessment activities occurring in many classrooms, and are therefore more more appealing and useful to educators. The extent to which either the *Victoria English Profiles* or *NCA* represent criterion-referenced approaches to assessment is a matter of debate. When using the *Victoria English Profiles* teachers are not required to consider each indicator in isolation. In contrast, teachers must address each *NCA* statement of attainment individually, although the statements do not, in and of themselves, suggest criterion levels of achievement. Yet, the two systems are criterion-referenced in that students are evaluated in relation to indicators rather than to each other. This suggests a need to redefine criterion-referenced as it relates to profiling student achievement in language and literacy and encourage teachers to adopt criterion-referenced perspectives to the rating of pupil achievement.

In the case of the *Victoria English Profiles*, attention to reliability has focused on the consistency with which teachers' judge their students' achievement. In the case of *NCA*, attention has focused on the reliability of the standard tasks. The reliability of teacher assessments has received significantly less attention. The role of moderation needs to be clarified in relation to both systems. While the construct validity of the *Victoria Profiles* has been supported empirically, the apparent links between assessment and instruction, and the links between the indicators and the underlying curriculum provide strong evidence of content validity. Neither the content validity nor the construct validity of *NCA* has been established satisfactorily, particularly where the standard tasks are concerned. In the absence of satisfactory evidence, it is difficult for users to place confidence in the system.

Clearly, a profiling system that is unmanageable is unsatisfactory from the point of view of administrators, teachers and pupils. The *Victoria English Profiles* can be used without undue difficulty since the system is directly linked to classroom practice. Moreover, the paperwork involved in recording and reporting is minimal. In contrast, the standard tasks linked to *NCA* take time to administer and score. In the case of teacher assessments, teachers are often required to maintain extensive records.

In this chapter, we have attempted to highlight some of the factors that should be considered in evaluating profiling systems. We contend that, if these factors are considered by developers and users of profiling systems, then such systems have the potential to meet some of the assessment needs in language and literacy in tomorrow's schools.

References

Abruscato, J. (1993). Early results and tentative implications from the Vermont portfolio project. *Phi Delta Kappan*, 74, 474-477.

Afflerbach, P.P. (1994). Large-scale authentic assessment. In S.W. Valencia, E.H. Hiebert, & P.P. Afflerbach (Eds.), *Authentic reading assessment* (pp. 193-196). Newark, DE: International Reading Association.

Australian Education Council. (1994). *English - A curriculum profile for Australian schools.* Carlton, Victoria: Curriculum Corporation.

Broadfoot, P. (1987). *Introducing profiling: A practical manual.* London: Macmillan.

Calfee, R., & Hiebert, E. (1991). Classroom assessment of reading. In R. Barr, M.L. Kamil, P. Mosenthal & P.D. Pearson (Eds.), *Handbook of research on reading* (Vol. 2, pp. 281-309). New York: Longman.

Cronbach, L.J., Gleser, G.C., Nanda, H., & Rajaratnam, N. (1972). *The dependability of behavioral measurements.* New York: Wiley.

Dearing, R. (1994). *The National Curriculum and its assessment: Final report.* London: School Curriculum and Assessment Authority.

Department of Education and Science. (1988). *Report of the task group on assessment and testing.* London: Department of Education and Science.

Durrell, D.D., & Catterson, J.H. (1980). *Durell analysis of reading difficulty.* New York: The Psychological Corporation.

Dwyer, J. (1992). System-wide assessment: Profiling performance. In C. Bouffler (Ed.), *Literacy evaluation* (pp. 28-40). Newtown, NSW: Primary English Teachers' Association.

Gipps, C., & Stobart, G. (1993). *Assessment: A teacher's guide to the issues* (2nd ed.). London: Hodder & Stoughton.

Glazer, S.M., & Brown, C.S. (1993). *Portfolios and beyond: Collaborative assessment in reading and writing.* Norwood, MA: Christopher Gordon.

Goodman, Y., Watson, D., & Burke, C.L. (1987). *Reading miscue inventory: Alternative procedures.* New York: Richard C. Owen.

Great Britain. (1988). *Education reform act: The curriculum and its assessment.* London: Her Majesty's Stationary Office.

Griffin, P. E. (1990a). *Developing literacy profiles.* Paper presented at the Thirty-fifth Annual Convention of the International Reading Association, Atlanta, GA.

Griffin, P.E. (1990b). Profiling literacy development: Monitoring the accumulation of reading skills. *Australian Journal of Education*, 34, 290-311.

Griffin, P., & Nix, P. (1991). *Educational assessment and reporting: A new approach.* Sydney: Harcourt Brace Jovanovich.

Griffin, P., & Roe, K. (1988). *The Victorian 100 school study.* Melbourne: Victoria Department of School Education.

Guskey, T.R. (1994). What you assess may not be what you get. *Educational Leadership, 51,* 51-54.

Haertel, E. (1992). Performance measurement. In M.C. Alkin (Ed.), *Encyclopedia of Educational Research* (6th ed., pp. 984-989). New York: Macmillan.

Hester, H.L., Ellis, S., & Barrs, M. (1993). *Guide to the primary learning record.* London: Center for Language in Primary Education.

Hiebert, E.H., & Calfee, R.C. (1992). Assessing literacy: From standardized tests to portfolios and performances. In S.J. Samuels and A. J. Farstrup (Eds.), W*hat research has to say about reading instruction* (pp. 70-100). Newark, DE: International Reading Association.

Hiebert, E.H., Valencia, S.W., & Afflerbach, P.P. (1994). Definitions and perspectives. In S.W. Valencia, E.H. Hiebert & P.P. Afflerbach (Eds.), *Authentic reading assessment: Practices and possibilities* (pp. 6-21). Newark, DE: International Reading Association.

Hitchcock, G. (1993). *Profiles and profiling: A practical introduction* (2nd ed.). Harlow, Essex: Longman.

Hutchison, D., & Schagen, I. (1994). *How reliable is national curriculum assessment?* Slough, Berks: National Foundation for Educational Research.

James, M., & Conner, C. (1993). Are reliability and validity achievable in national curriculum assessment? Some observations on moderation at Key Stage 1 in 1992. *The Curriculum Journal, 4,* 5-19.

Linn, R. L., Baker, E.L., & Dunbar, S.B. (1991). Complex performance-based assessment: Expectations and validation criteria. *Educational Researcher, 20,* 15-21

Madaus, G., & Kellaghan, T. (1993). The British experience with authentic testing. *Phi Delta Kappan, 74,* 458-469.

Marzano, R.J. (1994). Lessons from the field about outcome-based performance assessments. *Educational Leadership, 51,* 44-50.

Masters, G.N. (1988). The analysis of partial-credit scoring. *Applied Measurement in Education, 1,* 279-297.

Meisels, S.J., Dichtelmiller, M., Dorfman, A., Jablon, J.R., & Marsden, D.B. (1993). T*he work sampling system.* Ann Arbor, MI: Rebus Planning Associates.

Mossensen, L., Hill, P., & Masters, G. (1987). *Test of reading comprehension* (TORCH). Melbourne: Australian Council for Educational Research.

National Union of Teachers and School of Education, University of Leeds (1993). *Testing and assessing 6 and 7 year olds: The Evaluation of the 1992 Key Stage1 national curriculum assessment (Final Report).* Leeds: NUT.

Paris, S.G., Calfee, R.C., Filby, N., Hiebert, E.H., Pearson, P.D., Valencia, S.W., Wolf, K.P., & Hansen, J. (1992). A framework for authentic literacy assessment. Th*e Reading Teacher, 46* (2), 88-99.

Pole, C.J. (1993).*Assessing and recording achievement.* Buckingham: Open Univeristy Press.

50

Popham, W.J. (1980). Domain specification strategies. In R.A. Berk (Ed.), *Criterion-referenced measurement: The state of the art* (pp. 15-31). Baltimore, MD: Johns Hopkins University Press.

School Examinations and Assessment Council. (1993a). *Assessment handbook: English* (Key Stage 1). London: Author.

School Examinations and Assessment Council. (1993b). *Children's work assessed: English, mathematics and science.* London: Author.

School Examinations and Assessment Council. (1993c). *Standard assessment task booklist and running records* (Key Stage 1). London: Author.

Shepard, L. A. (1990). Inflated test score gains: Is the problem old norms or teaching to the test? *Educational Measurement: Issues and Practices, 9,* 15-22.

Shorrocks, D., Daniels, S., Frobisher, L., Nelson, N., Waterson, A., & Bell, J. (1991). *The evaluation of national curriculum assessment at Key Stage 1 1990/ 1991* (ENCA 1 Project). London: School Examinations and Assessment Council.

Shorrocks, D., Daniels, Stainton, R., & Ring, K. (1993). *Assessing six- and seven-year olds at key stage 1: A report on the 1992 key stage 1 assessment.* Leeds: National Union of Teachers/School of Education, University of Leeds.

Shorrocks, D., Frobisher, L., Nelson, N., Turner, I., & Waterson, A. (1993). *Implementing national curriculum assessment in the primary school.* Sevenoaks, Kent: Hodder and Stoughton.

Tierney, R.J., Carter, M.A., & Desai, L.E. (1991). *Portfolio assessment in the reading-writing classroom.* Norwood, MA: Christopher-Gordon Publishers, Inc.

Valencia, S.W., & Place, N. (1994). Portfolios: A process for enhancing teaching and learning. *The Reading Teacher, 47,* 666-669.

Valencia, S.W., Hiebert, E.H., & Afflerbach, P.P. (Eds). (1994). *Authentic assessment: Practices and possibilities.* Newark, DE: International Reading Association.

Victoria Department of School Education. (1991). *English profiles handbook: Assessing and reporting students' progress in English.* Victoria, Australia: Author.

Weiss, B. (1994). California's new English-language arts assessment. In S.W. Valencia, E.H. Hiebert, & P.P. Afflerbach (Eds.), *Authentic reading assessment* (pp. 197-217). Newark, DE: International Reading Association.

Wiliam, D. (1993). Validity, dependability, and reliability in national curriculum assessment. *The Curriculum Journal, 4* (3), 335-350.

Assessment of Reading Attitudes: Validity Issues

Mary M. Brittain
Virginia Commonwealth University

Clay V. Brittain
Army Training Support Center
Fort Eustis, Virginia

Reading depends upon cognition. It also depends upon attitudes. Thus, for teachers of reading, the assessment of reading attitudes may rival in importance the assessment of reading skills. A number of reading attitude scales and a variety of other methods for measuring reading attitudes are described in the educational research literature. Validity is the most important consideration with respect to all of these approaches to attitude assessment. In this paper we briefly discuss the basic nature of test validity and examine reading attitude assessment in terms of three validity related issues: (1) the sparsity of validation studies of reading attitude scales, (2) the greater emphasis in the existing studies on measuring reading attitudes versus defining the construct, and (3) the kinds of evidence which are relevant to the validation of reading attitude measurements. In regard to this last issue, none of the validation studies reviewed examined social and educational consequences in assessing the validity of reading attitude measurements.

Assessment of Reading Attitudes: Validity Issues

As Alexander and Filler (1976) have pointed out, reading is more than the exercise of cognitive skills. Attitudes also are involved. In discussing this same point, Dulin and Chester (1974) emphasized the importance of assessing reading attitudes. Teachers need to be concerned not only about whether students can read but also about whether they will read. Thus for the concerned teacher, the measurement of reading attitudes of students is as important as the measurement of their reading abilities.

The validity of reading attitude measurements is the subject of this paper. Validity is the most important consideration in evaluating any test. The basic issues of validity are the same for attitude scales as for tests of cognitive ability.

What does the test measure? What do the scores mean? The *Standards for Educational and Psychological Testing* (1984), issued jointly by the American Psychologocal Association (APA), the American Educational Research Association (AERA) and the National Council on Measurement in Education (NCME), state that the issues of validity in the use of questionnaires, attitude scales, and inventories are basically the same as the issues of validity in the measurement of aptitude and ability.

Conceptualization of Validity

Views on validity have changed substantially over the past several decades. The division of validity into content validity, predictive validity, and construct validity has given way to the view that validity is unitary. All validity is essentially construct validity. The emphasis in discussions of validity also has shifted from *tests* to *test scores*. Tests themselves do not have reliabilities and validities, only test responses do.

Changes in conceptions of validity can be seen in the treatment of validity in the different editions of *Educational Measurement* published by the American Council on Education. In the first edition (1951) Cureton discussed validity in terms of *tests*. The essential question of validity is how well a test does the job it is employed to do. In the third edition (1989) Messick discussed validity mainly in terms of *test responses and the scores which summarize these responses*. Test responses are functions not only of tests, or measuring instruments, but of the persons responding and the contexts in which they respond. It is of interest to note in this connection the change in title of the APA\AERA\NCME *Standards for Educational and Psychological Testing*. The 1974 version of the Standards was entitled Standards for *Tests*, while the 1985 version was called Standards for *Testing*.

Validity Issues

This paper will explore three validity-related issues in regard to the measurement of reading attitudes: (a) sparsity of validity studies reported in the research literature on reading attitudes,(b) emphasis on the *measurement* of reading attitudes versus their *definition.*, and (c) sources of evidence on the validity of reading attitude measurements.

Sparsity of Research Literature. The validity of reading attitude measurements has not been a salient topic in educational research. A search of ERIC for the period 1966 - 1993 revealed only 31 entries indexed under reading-attitudes **and** validity. This amounts to only slightly more than one study per year. This suggests that the validity of reading attitude assessment has not been a matter of intense or widespread interest.

Construct Measurement Versus Construct Definition. As Messick (1989) has noted, validity studies may have different points of origin. One may begin with a construct in search of proper measurement, or with test scores in search of proper meaning. Validity studies in the area of reading attitudes more often have been in the second category. That is, they more commonly have begun with reading attitude measurements than with reading attitude definitions. Two classic articles on social attitudes are germane to this point. One is Allport's chapter in Murchison's (1935) *Handbook of Social Psychology.* The other is Campbell's (1950) article, some fifteen years later. While both writers addressed the definition and the measurement of social attitudes, Allport was much more concerned with definition and Campbell with measurement. Allport cited some 30 definitions of social attitude and attempted to tease out the common threads running through them. He noted different kinds of attitudes; e.g., specific versus general, individual versus common, public versus private. He discussed differences between attitudes and related constructs such as interests, motives, and needs. Through this scholarly endeavor he derived a definition of social attitude as a state of readiness which is learned and which directs and motivates behavior. To be more exact, Allport defined social attitude as a mental or neural state of readiness, which is organized through experience and which exerts a directive and dynamic influence on behavior toward the object to which it was related.

In contrast, Campbell (1950) was not mainly concerned with definition. For him, attitude referred to behavioral consistency. The hallmark of social attitude was consistency in responses to social objects. Campbell's paper focused upon methods of measuring such consistencies and he categorized them in terms of whether they were structured or non-structured and whether they were disguised or non-disguised. Thus he came up with a fourfold taxonomy as follows: (a) non-disguised, structured (classic verbal attitude scales); (b) non-disguised, non-structured (free response interviews; and open-ended questionnaires; (c) disguised, non-structured (projective tests); and (d) disguised, structured (tests which appear to be objective tests of ability).

Studies of reading attitudes have been more in the Campbell mold than in the Allport mold; they are more likely to begin with method and scores to be interpreted than with a concept to be defined. The methods of measuring reading attitudes fall into all of Campbell's categories except the last one. But by far the most prevalent approach is the non-disguised-structured; i.e., attitude scales. Thus studies of the validity of reading attitude measurements have been largely studies of verbal scales assessing reading attitudes. What hypotheses are sustainable with reference to the interpretation and use of scores on reading attitude scales?

Sources of Evidence on Test Validity. Messick (1989) suggests that the kinds of sources of validity evidence are rather limited. One can do one or a combination of the following:

1. Look at the content of the test in relation to the domain of reference.
2. Probe individual responses to test items and tasks.
3. Examine relationships among responses to items, tasks, and parts of the test (internal structure of test responses).
4. Survey relationships of test scores with other measures and background variables (external structure).
5. Investigate differences in test scores and internal and external structures at different times, in different groups and settings, and under different experimental interventions, test requirements and motivational conditions.
6. Trace social consequences of interpreting and using test scores in particular ways, both intended effects and those unintended.

What sources of evidence are used in the validation of reading attitude measurements? A few of the studies identified in our ERIC search, but by no means a majority of them, sought to establish the relation of content of the attitude scale to content of the broader domain of reading attitudes. For example, to ensure that their reading attitude scale contained items representative of students' feelings toward reading, Tullock-Rhody and Alexander (1980) interviewed children and used their statements for items on the scale they constructed.

The most prevalent studies were those which examined relationships among responses to the attitude scales (i.e., internal structure). We refer here to the several factor analytic studies reported in the literature. The studies are rather consistent in identifying some half-dozen factors which comprise reading attitudes as measured by attitude scales. See for example Engin, Wallbrown, and Brown (1976); Wallbrown, Brown, and Engin (1978); Wallbrown, Singleton, and Levine (1982).

A number of the studies examined external structure. For example, Tullock-Rhody and Alexander (1980) compared scores on their reading attitude scale with teacher judgments about the reading attitudes of the children. McKenna, Stratton, and Grindler (1992) correlated scores on their reading attitude survey with scores on a social desirability scale. The purpose was to obtain evidence that the reading attitude scale was not in fact measuring something other than reading attitudes, i.e., the set to give socially desirable responses.

Two studies compared different ethnic groups with respect to scores on a reading attitude scale, thus making use of evidence from source number 5 above. Plake, Piersel, Harding, & Reynolds (1982) administered the Estes Reading Attitude Scale to fourth, fifth, and sixth grade groups which included both Anglo and Mexican-American children while Aaron, Seaton, & Moore (1980) administered the Estes scale to black children in the South. Plake et al. concluded that the Estes scale performed comparably in the two ethnic groups, but Aaron et al. found a substantial difference in performance on the Estes scale between black and white children.

Validation of Reading Attitude Measurements in Terms of Use

No study was found which examined the social and educational conse-quences as a source of evidence for the validity of reading attitude measure-ment. There would appear to be two major reasons for this. In the first place, the actual use of scores on reading attitude scales generally has not received much emphasis in the literature. McKenna and Kear (1990) argued that if attitude measurement does not influence instruction, then there is little point in doing the measurement. Perhaps teachers do make extensive instructional use of reading attitude scores. But it is not a topic extensively dealt with in the literature.

There is another plausible reason why validation studies have not been concerned with the use of reading attitude scores. It is only recently that social consequences of test use have begun to be incorporated into the test validity paradigm. This seems a bit perplexing given the view expressed by Cureton (1951) some forty-five years ago and quoted early in this paper that validity has to do with how well a test does the job it is supposed to do. What are the jobs that reading attitude scales are supposed to do? That question remains largely unanswered.

References

Aaron, R., Seaton, H.W., & Moore, D. W. (1980) Analysis of the Estes Scale for assessing the reading attitude of minority students. *Reading Improvement, 17*, 100-103.

Alexander, D., & Engin, A. (1986). Dimensions of reading attitudes of primary students. *Educational and Psychological Measurement, 46,* 887-901.

Alexander, J.E. & Filler, R.C. (1976). *Attitudes and Reading.* Newark, DE: International Reading Association.

Allport, G.W. (1935). Attitudes. In C. Murchison (Ed.) *A Handbook of Social Psychology* (pp. 798-844). Worcester, MA: Clark University Press.

56

American Educational Research Association, American Psychological Association & National Council on Measurement in Education. (1974). *Standards for educational and psychological testing.* Washington, DC: American Psychological Association.

American Educational Research Association, American Psychological Association & National Council on Measurement in Education. (1985). *Standards for educational and psychological testing.* Washington, DC: American Psychological Association.

Campbell,D.T. (1950). Indirect assessment of social attitudes. *Psychological Bulletin, 47,* 15-38.

Cureton, E.E. (1951). Validity. In E.F. Lindquist (Ed.), *Educational Measurement* (pp. 621-694), Washington, DC: American Council on Education.

Dulin, D. & Chester, R. (1974). A validation study of the Estes attitude scale. *Journal of Reading, 18,* 56-59.

Engin, A., Wallbrown, F., & Brown, D.(1976) The dimensions of reading attitude for children in the intermediate grades. *Psychology in the Schools, 13,* 309-316.

Estes, T. H. (1971). A scale to measure atttiudes toward reading. *Journal of Reading, 15,* 135-138.

McKenna, M. & Kear, D. (1990). Measuring attitude toward reading: A new tool for teachers. *The Reading Teacher, 43,* 626-636.

McKenna, M., Stratton, B. & Grindler, M. (1993). Social desirability of children's responses to a reading attitude survey. Paper presented at College Reading Association, St. Louis, MO

Messick, Samual (1989). Validity. In R.L. Linn (Ed.), *Educational Measurement* (3rd. Ed., pp.13-103), New York: American Council on Education and Macmillan Publishing Company.

Murchison, C. (Ed.). (1935). *A Handbook of Social Psychology.* Worcester, MA: Clark University Press.

Plake, B., Piersel, W., Harding, R., & Reynolds, C. (1982). The relationship of ethnic group membership to the measurement and meaning of attitudes toward reading: Implications for validity of test score interpretations. *Educational and Psychological Measurement, 42,* 1259-1267.

Tullock-Rhody, R. & Alexander, J. (1980). A scale for assessing attitudes toward reading in secondary schools. *Journal of Reading, 23,* 609-614.

Wallbrown, F., Singleton, B., & Levine, M. (1982). Further evidence concerning the dimensionality of reading attitudes. *Perceptual and Motor Skills, 54,* 1267-1280.

Wallbrown, F., Brown, D., & Engin, A. (1978). A factor analysis of reading attitudes along with achievement and scholastic aptitude. *Psychology in the Schools, 15,* 160-165.

"I Believe Learning is Concentrating, Figuring Things Out, and Sometimes Having Fun": Revisiting the Reading Clinic

Nancy B. Cothern

Indiana University/Purdue University Fort Wayne

With widespread acceptance of whole language theory has come the need to re-examine the purpose of and procedures used in university reading clinics. Formerly, the university clinic served the purpose of diagnosing and remediating reading deficiencies, and instruction was provided in tightly controlled settings with low pupil-teacher ratios. While this type of instruction provided specific direction for teachers, as well as abundant documentation of progress, it precluded students' taking initiative in their own learning.

This manuscript describes a language literacy program conducted annually on a university campus. Through design and completion of authentic research, elementary children are given an opportunity to play a vital role in their own learning - one typically not experienced in year-long classrooms. As a result of participation in the Literacy Workshop for Children, learners express new beliefs about learning; specifically, that learning is a social, collaborative, decision-making process in which their participation matters.

In moving toward more language-centered learning, one must consider how the role of the learner has changed. Current research suggests that when a more active role in learning is assumed, students are establishing behaviors which will help them solve problems in future learning (Farr, 1992). These include the abilities to (a) recognize a task, (b) develop a strategy to accomplish the task, (c) determine when and where to seek assistance, (d) evaluate progress (Wade & Reynolds, 1989), and (e) apply the same or adapted process to another task (Wang & Palinscar, 1989). These steps, facilitated by use of multiple language processes, serve as recognition of students' existing knowledge of language. Ultimately, such affirmation contributes to higher quality learning experiences and facilitates a desire to continue learning for personal reasons (Collins & Cheek, 1993).

Given this pro-active view of learning, it is appropriate to encourage use of language processes in developing existing areas of interest (Collins &

Cheek, 1993). By acknowledging students' interests, educators demonstrate a value of learning and of the learners themselves (Glasser, 1992). This is the basic premise of the Literacy Workshop for Children (LW), conducted annually on the urban campus of a mid-western university.

Three theories related to the reading process support the LW: first is Rosenblatt's Transactional Theory (1976) where text, reader, and feelings transact to form a personal meaning of text. Second is Mathewson's (1985) model of the reading process, as it suggests that attitudes influence comprehension of text, thereby increasing personal utility of information. High-interests which develop from personal experiences underlie feelings and prompt learners to pursue specific tasks. The interaction between task and attitudes then facilitates comprehension - understanding which allows for transfer of textual information to other learning events. Further examination of research concerning the role of attitude in learning leads to the third theory: Liska's (1984) belief-based model of attitude development. This model describes attitude development as a primary motivator of behavior. Briefly, Liska describes attitude as being dependent on a long-term "average" of beliefs (which are routine, spontaneous evaluations) pertaining to a specific event or idea. Liska's model is cogent to this discussion, in that attitude toward language literacy may motivate children to use language processes to increase information about high-interest topics.

Recognition of children's individual interests - a major component of the LW - ensures development and use of language-centered approaches to investigate interests. By its nature, such process-oriented learning requires students to think about thinking - about their own learning. By using the inner-voice to explore this process, a student is learning to take responsibility for learning (Kuhrt & Ferris, 1990). As a result, organization of short and long term projects in the future may be positively influenced. This notion is based on research on journal writing, specifically, that journaling (in this case, a LW project log) documents decision-making behaviors, problem solving options, and effects of both (Cothern, 1993; D'Arcy, 1987; Macrorie, 1987). Ultimately, the journal or log affirms the responsibilities assumed by the learner. Given that learners' experiences interact reciprocally with tasks, and that attitudes determine willingness to initiate the association, it seems likely that designing and completing high interest projects would be the ideal vehicle for personalized language development.

The instructional approach most often employed in the LW is individualization. After initial language literacy assessments are complete, children are grouped according to interest, rather than age or ability, and are assigned a graduate student mentor who shares a similar interest. Reading, writing, speaking and listening are then developed through group specific, high-interest activities and through project development. The children leave the LW with a project and log - a personal and tangible "history" of the process of authentic research.

Populations Served by the Workshop

The LW serves two populations: graduate students earning a reading endorsement, and local children recommended by teachers, parents, or other interested adults. Newspaper advertisements, campus papers, public service announcements, descriptive pamphlets, and word-of-mouth establish that to be eligible, a child must have completed K, 1st, 2nd, 3rd, 4th, or 5th grade, and be described as *aliterate*, or a "reluctant reader" (a child who does not read for pleasure or information, regardless of ability).

Getting Started

The pre-requisite course for the LW focuses on language arts assessments appropriate for elementary aged children; it is during this course that graduate students are trained regarding LW procedures and assessments. The first three days of the workshop (before children arrive) are devoted to concentrated review of assessments. Students present one or more assessments to the group, along with a typed summary of procedures for administering and scoring the tests. Then, they are given the option of practicing administration of tests to other graduate students, family members, and/or friends (none of the assessments require formal training).

Individual assessments are used to tentatively group children, design basic instructional approaches, and prepare case reports for parents and future teachers. Observational records confirm group appropriateness and provide additional information for planning high interest group activities. Assessments administered by graduate students address cognitive abilities, visual and auditory discrimination, comprehension, knowledge of story structure, spelling development, reading and writing attitudes, beliefs about learning, and interests. These assessments were chosen because they adhere to the philosophical framework of the LW (in terms of utility of knowledge gained, as well as method of acquiring information), are relatively simple to use, are representative of those used by many classroom teachers, and generally require little time to administer and score. Each adheres to current theory suggesting that the testing experience should be a positive one for children, as well as one which provides an illustration of the total child (Pearson & Stillman, 1993; Valencia & Pearson, 1987). Together, the assessments provide information useful in grouping students (interest inventory, learning styles inventory), planning interest specific lessons with ability specific follow up activities (reading/writing attitude scales, informal reading inventory, diagnostic reading test, features list, dictated story, IQ, auditory and visual discrimination), as well as the nature and availability of resources available for support of academic growth (belief statements, interest inventory, attitude scales). When combined with LW observations, graduate students are able to use this information to create a detailed plan for language literacy development which is to be implemented by a team composed of the child, parents, and teacher.

Daily Operations of the LW

Children attend daily from 8:30 - 11:45 a.m., and two Open Houses are scheduled for families to observe and discuss progress (at start and end). On arrival each morning, students participate in a story shared by a guest reader (people from the community or university, parents, graduate students, or other interested adults/families), followed by independent project work time, mentor visits, and/or visits to the computer lab. A time-line of LW activities is presented in Table 1.

As noted above, children are assigned to a group of five to ten peers who share similar interests. Three to five graduate students are randomly grouped and rotate from classroom to classroom on a weekly basis, ensuring opportunities for all students and children to work together. Each child is assigned a graduate student who serves as a mentor, providing suggestions and ensuring that materials are requested and delivered to the appropriate person. See Table 2 for the daily schedule.

A wide variety of materials are used; all are determined by interests and projects. Tuition paid by graduate students, as well as that paid by children ($125.00 each; a few scholarships are donated by philanthropic organizations and local businesses), provides for materials and staff, including a Literacy Workshop Materials and Computer Coordinator (who secures supplies and coordinates computer activities) and an Assistant Director (who oversees LW scheduling and assists in evaluation of graduate students). Children attend the Computer Lab in groups of approximately ten, allowing for one-to-one use of computers with two to four adults for assistance. Use of open-ended software is encouraged, with particular emphasis on word processing and problem solving software. The lab includes a wide variety of programs, so that interest specific software is available for almost all children. Additionally, all students compose at the computer, rather than on paper; revise and edit, then print copies of their own work.

Table 1
Timeline of Literacy Workshop Activities

Week 1	Open House Assessments (children attend 1 morning) Group children according to learning interests Assign graduate student mentors to children
Week 2	Begin daily activities (children attend daily): - story reading - computer lab (alternate days; for project related work only) - review projects from previous years - decide on and plan project
Week 3	Continue daily activities - story reading - computer lab time, as needed - complete project calendar - acquire materials for project - begin project
Week 4	Continue daily activities - story reading - computer lab time, as needed - work on project - revise calendar daily (as needed) - write project journal entries
Week 5	Continue daily activities - story reading - complete projects - revise calendar daily (as needed) - write project journal entries - Open House (last day for children)
Week 6	Complete case reports Conduct Parent conferences

Table 2
Daily Schedule

8:30	Guest Reader Announcements
9:00	Move to rooms for high interest group activity
9:45	Independent reading and/or writing time
10:05	Break
10:20	Meet with graduate student mentors to review progress
10:35	Project work time Computer lab as needed
11:30	Review calendar and write daily log entry
11:45	Dismissal

As materials are determined by projects, no formal prepared reading programs, managements systems, or kits are used. There is a heavy reliance on picture books, and several are read daily: the guest reader's choice for the whole group, small group readings in classrooms of about eight children (read by graduate students and/or volunteer children), and independent reading. Novels and picture books may be checked out by children for reading at home with family members. Other materials are usually brought in by students, and pertain to high interest activities designed for specific groups of children in classrooms. Past workshop activities for high interest group work have included cooking; study of bubbles, animals, and natural disasters; completing three dimensional art activities; sewing; and music. All of these included reading, art, and creative writing using all steps of the writing process. Fortunately, a well-equipped Learning Resource Center is available on campus, which assists by taking numerous photographs, audio/videotaping, and advising regarding artistic media options.

During the process of project completion, books pertaining to children's interests are purchased and students are encouraged to write and/or call professionals who may be able to offer assistance or grant interviews related to children's interests. Children's projects to date include but are not limited to the following: producing a claymation film; choreographing and performing dances; producing "how to" videos on baseball, football, soccer, and hockey; comparing sports-related statistics, then recording information in tabular form; authoring books; building models; writing and dramatizing poetry, and an historical skit of First Ladies; designing and building furniture, a birdhouse, a doghouse, and a model home; studying landscape architecture and creating models of plans; creating a three-dimensional mural of dinosaurs depicted in habitats; building and launching a rocket; studying guns and building a model gun from "junk"; making hair bows; compiling a written review of current software for children; writing and performing jump-rope chants; interviewing prominent authors on the telephone; composing several Garfield books; producing videos of "handi-capable" baseball and bowling; tie-dying t-shirts; studying animals and creating two-/three-dimensional displays; constructing a lighted model of a submarine; researching historical and/ or sports figures; compiling a photographic insect collection; and creating a model of a rain forest. Each day, children meet with mentors to review daily progress, and revise their project calendar as needed (see Figure 1). The routine contact between learners who are on a first-name basis emphasizes the cooperative and social aspects of acquiring knowledge and refining skills.

Graduate students and staff also complete projects, although theirs cannot be related to the profession of education. The purpose of this is for children to have the opportunity to experience working with teachers who are also actively seeking personally meaningful knowledge and/or skills. In traditional instruction offered during the academic year, children rarely share learning experiences with teachers - experiences in which the teacher is truly in the role of learner. The workshop offers children the chance to see, day by day, mature learning behaviors of mentors. Like the children, students discuss projects with a child or peer sharing similar interests, plan with calendars, and write daily project journal entries. Graduate student projects have included the following: planning and planting an herbal and a perennial garden; sewing curtains, dresses, maternity clothes; building birdhouses; painting gourds; writing poetry; decorating sweat shirts; designing and creating seasonal paintings; arranging dried flowers; writing a "Christmas Traditions" book; compiling a family cookbook; sketching vegetables; compiling a LW Literary Magazine, and designing and making miscellaneous crafts. At the final Open House, all project-related writing is displayed, all books used as references, and completed projects. During the Open House, children share their projects with family members, guests of new friends made during the LW, and university employees who join families in viewing children's and students' work. Interestingly, children's comments in sharing their mentors' projects

64

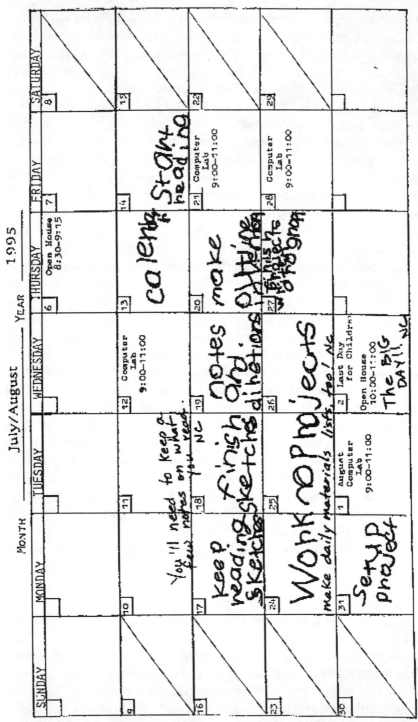

Figure 1. Sample Project Calendar

Table 3A
Background Information

Student: Katie, 12 years of age (entering 6th grade)

Reading Levels: 5th (independent; 6th (instructional), 7th (frustration), 8th (listening)

Comprehension: generally below level, although her well-developed general knowledge base seemed to facilitate understanding

Attitudes: school reading - negative; recreational reading - positive; writing - neutral

I.Q.: 102

Features List: transitional speller

Dictated Story: high use of "book language", appropriate volume, pitch, rate of speech; all story elements present except resolution/theme

Interests: enjoys family activities, even though her brother is "hard to take sometimes"; wishes that both parents did not have to work; has friends at school, but few in her neighborhood; enjoys reading/drawing about nature - rainforests in particular

---

are no less enthusiastic than when sharing their own projects.

The last week of the LW is devoted to parent conferences, during which the formal case report is discussed. The case report is comprehensive, including a description of the testing environment, the child's behavior during testing, bibliographic information and a brief description of each assessment, scores, a list of strengths and areas to be developed, and recommendations for the child, parents, and teacher (See Tables 3A and 3B).

As seen in Table 3B, recommendations are interrelated, so that each party has an opportunity to contribute to each activity. The team approach used in recommendations encourages transfer of learning from school to home and from subject to subject, illustrating to children how interests and academics overlap, providing support for one another.

Tabel 3 B
<u>Sample Recommendations</u>

Activity	Child	Parent	Teacher
nature walk	Draw a route for a neighborhood nature walk; invite a few school friends, if possible	Plan natural snacks to be eaten during/ after the walk; mail invitations created by Katie to school friends during class	Plan class nature walk; ask Katie & friends to map route and serve as guides; share nature picture books
family meal	Plan a special meal for tired, working parents; solicit help from brother; survey parents for favorites; find recipes for approval; organize area; prepare meal	Assist in securing ingredients and organizing work area; review safety rules; dress for the meal; write thank you note to children	Provide bibliotherapy about sibling relations and working parents; plan a writing lesson involving interviewing of family members; then develop & host a "Getting to Know You Newscast" for visitors who are invited to lunch
letter writing	Read magazines focusing on the environment; choose an area of concern and write a letter to an elected official stating concerns	Purchase print sources for environmental information; attend a local Audubon/Sierra Club meeting; assist Katie in securing name/address of appropriate offical; proof letter	Collect printed information on area(s) of students' concerns (current events); plan a panel discussion including elected officials and/or representatives from local organizations; write a class editorial to be submitted to local paper

Examining Effects of the LW

Belief statements, the primary means for evaluating effects of the LW, are collected pre-/post workshop, then examined for differences (Cothern, 1989). Children are asked to sit/lie comfortably, with eyes closed, and are led through several deep breathing exercises to increase relaxation and decrease attention to distractions. Then the examiner asks children to imagine their classroom from last year. All senses are involved by asking them to imagine the classroom from sitting in a desk, standing in the doorway, and from group areas; to picture the teacher's face and hear his/her voice; to recall aromas in the room, and to think about favorite lessons and subjects. After approximately three minutes of imaging to verbal prompts, graduate students approach the children individually and ask them to complete the sentence, "I believe learning...". The graduate students write the child's responses on paper. The same procedure is used post-workshop, except the imaging questions pertain to the activities, teachers, and building used in the workshop. Responses are then evaluated for differences. Specific procedures and sample belief statements are discussed in proceeding paragraphs.

Initial analyses of stated beliefs indicate that students view LW learning as being significantly different from school learning. Category development was data driven, and all beliefs were categorized as representing one of five levels (first being lower-level and five being higher-level). The first level of is *no evidence of learning*, which includes comments which do not reflect learning new information or expanding knowledge; and non-specific mentioning of subject areas or units of study (examples: Learning is important to my future. Handwriting is fun.) The second level, *social aspects of the learning environment*, includes non-specific comments about peers and/or teachers which are unrelated to acquiring and/or expanding knowledge (examples: She gave us tests that were too hard. Bill was my best friend in the class). Third, *learning as a process*, including comments focusing on decision making, problem solving, relationships between knowledge, and/or learning over time (examples: Learning is deciding what to do. Learning here was kind of weird and hard to do but it was fun when it was done). The fourth level, *learning as dependent on environment* (texts, experiences, and/or other learners), is characterized by comments about relationships between bodies of knowledge, previous learning, cooperative learning, peer-tutoring, peer-evaluation (examples: You must know how to read a paper or a book so you can help each other. Writing on the computer helps me know about what I read). Fifth, *learning as enabling*, includes comments about effects of learning, both personal and societal, short or long term (examples: When my friends learn, I learn. I did finish my project and now I like to read).

The categories above were developed as a result of examination of data collected over three years. Categories were ranked to indicate level of involvement (one representing lowest level and five representing highest level). The development and ranking of levels is based on an existing scale to measure degree of aesthetic involvement literary experiences (Many, Wiseman, & Altieri, 1992) and levels address behaviors necessary for problem-solving in future learning (Farr, 1992). More specifically, level one represents lack of awareness of tasks, level two addresses recognizing a task, level three addresses development of strategies to accomplish the task, level four addresses the need to determine when and where to seek assistance, and level five addresses self- and peer-evaluations of progress (Wade & Reynolds, 1989). In theory, advancement through the five levels develops children's abilities to apply the same or an adapted process to another task (Wang & Palinscar, 1989).

The categories above emerged consistently in pre-/post-LW belief statements, although approximately five percent of student responses were not used due to incoherence or illegibility. Most often, comments representing categories one and two, were recorded pre-LW (72% pre; 35% post), while comments in categories three, four, and five were found in post-LW beliefs (23% pre; 60% post). Sample pre-/post-LW belief statements of participants aged 7-12 are found in Table 4.

Post-LW comments reveal that children valued the opportunity to make decisions about their learning, that they sometimes learned with and because of others, they valued the process of interacting, and appreciated the responsibility such interaction holds. These comments reveal a crucial self-awareness in the learning process (Garner, 1987), one which is apparently not prominent in LW students' regular school learning. Given children's comments, it is possible that project-associated writing may serve as a vehicle for understanding how and why learners elect to pursue specific tasks. Ultimately, the project log becomes a tangible record of learning (Calkins, 1991; DeFina, 1992). As a participant-observer in this process, learners are simultaneously observing, modeling, practicing, and evaluating mature learning habits which require facile use of language processes. Given the long-term goal of education - the creation of life-long learners - it is reasonable to assume that such a process-oriented, language-based learning collaboration is an ideal place to begin.

It should be noted that the program described above is not ideally suited to the traditional academic year as currently structured. Studies of other

Table 4
Sample Belief Statements from Children Aged 7 - 12 Years

Pre-Literacy Workshop	Post Literacy Workshop
Handwriting is fun.	I got done with my project and now I
I play the computer.	like to read.
I like Tom.	
I like Math the most at school	I believe learning is concentrating,
My teacher was nice.	figuring things out and sometimes
I learn at lot of things at my school.	having fun.
I was good at Math.	I believe learning is about stories of a
I believe learning is important to	long time ago.
my future.	I read the baseball book and now I
The librarian was boring.	read more books.
Gym is cool, too.	My favorite thing about learning
I believe learning is a nuisance.	is drawing.
I believe learning is something	We are doing different things to
everybody needs.	learn with different people.
She gave us tests that were too hard.	I think learning is a little fun
We have to read a lot.	because my project was
We did take-aways and plusses.	very, very, very, very,
You have to sit at a desk all day	very, very fun to do!
and say yes or no.	You must know how to read
I like to eat lunch.	paper or a book so you can help
I'd rather be cleaning my fish tank	each other.
or skate boarding.	Learning is different from knowing.
Science is cool.	Learning is deciding what to do.
I believe learning is a little fun.	Learning only gets better when
	there's no worksheets.
	Learning my project was hard.
	I believe learning here is weird - kind
	of different.
	I feel proud of my project because I
	did do much good work.
	When my friends learn I learn.

process-oriented literacy strategies indicate that transfer of learning may occur with occasional implementation (Cothern, 1989; 1993). In the regular school climate, normal constraints of budget, space, materials, and pupil-teacher ratio preclude on-going use of projects. Rather that omitting such rich learning experiences, projects may be completed on a semester or quarterly basis, perhaps by groups of like-minded children, and referred to regularly during routine instruction.

Evidence of the theoretical soundness of the LW can be found in belief statements collected over the three years the LW has been conducted. Children state that learning in the workshop is different than that experienced in school: workshop learning is process-oriented, social in nature, requires decision-making, and has short- and long-term effects. While parent comments are fewer and generally less specific, several have indicated that their children are more organized, more willing to start, better able to complete long term tasks , engage in more non-fiction reading to support content area assignments, and are more easily engaged in literary activities, in general:

> "Chris didn't like the writing he had to do to finish his project, but this year he has had to write more in social studies and science. I think the reading program taught him how to use writing in these areas."

> "The work they did on their projects seemed to be one of the most important parts of the workshop. They are so pleased and proud of their finished products."

> "The planning and organization he had to do each day carried through his daily school work."
> "The program was great! Tiffany reads more and actually wants to read."

> "Jenny seemed more organized this year. Maybe she's growing up, but I think her projects at the literacy workshop helped her know how to go about things better."

> "Claire has really enjoyed this program. I can really see an improvement in her writing ability and her confidence in reading and writing."

Children who are not motivated will not put forth the effort to learn. If literacy is to be developed, learners must be willing to undertake investigations requiring that they gain and apply knowledge which is cumulative in nature and of substance. Educators who demonstrate to children that learners themselves are valued - and the obvious place to begin is by valuing children's interests - are a giant leap closer to facilitating life-long, mature learning behaviors in their students.

References

Calkins, L. (1991). *Living between the lines*. Portsmouth, NH: Heinemann.

Collins, M., & Cheek, E. (1993). *Diagnostic-prescriptive reading instruction: A guide for classroom teachers*, (4th ed.) Madison, WI: Brown and Benchmark.

Cothern, N. (1989). The effects of personal journals on fourth grade students' attitudes toward reading and writing. Unpublished doctoral dissertation, Louisiana State University, Baton Rouge, LA.

Cothern, N. (1993). E.R.M.A.A.: A strategy affirming the individuality of response. *Reading Research and Instruction, 32*, 1-14.

D'Arcy, P. (1987). Writing to learn. In T. Fulwiler (Ed.), *The journal book*. (41-46). New Hampshire: Boynton-Cook.

DeFina, A. (1992). *Portfolio assessment: Getting started*. New York: Scholastic.

Farr, R. (1992). Putting it all together: Solving the reading assessment puzzle. *The Reading Teacher, 46*, 26-36.

Garner, R. (1987). *Metacognition and reading comprehension*. Norwood, NJ: Ablex.

Glasser, W. (1992). *The Quality School: Managing students without coercion*. NY: Harper.

Kuhrt, B., & Farris, P. (1990). Empowering student through reading, writing, and reasoning. *Journal of Reading, 33*, 436-441.

Many, J. E., Wiseman, D. E., & Altieri, J. L. (1992). Enabling complex aesthetic responses: An examination of three literary discussion approaches. In C. Kinzen & D. Leu (Eds.), *Literacy research theory and practice: Views from many perspectives,* (pp. 283 - 290), Forty first Yearbook of the National Reading Conference.

Macrorie, S. (1987). Foreword. In T. Fulwiler (Ed.), *The journal book*. New Hampshire: Boynton-Cook.

Mathewson, G. (1985). Toward a comprehensive model of affect in the reading process. In H. Singer & B. Rudell (Eds.), *Theoretical models and process of reading* (3rd. ed., p. 841-856). Newark, DE: International Reading Association.

Pearson, P. D., & Stallman, A. (1993). Approaches to the future of reading assessment: Resistance, complacency, reform. *Technical Report No. 575*. Urbana, IL: Center for the Study of Reading.

Rosenblatt, L. (1976). *Literature as exploration*. New York: Harcourt Brace & World.

Valencia, S, & Pearson, P. D. (1987). Reading assessment: Time for a change. *The Reading Teacher, 40*, 726-32.

Wade, S., & Reynolds, R. (1989). Developing students' metacognitive awareness may be essential to effective strategy instruction. *Journal of Reading, 33*, 6-15.

Wang, M., & Palincsar, A. (1989). Teaching students to assume an active role in their learning. In M. Reynolds (Ed.), *Knowledge base for the beginning teacher*. NY: Pergamon.

73

Section Two

Literacy Assessment Through Portfolios

Involving Graduate Students in Personal Literacy Evaluation Through the Use of Portfolios

Diane D. Allen

University of North Texas

Portfolio assessment is a means of assessment used to determine reading and writing proficiency. In this chapter, graduate students were led through a process of developing their personal reading and writing portfolios as a means of learning how to guide their school students in portfolio development.

For years educators at all levels have used standardized test scores to explain and document student performance in the areas of reading and writing. These tests reflected the belief that reading could be broken down into discrete skills which could be measured by multiple choice test items. However, research now supports the view of reading as an transactive, constructive process (Rosenblatt, 1978, 1983; Halliday, 1975). This view has forced educators to address the weaknesses of such standardized assessment tools.

Standardized tests, similarly constructed class tests, and worksheets do not give a complete picture of the growth of readers over time in authentic situations (Wixson & Peters, 1987; Wiggins, 1993). Because they are timed, such tests often penalize slower readers and writers. Moreover, such tests provide little information that helps teachers and/or parents to understand how children approach print and attempt to make sense of the process. This need for alternative assessments has led educators to investigate the use of portfolios to document readers' growth and development in reading and writing (Goldman, 1989; Glazer & Brown, 1993).

Research indicates that using personal portfolios as an alternative to standardized measures provides a broader picture of student growth in literacy learning (Anthony, Johnson, Mickelson, & Preege, 1991; Glazer & Brown, 1993; Kritt, 1993), especially that of slower readers and writers (Jongsma, 1989; Simmons, 1990). Studies by Jongsma and Simmons indicated that those students who scored lowest on standardized, timed tests of writing skills ranked among the average writers when given the opportunity to select and submit writing samples collected during the school year.

If portfolios are to become a means of assessment and evaluation in a majority of elementary classrooms, then more teachers will need to become familiar with their design and use. To that end, several universities have begun experimenting with portfolio use in undergraduate teacher preparation (Hauser, 1994; MacIsaac & Jackson, 1994; Murnane, 1994) and graduate programs (MacIsaac & Jackson, 1994; Palmer, 1994).

Portfolios have been used in a variety of ways at the university level. They have been used as assessments for growth in individual coursework (Stowell, McDaniel, Rios, & Kelly, 1993; Hauser, 1994; Murnane, 1994) and as exit assessments for programs of study (MacIsaac & Jackson, 1994; Palmer, 1994). Regardless of the format or purpose of these portfolios, providing undergraduate and graduate education students with opportunities to experience the development and use of portfolios is crucial to the implementation of portfolios by these students in their own classrooms.

Course Description

The activities described in this paper were conducted with a master's level reading assessment/evaluation course. As part of the course requirements, each graduate student worked individually with an elementary student for 10 one hour sessions. These sessions were conducted under the supervision of the course instructor at the university reading clinic. The graduate students developed portfolios with the children in an effort to provide evidence of the children's growth in reading/writing during the term. Therefore, it was important for the graduate students to develop an understanding and an appreciation of portfolios for assessment purposes.

Seven female graduate students participated in the portfolio project. Six of these were elementary classroom teachers; one was an instructor at a junior college. None of these teachers reported the use of portfolios in her own classroom; several expressed lack of knowledge of the concept.

The overall purpose of this course was to introduce the students to the use, development and benefits of a variety of portfolio formats they could use in their own classrooms. Several activities designed to promote this understanding are described in the next section.

Activities

Activity One

At the initial class meeting I introduced the concept of personal literacy portfolios by using my own personal literacy portfolio as an example. As an introduction I told the students some "standard" information about my educational background including information about my degrees, number of years as a classroom teacher, number of years as a reading specialist, and number and types of experiences in higher education. After my introduction I asked the class to break into two groups. Their task was to write down things they could infer about me as a reader/writer from the information I had provided in the brief introduction. Also, they were to decide what information they needed or wanted to know about me as a reader/writer. Each group had an opportunity to share their responses with the class. The class agreed that it was difficult to know much about my personal and professional literacy from just a few bits of data. At this particular time I refrained from providing any feedback to either the statements or the questions. However, I did point out that we often make judgments about children's reading/writing abilities based on such limited information.

The next part of this activity involved the two groups again. I gave each group a copy of my personal portfolio (developed and abridged for this course) which contained documentation of my personal and professional literacy endeavors. The artifacts included a list of children's books in my personal library; a personal reading list; my public library card; professional journals to which I subscribed; other professional journals which I surveyed monthly; a "to do" list; a list of people to whom I write regularly; and copies of professional articles and memos which I have written. I explained that one purpose of portfolios was to document or provide evidence of the person's reading/writing strengths and weaknesses. A second purpose was to provide direction for future growth. In the group they were to discuss once again what they could learn about me as a reader/writer from my literacy portfolio. Several questions helped to focus their discussions. (1) What artifacts were present and what did they suggest? (2) What questions from the previous activity could now be answered? (3) What new questions did the students have about me? (4) For what other areas of reading/writing did they need information?

The discussions in each group were animated, and all members were actively involved. A spokesperson from each group presented a profile of me as a reader and writer to the class. As each made her presentation, she had to point out the artifact(s) from the portfolio that helped the group reach that particular conclusion. Each group also made suggestions as to the future direction both my personal and professional reading and writing might take. As expected, the identification of suggestions was difficult for both groups. Students found it risky to make such suggestions to a professor/teacher who would ultimately award a course grade.

Discussion revealed that the students in this class learned three important things from this activity. First, they learned that by examining the artifacts in my portfolio they were able to infer much about me as a reader/writer. They learned what I liked to read and write as well as the extent to which I participate in reading and writing. This gave them clues from which to draw conclusions about my abilities and interests as a literate person. The "standard" data gave a rather flat perspective of me; the portfolio made me seem more real.

Secondly, when the two groups presented their profiles to the class, they discovered that each group had drawn some different conclusions from the same material. They had to ask me, the reader/writer, what I intended when I included the information. It was important to consider why I had selected some documents and not included others. Thus, these teachers discovered that readers and writers must be included in the evaluation of their personal portfolios in order for teachers and others to draw valid conclusions about the contents.

Finally, these graduate students acknowledged the importance of viewing all types of reading/writing activities when evaluating or assessing a student. They realized that standardized measures rarely document the constructive, transactive nature of the reading process.

Activity Two

For the second class meeting the students were asked to create their own literacy portfolios. They were encouraged to organize and package their portfolio in any way; however, the majority of the students followed the example which I had presented at the first class meeting.

Student shared their portfolios with a partner. They chose partners they had not known previously so that the portolio information would be new to them. Each student was asked to study their partner's portfolio, list information learned about the person related to reading/writing, and list questions designed to help gather more information or to clarify portfolio contents. After studying each other's portfolios, the partners met for the purpose of answering the aforementioned questions.

During the second part of the activity each student introduced her partner to the rest of the class based upon information obtained from the portfolio. The students were surprised at the wealth of information they learned about each other from a variety of documents. The artifacts themselves were varied and included such things as lists of books read and reactions to those books, professional journal covers, lesson plans, cookbook pages, checkbook registers, personal poetry, letters written to the editor of a local newspaper, and letters to families and friends. The students were often surprised as well by the inaccurate conclusions reached by their partners and realized the need for the inclusion of their own evaluation of their work.

Activity Three

Although I had already planned this activity, it occurred almost as a natural progression from the second activity. I asked the students to review their personal portfolios and to write one page describing themselves as readers and writers and to explain why this portfolio was representative of their literacy. This would serve as the introduction to the literacy portfolio.

These summaries/evaluations were quite revealing. The most valuable piece of information gained from reading them was that several members of the class did not perceive of themselves as readers. Some actual quotations from these papers illustrates this:

> "I would like to spend more time on personal reading in a sense that I want to train myself to make personal reading a daily event. I feel that my lack of reading experience has hurt me educationally...."

> "I'm not the type of person to pick up a novel and read."

Most of these students revealed that they are writers of functional text, such as notes, lists, recipes and lesson outlines. As one student stated, "I'm a note writer....I have never been fond of writing papers or poetry." Only two people considered themselves "real" writers. One student has written a poem which she uses to introduce herself to each new class that she teaches. The other writer in our group frequently pens political brochures and letters to the editor.

Lastly, it was encouraging to me that all of the students expressed the desire to expand their reading and writing. However, most mentioned the time constraints of being both a teacher and a student as an obstacle to reading or writing more. One student described her dilemma this way:

> "As a reader I'm working on learning to enjoy books more for pleasure than an assignment but find little time between school and teaching. I do enjoy books where I can read short excerpts that only take a few minutes."

After our discussions about finding more time to read and write professional as well as personal texts, the students identified and recorded personal growth goals. These goals were placed in their portfolios and will be the measures by which they determine their own literacy growth in the future.

Summary

The graduate students enrolled in an assessment course were introduced to the development and use of personal literacy portfolios through three activities. They examined the instructor's personal portfolio and made observations related to her reading and writing; they created their own literacy portfolios; and they reflected upon and described themselves as literacy learners.

Each graduate student used her personal literacy portfolio to introduce the concept of the portfolio to to the child they tutored in much the same way that I used my personal portfolio at the beginning of the semester. This introduction helped the children to visualize ways in which they might work with their tutor to create their own portfolios of the work completed in the tutoring sessions.

All of these activities proved valuable to this group of graduate students. They learned to evaluate their own literacy and to set goals for expanding their reading and writing. By using what they had learned from the development of their own literacy portfolios they were able to assist young readers who had not previously been very successful in reading develop their own portfolios and begin to evaluate their own reading growth.

References

Anthony, R. J., Johnson, T. D., Mickelson, N. I., & Preece, A. (1991). *Evaluating literacy: A perspective for change.* Portsmouth, NH: Heinemann.

Glazer, S. M., & Brown, C. S. (1993). *Portfolios and beyond: Collaborative assessment in reading and writing.* Norwood, MA: Christopher-Gordon.

Goldman, J. P. (1989). Student portfolios already proven in some schools. *School Administrator, 46,* 11.

Halliday, M. A. K. (1975). *Learning how to mean.* New York: Elsevier North-Holland.

Hauser, J. (1994). Teacher preparation curriculums and portfolio assessments. Paper presented at the Linking the Liberal Arts and Teacher Education Conference, San Diego.

Jongsma, K. S. (1989). Portfolio assessment. *The Reading Teacher, 43,* 264-265.

Kritt, D. (1993). Authenticity, reflection, and self-evaluation in alternative assessment. *Middle School Journal, 25*, 43-45.

MacIsaac, D., & Jackson, L. (1994). Portfolio use within the College of Education at the University of Northern Colorado: Current practices and future directions. Paper presented at the Linking the Liberal Arts and Teacher Education Conference, San Diego.

Murnane, Y. (1994). Portfolio use in higher education: A primer. Paper presented at the Linking the Liberal Arts and Teacher Education Conference, San Diego.

Palmer, B. M. (1994). Trends in assessment: The M.Ed. portfolio. Paper presented at the College Reading Association Conference, New Orleans.

Rosenblatt, L. (1978). *The reader, the text and the poem.* Carbondale: Southern Illinois University Press.

Rosenblatt, L. (1983). *Literature as exploration.* New York: Modern Language Association.

Simmons, J. (1990). Portfolios as large-scale assessment. *Language Arts, 67*, 262-268.

Stowell, L. P., McDaniel, J. E., Rios, F. A., & Kelly, M. G. (1993). Casting wide the net: Portfolio assessment in teacher education. *Middle School Journal, 25*, 61-67.

Wiggins, G. (1993). Assessment: Authenticity, context, and validity. *Phi Delta Kappan, 74*, 200-214.

Wixson, K., & Peters, C. (1987). Comprehension assessment: Implementing an interactive view of reading. *Educational Psychologist, 21*, 333-356.

Teachers as Learners: Experiencing Self-Evaluation, Portfolios and Rubrics

Michael P. Ford

University of Wisconsin - Oshkosh

For many different reasons, educators at all levels of education are exploring the use of portfolios (Ohlausen, Perkins & Jones, 1993). Not surprisingly, an increasing number of teacher educators are discussing the use of portfolios within their programs (French & Foster, 1992; Mosenthal, Daniels & Merkkelsen, 1992; Ohlhausen & Ford, 1992; Stowell, 1993). While conceptualizations of these portfolios differ, the time has come for teacher educators to practice what we preach (Stahle & Mitchell, 1993) and to encourage students to do as we do (Vogt, McLaughlin, & Rapp Ruddell, 1993) by using portfolio assessment in our university courses.

My Context

I began experimenting with portfolios in 1990. My primary use of portfolios as described in this article is within the context of a graduate course entitled "Whole Language: Issues and Implications." It was during the teaching of the course that I first began using portfolios. I wanted to present the use of portfolios to the class and concluded that the best way to do this was to actively involve my students in using portfolios to document their learning. I discovered that portfolios were not only an effective way for my students to access content, but also a way for me to align my assessment with my instructional beliefs. The portfolio was also a success vehicle for making students responsible for their own learning. It encouraged students to not only document, but direct their learning. During the 1994 spring semester, I was able to closely examine students as they encountered the portfolio process. I will begin by describing the implementation of portfolios in this class and then present profiles of three students' use of portfolios.

As we acknowledged this preoccupation with grades and how it often influences what we did as learners and teachers, we shifted our attention to developing a frame for working within this constraint. We examined the concept of rubrics (Routman, 1991) and began to co-construct a rubric to help guide learning in the course. Students identified behaviors they believed constituted "A" level performance in a graduate course. These lists of expectations were compiled into a list of 39 behaviors. These became the basis for discussions as we worked to reach consensus on a rubric that would be used in the course. The behaviors were organized into five categories: (a) acquires knowledge inside and outside the classroom, (b) applied what has been learned, (c) shares knowledge with others, (d) empowers and engages self, and (e) displays a positive attitude toward learning. Students agreed on the qualifying labels "consistent" and "inconsistent" to judge the behaviors and that a student must show consistent behavior in four of the five categories to receive an "A" in the course.

The rubric provided a foundation for discussions on how to develop a learning portfolio. In the past, I had assumed that the teachers with whom I worked had little knowledge about the portfolio process (Johns & VanLeirsburg, 1991). Since then, however, the intense focus on classroom use of portfolios as an alternative assessment technique (Cramer, 1993; DeFina, 1992; Tierney, Carter & Desai, 1991) has caused most students to enter my course with some knowledge of portfolios. Thus, I shifted my initial discussion from defining portfolios to describing the four different types: moving vans, activity-based, goal-based and reflective (Vavrus, 1990). The learning portfolio in this course was intended to be more than just a collection of "stuff" or a collection of activities prescribed by the instructor (Stahle & Mitchell, 1993). I wanted to move students toward the use of a reflective or goal-based portfolio, wherein reflective "captions" are attached to each piece of evidence. This encouraged students to think about the portfolio as more of a process than a product.

The process of developing this type of learning portfolio began with self-assessment. Students were asked to reflect on their knowledge of language, their current classroom practices and their personal habits as language users. This examination, with consideration of the rubric behaviors, allowed students with consideration of the rubric behaviors, allowed students to develop personal goals toward which to direct their learning. In class, we discussed how learners could provide evidence that they were making progress toward the goals and satisfying the rubric standards. Students identified a number of ways to document their growth and change during the course (reading logs, response journals, samples of children's work, etc.). Following this discussion, students were invited to embark on the process.

Students were encouraged to start the process as quickly as possible. I asked students to bring "embryonic" portfolios to class and share these in-progress portfolios with partners, thus providing an opportunity for students to assist each other in clarifying the process. I also asked students to write an initial "Dear Reviewer" letter to provide information about their goals and plans for documenting progress towards those goals. This also allowed me to provide individual feedback to students be fore their portfolios were finalized.

The learning portfolios played an integral role in the class. Students learned about alternative forms of assessment through direct experience and saw how the line between instruction and assessment could be blurred in their own classrooms. As students continued to develop their portfolios, I involved them in peer sharing, provided opportunities to ask questions, and conducted mini-lessons as needed.

For example, we spent time examining the role of captions. We analyzed how some learners used their captions to not only identify their evidence, but also to contextualize and connect it to their goals to show growth and change. About midterm, I asked them to write a second "Dear Reviewer" letter discussing their progress. They submitted this with their portfolios allowing me to review what they had done so far. I provided extensive feedback in a "Dear Learner" letter and scheduled conferences to discuss their progress in terms of their goals and the rubric standards.

Most students were well on their way to directing and documenting their own learning. We continued to provide class time for sharing. We discussed issues such as the possibility of changing or omitting certain goals (concluding since the process is dynamic that this is possible.) As the semester ended, closure was needed. Students assembled their evidence, reflected upon it and graded themselves based upon the learning that resulted from their participation in the course. At this point, the students prepared a final "Dear Reviewer" letter that provided a written rationale for their grading decision. The instructor emphasized the need to provide evidence supporting the rationale and reminded students to use the rubric as a guide in making their grading decision. I met with students individually so they could share their evidence with me and discuss their grading decisions. Following each conference, I collected the portfolios and provided additional written feedback.

This type of learning portfolio differed from common conceptualizations of portfolios as often used in teacher education programs. This was not a notebook in which students collected and gathered everything they could find, a showcase where they presented their best work, or a collection of predetermined assignments. This portfolio was a way for students to document growth and change that resulted from participation in the course. Students determined their goals based on self-assessment, documented their progress based on evidence they selected, and determined their final grade based on that evidence and group determined standards.

It was a way of inviting students to take control of their learning. The portfolio was not just another final product left with the instructor to be graded, but represented the final step of a recursive process beginning and ending with self-assessment.

This type of assessment requires instructors to reexamine their role within the learning environment. Initially, the instructor must act as a catalyst to get students to self-assess and set goals. Instructors may model these processes by initiating their own portfolios. Instructors may share sample portfolios from previous students or even invite those students to share their portfolios with the new students. The instructor should also provide opportunities for students to share their initial efforts with one another so that they can work together to answer questions as they start the process. Finally, the instructor needs to provide early response to students to assure them that they are on the right track. In the initial stages, the challenge for the instructor is to clarify the process without directing it.

Time and response are critical to the portfolio development process. The instructor should provide time for the portfolio process to become an integral part of the class routine. The instructor also must respond to each student's portfolio and/or structure the opportunity for peer response. At the end, the instructor assumes the role of an outside reviewer. If conferences are used, the instructor often becomes the audience for students as they present their final portfolios. Without conferences, the instructor must examine the portfolio as it stands on its own merits. At this point, the primary role of the instructor is to review (and if necessary, challenge) the self-assessment decision of the student.

The Study

This study focused on three graduate students (within a class of six) as they encountered the portfolio process for the first time. Each was asked to complete a learning portfolio as a self-evaluation component for a fourteen-week graduate reading course. The portfolio component accounted for 70% of their grade while attendance and participation accounted for 30%. I was interested in learning what goals they would select to direct their own learning, how they would document that learning, and how they would evaluate their learning in the end. Data were collected on an ongoing basis as the instructor met with the students. A variety of sources were used including pre and post responses to survey questions regarding self-evaluation, portfolios and rubrics; comments re corded during class discussions and individual conferences; anecdotal information about individual students recorded in a field notebook; and examinations of items shared by students in class and in their portfolios.

The primary data sources for this study were the students' learning portfolios. Each portfolio was carefully reviewed twice during the course; in-progress portfolios were reviewed at the halfway point and final portfolios were examined at the end of the semester. Close examinations of the portfolios included noting descriptions of the format; king, quantity and quality of the evidence; and degree of captioning and/or reflection within the portfolio. I relied primarily on these data to compile brief case studies of each student and to tell the story of how each student moved through the portfolio process. I examined these stories to find common threads and contrasts between these cases and between my work and the work of other teacher educators.

Dominic

The Plan. Dominic was a veteran secondary teacher who after spending much of his career in technical education was not teaching English. He decided to take this course as his final elective in the masters degree in reading program. Dominic's interest in whole language was two-fold. His primary interest was in "elements of whole language instruction that could be used in the high school classroom as a part of different content areas when the system in the school is not whole language based." In addition, his involvement with graduate work in reading meant that many of his colleagues would ask him to explain what elementary teachers were doing in their whole language class-rooms. Dominic wanted to be able to provide articulate responses to these questions. To document his learning, he identified five tasks: (a) journaling after each class session, (b) collecting practical ideas, (c) writing short reviews of journal articles, (d) bringing materials and ideas to class, and (e) becoming involved with the district reading committee and staff development opportunities. Each task had potential to also provide evidence satisfying the rubric standards.

The Portfolio. Dominic's "Whole Language Portfolio" was continued in a white expandable folder. It contained five separate folders labeled assessment, application and practice, professional involvement, journal, sharing and knowledge acquisition/research. The assessment folder primarily contained documents related to self-assessment required throughout the portfolio process (i.e., Dear Reviewer Letters, instructor responses, final statement). In the application and practice folder, Dominic included samples of student work to illustrate one significant change in his practice. This change involved shift from the use of a discussion-study guide-essay exam format to the use of a reader-response format in his teaching of the novel *Lord of the Flies*. He also included materials collected to set up guidelines for using writer's workshop and thematic instruction in the future. The professional involvement folder contained evidence documenting his activity with the district language arts committee including captioned memos and materials from meetings. In the journal folder, Dominic included his response journal containing weekly reflections on his reading and thinking related to class issues and ideas, including responses to his self-selected outside text Nancy Atwell's *In the Middle* (Atwell, 1987) The sharing folder contained two portfolio-related new articles he shared in class. The knowledge folder contained two journal articles with attached reactions and one set of eight related ERIC abstracts "that best represent my own interests and needs" with brief reactions. Each folder contained a letter explaining the evidence inside. All the evidence was captioned with explanations of what it was and how it indicated progress toward his goals.

The Evaluation. Dominic awarded himself 63 out of 70 points, rating his performance on the lower end of the A range (90%). He acknowledged that his goals had expanded "to include things that I could use in my own classes regardless of the programs used in the school." In his rationale, he directly linked evidence in his portfolio to all five of the rubric standards. For example, he offered his journal as evidence that he had applied what he had learned (standard #2) and had been consistently engaged throughout the course (standard #4). He indicated when he had been successful at accomplishing his goals and when he had fallen short. In describing his research efforts, he admitted that he "did not get as much of this" as he had liked with time and distance interfering with his ability to get access to the library. He concluded that he had "shown consistency in all five areas of the rubric and as a result should receive an A." Dominic observed that portfolios "are the practical way to evaluate whole language/ workshop courses...the portfolio guided my learning and directed me to set my own goals" though he admitted that this type of self-evaluation might not be "feasible in the high school"

Belinda

The Plan. Belinda was a veteran first grade teacher in a small rural school. She fully embraced the whole language movement. She stated:

> I love whole language! It makes so much sense for so many reasons. The more I learn about it and implement it in our classrooms, the more sense it makes.

Prior to the class, she had taken many steps in moving her practice in that direction. She was taking the class for her own professional development having previously completed a masters degree in reading.

In her initial "Dean Reviewer" letter, Belinda identified four key goals all related to improving the teaching of skills within her whole language classrooms: (a) promoting vocabulary development, (b) teaching sight words, (c) integrating spelling, and (d) integrating phonics. She planned to address those issues by developing two "whole language units," one on the environment and the other on fairy tales. She also wanted to set up a writers' workshop in her room. Within these changes, she would also use portfolios and self-assessment techniques. Belinda's potential evidence would include unit lesson plans, teacher observations, tape recordings of student oral readings, video taping of student projects, and samples of student work.

Following some initial comments, Belinda altered her plan. She (a) added the implementation of portfolios and (b) student self-assessment techniques as goals. She outlined a procedure for developing portfolios that made it independence of her unit planning goal. She combined her four goals related to skill instruction into one goal and dropped the idea of developing a fairy tale unit and writer's workshop. By midterm, Belinda had focused her goals upon unit planning, spelling, and phonics instruction, and portfolios and self-assessment.

The Portfolio. The "Portfolio of Belinda" arrived in a three-ring notebook decorated with a cow — a favorite symbol of hers. Three sample books created by her students were handed in separately. Her portfolio was organized into eleven sections. The first section "Reflections" contained the required self-evaluation documents. Section two "Whole Language" contained a statement of her beliefs about whole language. Sections three, four, and five contained evidence of three related theme units implemented during the course: the environment, rain forest, and endangered animals. Each section presented evidence including the unit plan, plans and activities for addressing spelling within the unit, materials used during the unit, samples of home involvement activities, plans for math and science connections, and examples of completed student work. Sections six and seven represented her reflections upon spelling and phonics within her first grade program. Each section began with a synthesis statement and included samples of materials used in her instruction. Belinda also included outside resources (for example, four bibliographies of materials) that she had collected. Section eight was focused on portfolios. It also began with a synthesis statement and included three sample student portfolios. Section nine explored assessment in general and included an overview statement as well as fourteen different assessment forms (reading and writing logs, self-evaluations, etc.) she had created for classroom use. In section ten, she reflected upon her use of writers' workshop and included an overview statement and a description of her writing program. The final section contained 11 double-sided pages of photographs depicting aspects of her classroom environment and instructional program.

It was apparent in reviewing Belinda's portfolio that she had put forth tremendous effort in documenting what she did in her classroom. Each section began with overview statements providing evidence she had been reading and thinking about each topic. She synthesized the ideas of others and modified them for her classroom. Individual pieces of evidence, however, were usually not captioned. Because of this, it was more difficult to get a sense of how the evidence she had assembled illustrated her growth and change. It was difficult to separate what she had been doing before the class from what she was doing differently because of the class.

The Evaluation. "I think my grade for this class should be an A! I have learned an A worth of stuff from you, my research and others in the class." Obviously Belinda was pleased with the outcomes of her participation in this class. Her rationale for her grading decision began with an examination of her personal goals. She identified changes in her phonics and spelling programs and the addition of portfolios and self-assessment as her greatest changes. She described the impact of those changes on her students — better engagement, more confidence, greater self-awareness, and growth as readers and writers. Belinda also looked at the rubric to further support her evaluation decision.

> I feel that I have been consistent in our class rubric...I am applying that knowledge daily which is a way of empowering and engaging myself., I have tried to share some of my experiences and have brought in information to share...and I always see myself as an individual with a positive attitude.

In the end she had gone beyond the goals she had set for herself (even re embracing the goals of implementing writer's workshop), documented efforts in each area and used that to support her self-evaluation decision.

Belinda overtly voiced her positive feelings about the portfolio process. "Because of our discussions, I have examined my beliefs and have done much self-assessment...I never had a class that has made me do more thinking." This belief in self-assessment translated to classroom practice with the addition of portfolios and the inclusion of self-assessment techniques in their whole language classroom.

Bonnie

The Plan. Since Bonnie was a recent graduate of our teacher education program, this was the second time I had worked with her. She had been teaching a third and fourth grade combination class at a Christian school for two years. She admitted that she usually goes "by the book," using teacher texts for most of her subject areas. Bonnie's initial steps toward whole language included eliminating her English textbook and substituting her own writing program. She had just begun to use trade books in her reading instruction and she had made some initial steps toward integration through the use of a mini-unit on sandwiches. She acknowledges that she wasn't sure "this was really meaningful, but the class loved it." She had just completed a space theme with a "looser" organization "but only in a limited way." Bonnie was interested in moving further along on the continuum.

In her initial "Dear Reviewer" letter, Bonnie wanted to center her instruction (and her focus in this course) on "teaching theme units across the curriculum." She wanted to be able "to implement practical ideas learned from this course" in her classroom. She expressed a desire to explore issues related to motivating students through choice and active involvement. She also wanted to be able to share this information with other interested teachers in her school. Bonnie commented that she would track progress toward these goals by maintaining an ongoing journal containing samples of items to substantiate the entries. Since her initial letter did not include specific goals, Bonnie later defined her expected outcomes generally as implementing practical areas from this course in her classroom, gaining knowledge to share with other educators in her school and reevaluating her educational philosophies. She sees these goals as compatible with the rubric behaviors.

The Portfolio. Bonnie's portfolio came in a very large brown artist's folder. It contained a pocket folder as well as a number of separate items captioned and placed loosely in the folder. To document her change, Bonnie included copies of her new and old schedules to show her change, Bonnie included copies of her new and old integrated block; a survey she developed (based on an idea from Regie Routman's *Invitations)* to use with students to learn more about them; samples from students' reading logs students would complete choice reading time; examples of students' work from the endangered animal theme; and a copy of a parent letter describing a theme project that would be graded according to a scale developed by the students.

The heart of Bonnie's portfolio was the pocket folder containing her self-assessments and her response journal. Entries in the twenty-one page response journal were organized around the rubric standards. Each entry was labeled according to the standard for which it provided evidence. For example in one entry she examined herself as a reader in response to an assigned reading about good readers. She labeled the entry as evidence that she was satisfying goal number four — engaging self and examining personal habits. An entry describing how she allowed her students to design a new classroom arrangement was labeled "Goal 2: Applying what has been learned." Though the entry described what she did, it did not discuss how this project connected to something she had learned. In general, however, in reviewing her entries, she did provide evidence that she was reading and thinking about issues and ideas related to class and attempting changes in her classroom. Her endangered animals unit not only provided for a greater degree of student choice and control, but also culminated in a social action project unit wherein students made and sold buttons to raise funds to donate to environmental organizations. This seemed a significant step forward from her initial step into integration with her sandwich mini-unit.

The Evaluation. Bonnie addressed each of the rubric standards in supporting her self-evaluation decision. She pointed out that what she had read indicated that she had consistently acquired new knowledge. She had applied this knowledge through a variety of classroom changes including her endangered animals unit, word wall, improved schedule, survey for next year, orders for new trade books and plans for next fall. Her goals included: developing her Wisconsin history unit as literature-based and student interest-driven, planning one theme per month in her classroom, and setting up an observation plan for students. She had shared her knowledge with others including her principal and other teachers. She related that her principal "was concerned about themes for the classroom until I could show her that they fit into our curriculum goals." The principal videotaped her class "and could really see the learning going on as students wrote and commented on what they were reading." Her third grade colleague also implemented ideas Bonnie had shared from class such as a reading log and reading/ writing rubrics. Bonnie did admit, however, that she was not sure that she " always had a positive attitude toward everything I had read or found out about whole language, but I did learn and it did stretch my brain." She also looked at her personal goal of expanding her use of thematic instruction and concluded that "she felt more confident about getting up themes for next year based on what I learned in this course" listing some possible themes to research during the summer. In looking at her learning, Bonnie stated her performance an A (66 out of 70 points). She noted that "as always, the more I learned, the more I realized how much I need to continue to learn."

Common Threads and Contrasting Colors

Analysis of these student portfolios revealed that all three were capable of assessing their knowledge, practice and habits. There were all capable of setting goals that closely related to their needs as learners. There were all capable, sometimes with guidance, of documenting their own growth and change. And they were all able to provide evidence to support their self-evaluation decisions. With appropriate support, they were able to direct and document their own learning.

The portfolios also revealed that students selected a wide variety of personal goals. Even when their goals were similar (both Bonnie and Belinda focused on thematic instruction), their previous experiences and present contents often caused their paths of inquiry to be different. As Stowell (1993) concluded: "In any professional, each individual brings his or her own particular expertise to each event" (p.14).

Likewise, the means students chose to document their learning was often different. While certain types of evidence were found in all portfolios (samples of student work to show changes in practice), other evidence such as the photo journal illustrated specific goals for one individual. This was similar to the likenesses and differences that French and Foster (1992) found in their analysis of clinical portfolios maintained by teachers in a reading center. Even when the sections of the portfolio were teacher-determined and the teacher educators professed a belief in providing graduate students with a structure, contents of portfolios still varied from learner to learner. Thus, portfolios allowed learners to document growth and change in ways that reflected who they were as individuals. This potential for personalizing assessment is arguably one of the most significant advantages of this process (Ohlhausen & Ford, 1992).

In the end, students reviewed themselves as "A" learners. Some have suggested that high grades may be related to the clear identification of outcomes at the beginning of the semester and the constant monitoring of the learning process (Vogt, McLaughlin & Rapp Ruddell, 1993). The rubric that framed Dominic and Bonnie's grading decisions provided a clear set of expectations. For Belinda, the rubric seemed less important then her personal goals in justifying her grading decision; but like the rubric, her goals also provided a clear set of expectations.

Some writers have questioned whether the portfolio process provided enough rigor for reviewers to distinguish between surface and substance (Ohlhausen, Perkins & Jones, 1993); however, in a study comparing distributions of grades prior to the use of portfolios with grades based on the use of portfolios. Vogt, McLauglin, and Rapp Ruddell (1993) concluded that distributions were "highly similar to patterns established with traditional grading practices" (p.9). They asserted that "the validity of the portfolio process does not appear to be as problematic" (p. ll). In that study, the teacher educator maintained control over the grading process. In my case, self-evaluation drove the grading process. I would only speculate whether Dominic, Belinda and Bonnie would have received similar grades if I had used more traditional measures. Perhaps the only reason teacher educators examine that question is because of the constraints within which we work—one that assumes validity in traditional grading practices. I believe I know more about what these learners had learned by reviewing what they had done in the portfolio process than I would have learned by reviewing traditional measures. In the end, I could conclude that they all had contextualized their learning, they participated in the assessment, and they were engaged in a process that showed them how to be independent lifelong learners.

References

Cramer, A. A. (1993). *Navigating the assessment maze with portfolios.* Clearinghouse (November/December), 72-74.

DeFina, A. A. (1992). *Portfolio assessment: Getting started.* New York: Scholastic.

French, M. P., & Foster, F. L. (1992). Portfolios in inquiry-oriented reading teacher education. In A. M. Frager & M. Miller, (Eds.), *Inquiry-oriented reading education.* College Reading Association.

Johns, J. L., & VanLeirsburg, P. (1991). *How professionals view portfolio assessment.* Literacy Research and Reports No. 10. Dekalb, IL: Northern Illinois University.

Ohlhausen, M. M., & Ford, M. P. (1992). The promise and process of portfolio self-assessment in teacher education classes. In A.M. Frager & J. Miller, (Eds.), *Inquiry-oriented reading education.* College Reading Association.

Paulson, F. L., Paulson, P. R., & Meyer, C. A. (1991). What makes a portfolio a portfolio? *Educational Leadership, 46,* 60-63.

Routman, R. (1991). *Invitations: Changing as teachers and learners K-12.* Portsmouth, N.H: Heinemann.

Stahle, D. L., & Mitchell, J. P. (1993). Portfolio assessment in college methods courses: Practicing what we preach. *Journal of Reading, 36,* 538 -542.

Stowell, L. (1993). *A team approach to teacher portfolios in teacher education.* Paper presented at the 43rd Annual Meeting of the National Reading Conference Charleston, SC.

Tierney, R. J., Carter, M. A., & Desai, L. E. (1991). *Portfolio assessment in the reading-writing classroom*. Norwood, MA: Christopher Gordon.

Vogt, M. E., McLaughlin, M., & Rapp Ruddell, M. (1993). *Do as I do: Using portfolios to evaluate students in reading methods courses*. Paper presented at the 43rd Annual Meeting of the National Reading Conference, Charleston, SC.

Authentic Assessment in a University Preservice Literacy Course

Deborah R. Dillon*
Brenda Dixey
Valerie Hall
Susan Nierstheimer
and
Tammy Younts
Purdue University

In this paper a team of five university instructors describes the development and use of several alternative assessments, constructed to measure preservice teacher education students' learning in a course titled "Teaching Reading in the Elementary Schools" and to model for these future teachers how they might measure children's learning in K-6 grade classrooms. The new assessments are grounded in the notion that to adequately prepare preservice teachers to work in schools where many children are at-risk emotionally and cognitively, new ways of thinking about teaching, how children learn, and how we assess learning are needed. Additionally, future teachers need to view learning, teaching, and assessment as integrated processes. What follows is a description of the new assessments developed to meet preservice teachers' needs.

Designing a New Course

In 1992 a university professor, a professional staff member, and three doctoral students (all former teachers) collaborated in revising an elementary reading course titled EDCI 306 "Teaching Reading in the Elementary Schools." The description for the course reads as follows: "This course combines study about theory and practice in the teaching of developmental reading at the elementary level. Major emphasis is placed on current methods and materials used in reading instruction. Lecture-discussions, small group work, and simulated teaching comprise the different course activities." Typically, EDCI

NOTE. Authors listed in alphabetical order; authors shared equally in the conceptualization and writing of this manuscript.

306 is the first literacy course undergraduates enroll in at Purdue University as they prepare to be elementary teachers. Students schedule the course as second semester sophomores or first semester juniors and approximately 120 students, divided into four sections of 30, take EDCI 306 each semester. EDCI 306 assignments and assessments were traditional, including multiple choice exams, quizzes, the development of lesson plans, and a final project.

As a precursor to revamping the assessments associated with EDCI 306, we systematically gathered students' written and verbal evaluations of course content and assessments and coupled these with our own emerging goals for students' learning. Students requested that EDCI 306 prepare them to think and act like practicing teachers as they learned important theory and practical knowledge. Critical to preparing students in the manner they requested was for the five instructors to model and use new forms of teaching, such as cooperative learning, and new forms of assessment, such as performance-based measures and portfolios. We wanted the new assessment measures we developed to integrate thinking, reading, and writing and to be realistic and interesting (Farr, 1992); we also wanted these measures to focus on the importance of self-evaluation (Graves, 1992). To achieve our goals we read about new assessment procedures, particularly those consistent with whole language philosophy (e.g., Atwell, 1987; Anthony, Johnson, Mickelson, & Preece, 1991). We also read the writings of researchers who have challenged literacy educators to examine new frameworks for authentic literacy assessment (e.g., Farr, 1992; Paris, Calfee, Filby, Hiebert, Pearson, Valencia, & Wolf, 1992). Finally, we explored the work of university teacher-researchers (e.g., Hansen, 1992; Kiefer & Morrison, 1994) who are using portfolios and other forms of authentic assessment in their college classrooms. Based on our readings and students' evaluations, we selected a holistic framework of evaluation where assessment is longitudinal, contextual, and collaborative; assessment is also focused on understanding students' attitudes, strategies, and uses of literacy (Sorenson, 1993).

The assessments, described more completely below, were consistent with authentic instruction (Newmann & Wehlage, 1993) in that the work was aimed toward production of discourse, products, and performance that had value or meaning beyond success in our particular course. For example, in the position paper assignment students were asked to explore relevant aspects of current knowledge as well as examine their own thinking (Black & Ammon, 1992). Learning to examine one's thinking is a step toward self-evaluation (Kremer-Hayon, 1993) and becoming a reflective practitioner (Schon, 1983). One of our goals as instructors is to foster the growth of our undergraduates as reflective teachers who make decisions based on critical judgment and awareness of their actions.

Based upon our reading and discussion of the research literature on assessment, we constructed the following assignments and assessments for EDCI 306:

1. a variety of journal articles and other issue-oriented readings, supplemented with two textbooks that focus on teacher development and change processes;
2. writing-to-learn activities such as learning log/journals, Buddy Journals, and pen pal letters to local elementary children;
3. two position papers;
4. a basal review and expository text analysis assignment;
5. a literacy reading and writing unit including microteaching a portion of it;
6. one quiz and two exams;
7. a personal literacy history portfolio; and
8. a professional literacy portfolio, which provided a record of each students' development as a professional in this literacy course and beyond into their preservice academic career.

The assignments and assessments developed for EDCI 306 were designed to address specific concepts or topics covered in the course. Additionally, students were expected to integrate knowledge from previous assignments and assessments into subsequent ones. By developing this interconnectedness, the assessments themselves became learning experiences for the students. We also encouraged students to learn from one another by completing assignments and some assessments in collaborative small groups. Finally, students were provided in and out-of-class time to complete the assignments and assessments.

An Overview of New Assignments and Assessments

In the following section we describe the various assignments and assessments we developed for EDCI 306 in their approximate chronological order. Additionally we provide the purpose undergirding each assignment and how it was used in the class.

Personal literacy history portfolio. The purpose of this assignment was to help EDCI 306 students connect what they were learning in class about literacy development with their past reading and writing experiences. We asked students to find artifacts or items representative of their past literacy learning and to reflect on how these artifacts were important in their development as literate adults. More indepth information about the literacy history portfolio will be presented in the next section of this paper.

Position paper #1. The purpose of the first position paper was to encourage students to reflect on their developing beliefs about how children learn to read and write. We wanted students to begin to think about practical applications of the theory they had read and discussed in class thus far. The students were asked to reflect on their beliefs and, based on these beliefs, to describe what instruction in their future classrooms might look like. They wrote specifically about concepts we had explored in the class readings and discussions such as classroom organization schemes, activities, and materials. The students also reflected on the various roles teachers and students might assume during literacy lessons. We intended for this assignment to serve as a foundation for a second position paper in which students would more specifically describe their evolving teaching approaches.

Exam #1. The first exam consisted of a series of short essay questions that focused on a variety of topics addressed in class thus far. For each question students were asked to react to the content in varying ways. For example, the instructors read a tradebook for young children aloud. EDCI 306 students were then asked to: "Define emergent literacy and then discuss three specific activities/lessons you would construct (using the tradebook read orally) to develop students' emergent literacy." A second question requested that students discuss several methods used to involve children in reading activities and then explain how the method would be incorporated into the classroom setting. The purpose of exam #1 was to pose questions that required not only content knowledge about literacy, but also practical application based on students' current understandings and their anticipation of a future classroom.

Quiz on word recognition. After reading Patricia Cunningham's 1991 book, *Phonics They Use: Words for Reading and Writing,* the students were asked to develop a lesson on a word recognition concept they had studied and wanted to "practice teach." As they planned their lessons, the students were asked to use professional resources such as their class texts, articles, and resource materials coupled with self-selected children's tradebooks. Each student developed a plan for his or her word recognition lesson outside of class and then presented the lesson to a small group of peers in a microteaching format. The shared nature of this activity allowed students to teach and listen to their peers' reactions to their activities. They also had the opportunity to see multiple ways to design and teach a lesson by observing other students.

Basal reader analysis. In order to prepare students for the kinds of published materials commonly used in the field, they were asked to review and critique a basal series. The instructors brought in basals that represented a variety of philosophies and publishers for this assignment. In addition to describing what they found, the EDCI 306 students were asked to evaluate the content and organization of the series and to speculate how they might adapt the series to meet the needs of their future students. Finally, they were asked to take a position on the feasibility of using the series to teach reading based on their belief systems. The basal review was completed and graded as a group project.

Position paper #2. In the second position paper, the students were asked to describe in detail a litcracy lesson on a typical day in their future classrooms. This write-up involved incorporating the students' new understandings about reading and writing gained since they wrote the first position paper. The new knowledge about approaches and materials had to be organized and described based on the students' newly informed and continually evolving belief systems.

Text analysis activity. The purpose of this assignment was for a small group of students to examine an expository textbook for content presentation and potential challenges to children's comprehension. Concurrently, students were to evaluate tradebooks that focused on the same content to consider how they might be used to supplement the classroom textbook.

Exam #2. Exam #2, a take-home test, was designed to integrate a variety of topics that had been studied over the course of the semester. Students selected expository and narrative texts for a lesson, designed reading and writing strategies to teach using the texts, and constructed an assessment activity to measure children's learning. More indepth information about exam #2 will be provided in the next section of this paper.

An Indepth Description of Two Assessment Activities

In the previous section of this paper we presented an overview of the assignments and assessments created for EDCI 306; we will now present an indepth description of two of these activities; the Personal Literacy History Portfolio and Exam #2. Following this description we will present EDCI 306 students' reactions and our reflections on the assessments and assignments.

Personal literacy history portfolio. The Personal Literacy History Portfolio was designed as a process-oriented activity that continued throughout the semester. In the first week of the course we described the portfolio and showed samples we had prepared to clarify the project. Specifically, we requested that students select three artifacts or examples of literacy learning from their past and write an explanation of the significance of each item. (See Figure 1 for a sample entry; an artifact selected by a student from her third grade writing journal and her reflection on what she wrote and her literacy development.) The first entry in the portfolio was due about six weeks into the semester; three additional entries were due the tenth week and three more the thirteenth week. This time frame allowed students the opportunity to contact their caregivers (e.g., parents, guardians, or others) for help in finding literacy history artifacts.

When the students brought their portfolios to class they could volunteer to share an entry with peers in small groups. The sharing sessions helped to illustrate the students' common experiences and the variety of literacy experiences in their backgrounds. The sharing sessions became a forum for growth, giving students a better understanding of their classmates. For some, it was an emotional catharsis. A sense of community developed in our college classrooms as the students learned to trust each other, revealing their past experiences and the meanings the experiences held for them. At the conclusion of each sharing session, the portfolios were collected for instructor evaluation. The portfolios took hours for each instructor to read because each one was unique and extensive. We often became so absorbed in the stories that we lost track of time as we read of students who had overcome great obstacles to gain access to a university education. Many students described humorous events involving siblings and literacy development.

Nine literacy examples with accompanying explanations and one summary reflection integrating all the entries constituted the total portfolio. Students' work was assessed based on their purposeful selection of entries and the quality of the descriptions and reflections constructed for each entry. We each wrote a reflective note to individual students, sharing our reactions to what was written and providing suggestions for deeper consideration on future entries.

The Personal Literacy History Portfolio assignment fulfilled several goals we had for EDCI 306. First, through the portfolio project, the EDCI 306 students *learned about themselves and their emerging literacy. They also began to consider the importance of facilitating their future students' literacy development.* For the first time students examined how their own literacy

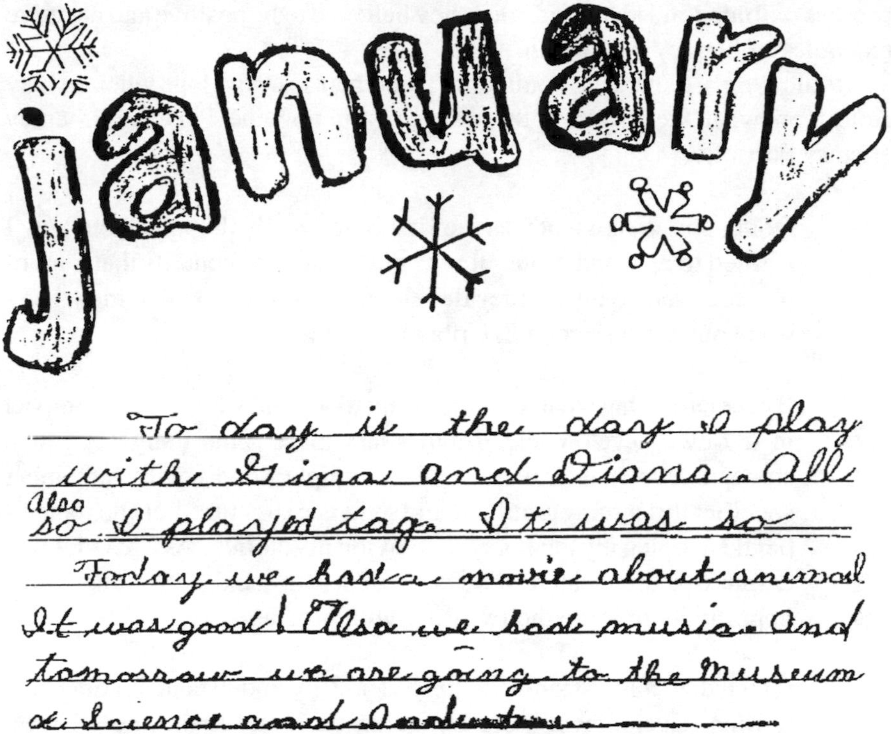

january

To day is the day I play with Gina and Diana. Also so I played tag. It was so
Today we had a movie about animal It was good! Also we had music. And tomorrow we are going to the Museum of Science and Indust

In the third grade, I got the chance to write and keep a journal. We started writing in our journals during the second semester, so I have entries from January to May. We would write it in daily. Usually, I would write about what I did that day, who I played with, what we played or something interesting that happened at home. My teacher would collect them weekly and make comments or corrections on them. I remember writing in this journal as if it were yesterday and I enjoy going back now and reading it. It's neat to note the progression I made, as I compare an entry from January to one I did in May.

Figure 1. Personal literacy history portfolio artifact

process unfolded and identified what they believed to be positive and negative examples of literacy instruction.

Following are students' comments from their learning logs wherein they reflect on what they learned through constructing the Personal Literacy History Portfolio:

> Doing this assignment was the first time I really thought about how I learned to read and write. It was nice to see the benefits that a lot of projects were to my literacy development, projects that to me when I was young just seemed like play and fun.

> By remembering what was important to me and what made an impact in my own development, I can stress these same things as I help students develop their literacy. For example, I don't really remember specifically learning grammar and sentence structure, but I do remember developing my ideas and displaying my stories. As a result, I will emphasize the creative processes of writing and give students the opportunity to share their writing with others.

> I feel that this assignment helped me to understand reading and writing development more by going back and seeing how I went through the stages and then combining that with what I have learned this semester.

As evidenced in these comments, the EDCI 306 students felt that by constructing a portfolio and reflecting on its contents, they discovered which activities were most valuable to their literacy development. Further, students learned the value of early literacy experiences. For example, one student commented: "I realize that how much and what one reads directly affects the reader." While examining their own emerging literacy, preservice teachers were able to realize the importance of providing a variety of literacy activities for young children.

The experience of preparing the literacy history portfolio helped some students realize the need to focus not only on children's cognitive learning but on children's affective development as well. As one student commented: "Reading has always been extremely important to me. It was sometimes the only way I could escape from the rigors of life. When I was growing up, I had a rough childhood. My parents were divorced when I was just ten, and I was moved back and forth from state to state and from parent to parent . . I guess you could say that in those years that I was growing into an adult, I read A LOT. I read to get away from my problems or to just have a better day."

Comments such as the one expressed above indicate how the EDCI 306 students recognized the significance of literacy in many aspects of their lives. The students appeared to take pride in their literacy development after examining their progress over the years. They stated that they wanted their future students to have positive literacy experiences and be commended for their work. Thus, while learning about their literacy development as children, the 306 students began to consider the literacy development of their future students.

Second, preservice teachers realized the importance of viewing the personal literacy portfolio as a means of *understanding each student and his/ her educational needs.* For example, one student stated: "Portfolios would also be a good way for both teacher and student to get to know each other better and the teacher can see the thinking processes of the child." Another student commented: "Their (my students') personal history portfolios can give me some insight into their reading and writing experiences, which in turn should help me teach these students more effectively than if I were unaware of their background." The process of developing a personal literacy history portfolio demonstrated to the students the insights a teacher can gain into a child's life, and consequently the improved instruction the teacher can provide.

Third, EDCI 306 students *shared emotional experiences with their caregivers* (parents/guardians) as they gathered artifacts for their portfolios. Students were often surprised by the collections that had been compiled by caregivers on their behalf. Some students had moved frequently and lost many items from their past. These students learned about themselves and their families as they struggled to reconstruct experiences through photographs and family discussions. As one student related: "I spent an entire evening going through storage with my mom to find such items. We were able to talk about my childhood. She told me things that I had forgotten and vice versa."

Caregivers enjoyed the opportunity of sharing this project with their son or daughter. The EDCI 306 students noted this in their comments: "I have thoroughly enjoyed doing this portfolio. My parents and I loved looking through my old papers and books and reminiscing about the past" and "I enjoyed talking to my mom about various items that I had collected to include in my portfolio . . . I think the assignment was as fun for her as it was for me." As students experienced for themselves the emotional bonding through the interactions surrounding this project, they realized the importance of involving caregivers in a child's education.

Fourth, while the EDCI 306 students engaged in the process of developing their own personal literacy history portfolios, they *thought about how they might use the literacy history portfolio in their own classrooms.* Students saw the value of having their future students share entries from personal portfolios in class. The following comments indicate the students' new ideas: "I believe that a portfolio like this would be very beneficial for children because it shows them where they were, where they are, and where they are going in their reading and writing abilities. They will be able to see the progress that they have made." Another student stated: "We (the student and I) will look at the student's progress together, and discuss what the child has learned that year. I will make it a point to show the students how much they have grown throughout the year. I want to give my students self-confidence as they leave my classroom to enter another level." A third student commented: "I think if they (children) can see their accomplishments, their self esteem and motivation will improve." The Personal Literacy History Portfolio was viewed by the preservice teachers as a vehicle to help future students observe their own literacy growth and gain confidence in their abilities.

Due to the memories stimulated by the literacy samples students collected, the EDCI 306 students were also able to recall emotions associated with different assignments. Students remarked: "Now that I want to be a school teacher I remember both the good and bad feelings I had from certain activities and (I think about these) as I am planning for my classroom" and "I can remember the best teachers were those that shared in my proud accomplishments and always encouraged rather than discouraged."

Recalling the feelings they had at the time of these literacy events, the EDCI 306 students made decisions concerning the types of assignments they planned to provide for their students. Several students thought of new ways to extend this assignment with young children, as noted in the following comments:

> This would be a good project for my students to be involved in, but not in the same depth. I would like for them to keep their things that they have done in a particular folder and I would like for them to write any books down that they liked during the course of the school year. When they put things in their folders, I want them to just jot down something they liked or disliked about the assignment.

Another student added:

It would be ideal if the child could take his portfolio from grade to grade, constantly expanding on the portfolio by adding entries and by reflecting on former work. The portfolio can be used as a wonderful assessment tool; a perfect way to document progress without grade labels, as well as a collection of very special memories!

In sum, the EDCI 306 students enjoyed learning about their own personal literacy histories and determined that they wanted their students to enjoy the benefits of this experience. We found the project to be a powerful cognitive and affective activity that allowed students to connect the theory and concepts they were learning in class to real life (past) experiences, and then back again to their developing ideas about what it means to be a teacher of literacy.

Exam #2. Although it might seem necessary to begin a semester with all the assessments developed and ready to administer, we found that the development of assessments came as we gathered as a group and defined what the goals and outcomes of instruction had been. By reflecting on how and what we had taught, we could best define what our desires were for student learning. In the case of the second exam, we felt that students had been exposed to a wide range of issues that addressed literacy instruction. Our goal was to prepare them to synthesize this information at a level that would enable them to move into a classroom situation and teach using an integrated, child-centered approach to instruction.

A week before it was due, students were given the exam which consisted of a map to be used in thinking about issues and collecting materials to use in constructing responses (see Figure 2). First, students were asked to select a content area textbook and identify a teachable topic within it. Second, students were asked to use the topic in the textbook and develop a theme for a unit, constructing a graphic organizer which could guide their teaching of the topic across the curriculum. Third, using the knowledge they had constructed during the Text Analysis Activity (an earlier course assignment), students were asked to analyze the textbook for characteristics of inconsiderateness. Fourth, students were to select a narrative tradebook that addressed the specified topic from the textbook, and an expository tradebook on the topic and describe how these materials would be used to enhance the textbook topic. Students also were to develop a mini-lesson on a reading strategy that would help students read the texts more successfully, describe ways of incorporating writing into the unit, and construct a form of assessment from which they could evaluate students' progress.

This take-home exam is designed to give you the opportunity to synthesize what you have learned in the last half of the semester. You will do this by gathering three texts that could be used to teach a particular topic. These texts should fit into the following categories: a copy of an excerpt from a content area textbook at the grade level you are interested in, a tradebook that is narrative in structure but focuses on the topic, a tradebook that is expository in structure that focuses on the topic. The three texts should be housed in a folder and turned in upon completion of the test.

We have provided you with a graphic organizer that delineates the various areas that you should discuss in the exam. You may use any materials along with your chosen texts that you wish as you write your response. The point breakdown for each area has been included for your information.

Analysis of Textbook Excerpt

You should discuss the textbook excerpt you have found in terms of Armbruster's characteristics of considerate texts. You will be given 8 points for showing how the text does not meet two of the characteristics of a considerate text. You will be given another 2 points for telling briefly how your choices of supplemental materials will enhance the text.

Strategies

Thinking about your thematic unit as a whole and the various texts you might use, talk about one reading strategy that could be useful to students in dealing with the texts. Tell what the strategy is, why it would help students with the reading, and very briefly how you would teach/introduce it. You will be given 8 points for the strategy section.

Theme/Topic

You will be given 4 points for choosing an appropriate theme/topic and the materials to support it. Your choice of tradebooks should reflect current, motivating texts that would enhance the textbook. The second part of this section involves a mapping of activities that could be used in a thematic unit. You will be given 6 points for showing creativity in integration of various content areas, use of different modes of learning, and activities that reflect child-centered teaching.

Writing

Looking at your thematic unit as a whole, describe two ways, other than the use of journals, that writing could be meaningfully used to enhance students' learning. You will be given 12 points for telling what each writing activity involves, when writing would occur in the lesson, and how the activity would enhance learning.

Assessment

Briefly describe one way that you could assess student learning. This learning can be topic knowledge or progress in reading and writing. You will be given 10 points for telling what the assessment would focus on and why information obtained would be helpful to you when planning future instruction.

Figure 2. EDCI 306: Exam #2

In constructing exam #2 we provided students with several choices, specifically, we asked them to define a topic and then choose appropriate texts, methods of teaching, and assessment tools. The challenge for us was to see how students answered the various elements of the exam in relation to the theoretical, contextual framework they had selected, and to assess the quality of their efforts. Another challenge for us was to account for the thinking processes students engaged in as they prepared their responses. These processes were as important as the products handed in when students completed the exam. We were able to get a picture of these processes when we facilitated the students' search for texts and materials to be used to write the exam, and when we discussed with students how they might organize various elements of the exam. Different from most forms of assessment, exam #2 offered students the opportunity to tailor the content of the exam to their own interests and strengths. They could also talk with peers and the instructors as they planned and revised their responses after sorting through feedback. In sum, there were many positive outcomes from exam #2 and our shift in general to more authentic assessment.

Conclusions: Reflections on the Assessments in EDCI 306

In reflecting back over the assessments designed for EDCI 306 we found that students felt more successful in their development as teachers of literacy based on their own self evaluation of their preparation. Students developed strong ownership for the ideas they generated, as evidenced by their willingness to share ideas and materials with their peers as they prepared assignments. Finally, students provided us with positive written feedback at the end of the semester. Several semesters after completing EDCI 306, students stated that they were able to use the actual materials and activities as they moved into the next literacy course which involved a teaching practicum. For example, Mike noted that he used authentic assessment measures in a corrective reading class where he tutored a child one-on-one: "I didn't (ask my student to just) do a lot of reading and writing and answering questions. (Rather, my student) was active. I based my evaluation on what she did; the process as well as the product." Jody, a former EDCI 306 student, reflected back on the authentic assessment knowledge developed in 306 as she experimented with ideas in a practicum course: "(I learned) ideas on how to find out information about kids and (ways to assess) without pen and paper."

It would be untrue to say that as instructors this form of teaching and assessment was easier in terms of time and mental effort. We spent many hours reading, discussing, and reacting to the assignments and assessments and the complexities associated with each one. As a result, we generated a list of the benefits to using authentic assignments and assessments, as perceived by EDCI 306 students and each of us as instructors. We found the following to be positive outcomes for the students in our classes in respect to the new assessments and assignments we designed: (a) course content and assignments were sequenced and integrated; (b) assignments served as examples for students for how they might use assessment in their own classrooms; (c) students were actively involved in motivating tasks, accomplished through social interaction in small groups; (d) students viewed the assignments and assessments as practical, real life activities that they would engage in as a teacher; and (e) students connected personally with the instructor, local elementary children, and to each other as professionals.

As instructors we found many benefits for using authentic assessment in the undergraduate curriculum. We found that our instruction became: (a) collaborative with students and other instructors; (b) student-centered and based on the needs of students; (c) informed by more authentic, rich sources of data gleaned through the assignments and assessments; and (d) highly motivating because of the personal relationships built with students, particularly as we read the personal life history portfolios.

Thus, the redeeming factor for the time and energy invested by both the instructors and the 306 students was the clear realization that all of us were actively learning about ideas and approaches to be used in future teaching. As instructors, we had grown in our ability to model teaching strategies and methods of assessment we believe in and advocate. We also felt that through this process we were able to get to know our students as individuals. Our goal is to continue to strive to develop our practices so that they adhere to a belief advocated by Dorothy Watson (1994) when she stated that she teaches as she does because: "This is the way I want the children I know and love to be treated, and . . . it's the way I want to be treated myself" (p. 607).

References

Anthony, R. J., Johnson, T. D., Mickelson, N. I., & Preece, A. (1991). *Evaluating literacy: A perspective for change.* Portsmouth, NH: Heinemann.

Atwell, N. (1987). *In the middle: Writing, reading, and learning with adolescents.* Portsmouth, NH: Heinemann.

Black, A. & Ammon, P. (1992). A developmental-constructivist approach to teacher education. *Journal of Teacher Education, 43,* 323-335.

Cunningham, P. M. (1991). *Phonics they use: Words for reading and writing*. New York: HarperCollins.

Farr, R. (1992). Putting it all together: Solving the reading assessment puzzle. *The Reading Teacher, 46* (1), 26-37.

Graves, D. H. (1992). Helping students learn to read their portfolios. In D. H. Graves & B. S. Sunstein (Eds.), *Portfolio portraits* (pp. 85-95). Portsmouth, NH: Heinemann.

Hansen, J. (1992). Teachers evaluate their own literacy. In D. H. Graves & B. S. Sunstein (Eds.), *Portfolio portraits* (pp. 73-81). Portsmouth, NH: Heinemann.

Kiefer, R. D. & Morrison, L. S. (1994). Changing portfolio process: One journey toward authentic assessment. *Language Arts, 71*, 411-418.

Kremer-Hayon, L. (1993). *Teacher self-evaluation: Teachers in their own mirrors*. Boston: Kluwer Academic Publishers.

Newmann, F. M. & Wehlage, G. G. (1993). Five standards of authentic instruction. *Educational Leadership, 50* (7), 8-12.

Paris, S. G., Calfee, R. C., Filby, N., Hiebert, E. H., Pearson, P. D., Valencia, S. W., & Wolf, K. P. (1992). A framework for authentic literacy assessment. *The Reading Teacher, 46* (2), 88-98.

Schon, D. (1983). *The reflective practitioner: How professionals think in action*. New York: Basic Books.

Sorenson, N. L. (1993). Holistic evaluation of literacy development: Framing the process. *Reading Research and Instruction, 32* (4), 66-75.

Watson, D. J. (1994). Whole language: Why bother? *The Reading Teacher, 47* (8), 600-607.

A Model for Preparing Preservice
and Inservice Teachers
To Interpret and Utilize Portfolio Assessment

Rebecca P. Harlin
Florida International University

Sally E. Lipa
State University College at Geneseo

From the author's research of preservice and inservice teachers' portfolio interpretation, the obstacles each group encountered during the process were identified. Using these findings as a guide, a model for familiarizing teachers with the portfolio process was developed. After field testing for three years in college classrooms and staff development workshops, a three-stage model was refined which establishes the theoretical framework for portfolios, systematic procedures for collecting, analyzing, and cross-checking data sources, and a format for developing a composite summary.

One goal of preservice and inservice literacy education is the development of authentic assessment practices. Although there are many professional sources suggesting appropriate ways to assess childrens literacy through assembling a portfolio, few of them help teachers approach the analysis of the data systematically. Seldom, if ever, are teachers encouraged to identify the theoretical framework against which the portfolio's contents will be compared. While data collection is difficult for some teachers, interpreting and summarizing the information is even more overwhelming for the novice. As the number of states and school districts mandating portfolios as a means of authentic assessment increases, the need for appropriate preservice and inservice education becomes evident.

Through three years of work with undergraduate and graduate elementary and reading education majors as well as staff development for inservice teachers implementing portfolio assessment, a three-part model was developed and revised. With each group of students and teachers, the model's utility in highlighting the process of compiling and interpreting portfolio documents was evaluated. Subsequent changes and refinements helped shape the model presented in this article.

Rationale

Well into the 1980's traditional views of assessment and teaching shaped the content of preservice and inservice teacher education. When the topic of evaluation was addressed in methods courses and workshops, considerable emphasis was placed on formal assessment, primarily multiple choice tests, decontextualized from both classrooms and teachers (Calfee, 1987; Teale, Hiebert, & Chittenden, 1987; Wixson, Peters, Weber, & Roeber, 1987). Assessment was product-oriented, reflecting both a narrow view of knowledge (Monroe, 1991) and an outmoded model of literacy (Kapinus, 1994; Winograd, Paris, & Bridge, 1991). This view of assessment coincided with the model of teaching as the transmission of knowledge to students and the belief that knowledge of subject matter, or book knowledge, was essential to becoming an effective teacher (Neilsen, 1990).

As new theories about literacy developed and were incorporated in methods courses, definitions of reading and writing, development of curricula, instructional approaches, and ways to evaluate literacy were transformed (Farr, 1992; Graves, 1991; Mosenthal, 1986). With the shift from product-oriented to process-oriented assessment, the range of literacy experiences included in evaluation models expanded (Afflerbach & Kapinus, 1993; Tierney, Carter, & Desai, 1991) and assessment and teaching became intertwined (Teale et al., 1987). Assessment was no longer decontextualized, based on one-shot evaluations and texts unlike those used in daily instruction. Instead, assessment became authentic in context and situation, continuous rather than periodic, multidimensional in the aspects of literacy tapped, and collaborative with students and parents participating (Valencia, 1990; Winograd et al, 1991). New views of assessment meant changes in the expertise teachers would need to be effective. Teachers' success with authentic assessment depends heavily on the depth of their understanding of literacy development and the school knowledge obtained from observing and teaching kids (Bird, 1989; Goodman, 1989; Taylor, 1991). Thus, the role and preparation of teachers metamorphosed.

Establishing the theoretical underpinnings of evaluation is essential to developing teachers' authentic evaluation practices for several reasons. Both preservice and inservice teachers may not see the connections between definitions of literacy, assessment, and approaches to instruction. Preservice and beginning teachers often fail to use the knowledge they do have in their day to day teaching (Zeichner & Gore, 1990) and in assessing students. Frequently, preservice teachers are unaware of the need for using their background knowledge of literacy and language development as well as the intuitive thinking stemming from teaching and observing children in identifying or recognizing what a good reader is (Goodman, 1989). Although new assessment practices place higher demands on teachers' professional judgment and require a continual sharpening of their skills, preservice teachers receive limited exposure to both aspects in their coursework (Calfee, 1987). Just as student teachers fail to implement the types of teaching strategies encouraged by their professors because the strategies are verbalized rather than modeled by the faculty (Ginsberg & Clift, 1990), the same can also be said of authentic assessment where the process is described in a lecture rather than demonstrated.

Inservice teachers may be unaware of the relationship between their beliefs about teaching, learning, literacy, and accountability indicated by what and how they choose to evaluate in their classrooms (Sorenson, 1993; Teale et al, 1987). Since new assessment approaches require inclusion of the child, teacher, and the local school, they also demand higher literacy levels and more reflection by the teacher (Graves, 1991). Along with greater emphasis on teachers' judgment and their understanding of children's learning and literacy (Tierney et al., 1991; Valencia, 1990), new assessment practices involve the need for revision in teachers' beliefs and utilization of assessment tools (Afflerbach & Kapinus, 1993; Valencia & Place, 1994).

Linking Theory, Strategies and Assessment

Since teachers' beliefs and understandings of literacy play an important role in authentic assessment, our model begins with establishing the theoretical underpinnings. For preservice teachers, this discussion takes place after models of literacy, language development, and instructional approaches including readers' and writers' workshop have been discussed, modeled, and experienced. For inservice teachers, particularly those whose literacy background has not been updated in several years, articles from professional journals are disseminated prior to the workshops. As suggested by recent articles on portfolio development, participants can begin with reading professional materials to establish a research basis for their beliefs (Daws, 1993; Johnston & Wilder, 1992).

Activating Theoretical Underpinnings

As a starting point, participants respond in writing to six questions about literacy, based on what fluent readers and writers do: What do effective readers do (1) before they read? (2) while they read? (3)after they read? What do effective writers do (4) before they write? (5) while they write? (6) after they write? Since the background of inservice teachers varies, it is usually easier for them to think about what it is that they, themselves, do as readers and writers. Usually, teachers are asked to list two or three behaviors or strategies for each question. This limitation of two to three responses keeps everyone focused and actively engaged in the process. At another time, we return to the six guide questions to address the emergent and beginning developmental levels since the strategies or outcomes would differ from those benchmarks of fluent readers and writers.

Next, a master list of the brainstormed behaviors is recorded as individuals share their responses with the group. For preservice teachers, the process is a metacognitive one as they tap their background knowledge. As professors, we can see which dimensions of literacy the group identifies that coincide with the background knowledge developed and modeled in the course. Not only does this process help provide the underpinnings for evaluation for preservice and inservice teachers, but it also establishes a common language all members of the group understand. When working with inservice groups who hold opposing beliefs (whole language versus skills orientation) this discussion usually demonstrates their common ground. Since authentic assessment, particularly portfolio assessment, is responsive to individual communities of teachers, administrators, and parents, the dimensions of literacy or outcomes valued by a particular locality are identified and maintained throughout the process (Graves, 1991; Monroe, 1991; Paris et al, 1992). Thus, the list of behaviors is subject to change from one community or workshop to the next.

Once individuals' ideas have been exhausted, we reach consensus through discussion and compile a final list of strategies or outcomes to serve as the framework for assessment of fluent readers and writers. For example, in response to the question, "What do effective readers do before they read?" the list might include make predictions from the title, activate schemata, or think about the author's other books.

Identifying Assessment Possibilities

To highlight or establish the link between background knowledge of literacy and the evaluation of literacy, our next step is to identify assessment possibilities for each of the strategies we listed. Beginning with the first strategy on the list, we ask, "How could you find out if a student did this?" As the group brainstorms possible sources of data or tasks, they are listed beside the strategy. For example, the behavior or expected strategy used by a fluent reader, "Make predictions from the title", might have several sources of data-a reading response journal, teacher's anecdotal records, or the child's DR-TA response sheets. What begins to emerge is that there are many possible sources, tasks, or opportunities that can be used to supply evidence. For preservice and inservice teachers, the array of choices surprises them -- there is not just one way of obtaining information.

When the total list of sources is reviewed, several facts become evident. First, teachers can see that most of the methods for collecting evidence about literacy can be obtained in the context of their classroom and throughout their normal instructional activities. Secondly, when their colleagues or peers share how they use a particular source or task, teachers discover a purpose for that same document they had not considered. Finally, some data sources may be richer than others. With reading response journals, for example, teachers can see that many behaviors or strategies may be tapped within that one source.

Developing Familiarity with Data Sources

In inservice workshop settings, there are always surprises for the presenter. Sometimes, we are informed that the audience is comprised of teachers with extensive whole language backgrounds and experience in authentic assessment and that they only need to know how to utilize their expertise in developing portfolios. Other times we are told that the teachers know nothing about assessment or literacy development (Fortunately, neither has been accurate). However, we do find that teachers' expertise and familiarity with samples, tasks, and anecdotal records varies widely within any group. This variability usually becomes evident as we discuss assessment possibilities. We may find that teachers are unable to suggest a possible match for a strategy or only a few members of the group are familiar with particular data sources, such as keeping conference notes or using retellings. For these reasons, we devote the next time segment to becoming familiar with a variety of data sources.

Additional advantages to introducing teachers to assessment possibilities at this stage are that they usually are more interested in increasing their repertoire and in having choices of tools. They are more likely to see the value in spending some time examining different sources because the need is obvious. From the list in Figure 1, sources of data are selected according to participants' needs and introduced one at a time. We provide children's examples/samples to share and to identify the types of information that can be tapped by each source. For tasks, we share the directions, scoring rubric, and approximate time for administration. Since teachers are usually fascinated by

Anecdotal Records	Reading Logs
Booklists	Reading Miscue Analysis
Conference Notes	Retellings (Oral and Written)
DL-TA Records	Running Records
DR-TA Records	Self-Evaluations
Discussion Questions	Semantic Maps
Interviews	Summaries
Journal Entries	Surveys
K-W-L	Tape Recordings
Learning Logs	
Projects/Presentations	

Figure 1. Sources of information usually found in portfolios.

what other teachers write, we have found considerable interest in teachers' anecdotal records. With these records, we share both negative (litanies of what the child cannot do) and positive examples (jargon-free observations) as well as several formats teachers use. Throughout this time we encourage teachers to share their ideas and expertise with assessment tools with the group.

The length of time spent exploring data sources and becoming familiar with what each entails is well invested. As in the first part of the model where the common language for describing literate behavior is established, participants now have a chance to clarify those behaviors and relate them to assessment. By using the terminology in these discussions, teachers feel more comfortable and sure of its meaning. By the end of this time, preservice and inservice teachers recognize what a strategy is as well as how and where they might see it.

Analyzing Portfolio Documents

Since the goal of portfolio assessment is constructing a composite picture of a child's literacy development, the second part of our model addresses the connections between documents. We use portfolio case studies of emergent, beginning, and fluent readers for this purpose. Each portfolio contains four types of documentation-structured tasks (cloze, Concepts About Print, etc.); children's reading and writing samples; teachers' anecdotal records; and children's self-reports (interviews, selfevaluations), representing both the child's and teacher's voices. To keep the task manageable, each portfolio's contents represent two months of data about the child, roughly equivalent to what could be gathered within one report card grading period.

After each member of the group receives a copy of the target child's portfolio, we review the portfolio's contents identifying each document, explaining the notations and the conditions under which the data were obtained. Although the portfolio documents are similar to ones reviewed in the previous workshop segment, sometimes it is necessary to clarify this information if the format is different from the samples they had seen.

Before Reading Strategies	Document Source
Activate schema	Metacognitive Strategy Index, Quest. #9
	Teacher's Anecdotal Records 11/22, 12/8 & 10
Make predictions	Metacognitive Strategy Index, Quest. # 1
	Teacher's Anecdotal Records, 10/31
Set purpose	Teacher's Anecdotal Records, 11/22
Select genre	Not found
Form questions	Metacognitive Strategy Index, Quest. #6
	Teacher's Anecdotal Records, 12/8 & 10
	Reading Response Log
	Learning Log
Think about author's other books	Reading Response Log
	Conference Log
Look at pictures	Metacognitive Strategy Index, Quest. #2

During Reading Strategies	Document Source
Look for answers	Learning Log
	Teacher's Anecdotal Records, 11/22, 12/8 & 10
Summarize	Reading Response Log
	Conference Notes
	Teacher's Anecdotal Records, 12/15 & 17
Utilize background knowledge	Teacher's Anecdotal Records, 10/31
	Metacognitive Strategy Index, Quest. #13
Read w/ purpose	Teacher's Anecdotal Records, 11/22 & 12/8
Make more predictions	Teacher's Anecdotal Records, 10/31
	Metacognitive Strategy Index, Quest. # 19
Check old predictions	Teacher's Anecdotal Records, 10/31

Figure 2. Preservice teacher's document analysis form.

By using the literacy framework established in the first part of the workshop, the analysis of documents is more systematic because teachers know what behaviors they are trying to find in the data. Teachers work individually reading and checking each document, noting strategies demonstrated by the child. For preservice teachers, this task is assigned to be completed by the next class meeting, but for inservice teachers, it is usually done at the workshop site. Next, they compile their information across documents and record their results on the literacy framework grid. In Figure 2, a partial listing of documents analyzed by a preservice teacher shows the format for compiling the information. We have found it essential that teachers work independently on their analysis because they have an opportunity to read and reread documents at their own speed and are better able to focus on the task. During this time, individuals also have a chance to develop their own impressions of the child's literacy development and a sense of the patterns that are emerging. In the next part of the workshop, individuals participate more actively and equally in the discussions and feel more confident stating their findings because they have had "think time".

Summarizing the Data

In the last part of the workshop, teachers focus on developing a portrait of the child, based on their document analysis. We begin the process by sharing individuals' lists in dyads or small groups. By identifying behaviors or strategies and substantiating sources, teachers develop and extend their knowledge base. They become more able to recognize evidence of the strategy in different forms, becoming less literal in their definitions. An awareness of how methods of collecting evidence about literacy relates to a child's proficiency develops as teachers realize that the child may perform differently on tasks that measure the same skill or strategy.

Throughout these discussions, teachers utilize cross-checking of documents within the portfolios and tap individuals' expertise or familiarity with some data sources. Moreover these discussions further serve the purpose of developing a common language for describing what the child **can do** as a reader and a writer. For some inservice teachers, this represents a transition away from a product-oriented stance in which assessment delineated what the child cannot do. Teachers begin to recognize fluctuations in the frequency of strategies across texts and classroom situations. By the end of the small group discussions, the group reaches consensus about the child's literacy proficiency.

Developing a Composite Summary

Within the small groups, teachers record their findings on a group composite record (see Figure 3) which lists questions to guide their discussion. The task is to reconfigure the information about what the child does before, during, and after reading and writing and develop a sense of the child's

DIRECTIONS: Use this worksheet to record observations about the literacy behaviors of the target child that you agree upon in your group and list which data sources you used to support your statements. Then make recommendations for a literacy program you feel would foster the student's growth. Last of all, indicate any additional questions you would now like to investigate and how you would go about seeking their answers.

1. What does the child have firmly established as a reader?

2. What is the child developing as a reader?

3. What is the child beginning to develop as a reader?

4. What does the child has firmly established as a writer?

5. What is the child developing as a writer?

6. What is the child beginning to develop as a writer?

Figure 3.   Group composite record form.

development on a continuum. There is a comfort level in the dyads or small groups which enables teachers to ask each other, "Do you see what I see?" In response to the guideline questions, teachers differentiate between the strategies the child uses consistently (across texts and situations), selectively (some contexts, but not all), or that are just emerging. Teachers also note the data sources/documents they used to support each strategy on the list. Through this task teachers develop a sense of literacy as both a process and a continuum, rather than a grade equivalent score or a percentile rank. (After our model was developed, many western New York school districts adopted report cards which replace letter grades with indications of the child's proficiency --(Not Yet; Beginning, Developing, Uses Independently/Consistently).

As their group's composite record develops, the link between assessment and instruction emerges. They begin to ask each other about the opportunities for strategy development a child may have in the classroom as well as the appropriateness of the teacher's instruction. In writing, this may become apparent as the group compares the comments recorded in the teacher's anecdotal records during small group instruction to the conference notes in writer's workshop and the child's samples. The group might think that the teacher's prompts are hindering the child's revision of a particular piece by focusing on the mechanics, rather than clarifying the meaning. When they examine the child's behaviors reading familiar text or her own language in a dictated story to samples from less familiar texts or genres, teachers begin to identify when a match or a mismatch occurs. How appropriate are the texts this child reads for pleasure and instruction? Are they too easy or too difficult? Throughout this discussion, teachers develop a clearer idea of the impact of instructional approaches and curricula on the child's chances for becoming a literate individual.

Thus, the final part of this task is to ask the group to make recommendations for a literacy program for the child whose portfolio they analyzed. Based upon what they have identified as consistent, selective, and emerging behaviors, the group lists instructional suggestions and opportunities they feel would foster the child's development in reading and writing. For both preservice and inservice teachers, this affords them a chance to tap their background knowledge of literacy instruction in arriving at their decisions. Throughout the process of developing the composite summary and recommendations, teachers are encouraged and reminded to use language consistent with the literacy framework and appropriate for parent conferences or next year's teacher.

Establishing Common Ground

At this time, the total group meets to share their findings and recommendations. To keep this process straightforward and equitable, the discussion begins with the behaviors or strategies the child demonstrated consistently. In turn, each group shares their list as well as their document sources and these are recorded on a chart. Subsequent groups add to the list only those strategies or sources not previously stated. Discrepancies among groups are resolved and consensus reached. The process continues for the child's selective and emerging strategies and instructional recommendations. Teachers find that their impressions of the child are actually quite similar, demonstrating how portfolios can portray a child to those without firsthand knowledge of him.

Next, we focus on the importance of balanced documentation within a portfolio. By this time teachers already recognize that the portfolio reveals as much about the teacher and her values as it does about the child. Although the case study portfolios are balanced in terms of documentation and input, issues arise about the number of documents-too many or too few of a particular type or from a given context. We also ask teachers what they wish had been contained in the sample portfolios and why. The time spent exploring issues of portrayal, distortion of a child's abilities, and the utilization of portfolios is essential to understanding the portfolio assessment process. Since teachers bear personal and professional responsibility for their assessment, we need to recognize and underscore that what has been omitted from a portfolio may be as important as the documentation that is included. If a child's portfolio represents him to others, then ethical issues of fairness and accuracy must be addressed.

Finally, we remind our preservice and inservice teachers that the literacy framework we developed at the beginning is subject to change. As teachers read professionally, explore literacy alternatives, observe children, and implement portfolio assessment, their theoretical framework will be shaped by these experiences. What they identified as important strategies for emergent readers this year may be replaced and revised in the future.

Conclusion

Our model immerses participants in the portfolio process, changing assessment from a static to an dynamic process. As teachers engage in their analysis and synthesis of data, they acquire a better sense of logistical considerations of time, document collection, and summarizing a class set of portfolios. Throughout the model, we emphasize teacher's judgment and understanding of children and literacy learning as prerequisite abilities for implementing portfolios or any form of authentic assessment. Thus, teachers are at the center and it is their metacognitive abilities, experience, and education that are critical. As teacher educators we have the responsibility to assure that they are prepared to meet the future challenges of teaching and assessment.

References

Afflerbach, P., & Kapinus, B. (1993). The balancing act. *The Reading Teacher, 47*, 62-64.

Bird, L.B. (1989). The art of teaching: Evaluation and revision. In K.S. Goodman, Y.M. Goodman, & W.J. Hood, (Eds.), *The whole language evaluation book,* (pp. 15-24). Portsmouth, NH: Heinemann.

Calfee, R.C. (1987). The school as a context for assessment of literacy. *The Reading Teacher,40*, 738-743.

Daws, D. (1993). Schoolwide portfolios. In *Student portfolios*, (pp. 33-45). National Education Association.

Farr, R. (1992). Putting it all together: Solving the reading assessment puzzle. *The Reading Teacher, 46*, 26-37.

Ginsberg, M., & Clift, R. (1990). The hidden curriculum of preservice teacher education. In R.W. Houston, (Ed.), *Handbook of research on teacher education*, (pp. 549-566). New York: Macmillan.

Goodman, Y.M. (1989). Evaluation of students: Evaluation of teachers. In K.S. Goodman, Y.M. Goodman, & W.J. Hood, (Eds.), *The whole language evaluation book,* (pp. 3-14). Portsmouth, NH: Heinemann.

Graves, D. (1991). When tests fail. In J.A. Roderick, (Ed.), *Context-responsive approaches to assessing children's language.* (pp. 9-19). Urbana, IL: National Conference on Research in English.

Johnston, J.S., & Wilder, S.L. (1992). Changing reading and writing programs through staff development. *The Reading Teacher, 45*, 626-631.

Kapinus, B. (1994). Looking at the ideal and the real in large scale reading assessment: The view from two sides of the river. *The Reading Teacher, 47*, 578-580.

Monroe, D. (1991). Qualities of a school district culture that support a dynamic process of assessment. In J. A. Roderick, (Ed.), *Context-responsive approaches to assessing children's language,* (pp. 97-104). Urbana, IL: National Conference on Research in English.

Mosenthal, P.B. (1986). Translating definitions of reading in research into practice. *The Reading Teacher, 39*, 476-479.

Neilsen, L. (1990). To be a good teacher: Growing beyond the garden path. *The Reading Teacher, 44*, 152-153.

Paris, S.G., Calfee, R.C., Filby, N., Hiebert, E.H., Pearson, P.D., Valencia, S.W., & Wolf, K.P. (1992). A framework for authentic literacy assessment. *The Reading Teacher, 46*, 88-98.

Sorenson, N.L. (1993). Holistic evaluation of literacy development: Framing the process. *Reading Research and Instruction, 32*, 66-75.

Taylor, D. (1991). From the child's point of view: Alternate approaches to assessment. In J.A. Roderick, (Ed.), *Context-responsive approaches to assessing children's language* (pp. 32-51). Urbana, IL: National Conference on Research in English.

Teale, W.H., Hiebert, E.H., & Chittenden, E.A. (1987). Assessing young children's literacy development. *The Reading Teacher, 40,* 772-777.

Tierney, R.J., Carter, M.A., & Desai, L.E. (1991). *Portfolio assessment in the reading-writing classroom.* Norwood, MA: Christopher-Gordon Publishers, Inc.

Valencia, S. (1990). A portfolio approach to classroom reading assessment: The whys, whats, and hows. *The Reading Teacher, 43,* 338-340.

Valencia, S.W., & Place, N. (1994). Portfolios: A process for enhancing teaching and learning. *The ReadingTeacher, 47,* 666-669.

Winograd, P., Paris, S., & Bridge, C. (1991). Improving the assessment of literacy. *The Reading Teacher, 45,* 108-116.

Wixson, K.K., Peters, C.W., Weber, E.M., & Roeber, E.D. (1987). New directions in statewide reading assessment. *The Reading Teacher, 40,* 749-754.

Zeichner, K. M., & Gore, J. (1990). Teacher socialization. In R.W. Houston, (Ed.), *Handbook of research on teacher education,* (pp. 329-348). New York: Macmillan.

The Challenge of Change: The M.Ed. Portfolio

Barbara Martin Palmer
Marie E. Holahan
and
Judy Ramoy Johnstone
Mount Saint Mary's College

Portfolio development as a means of assessment has many definitions at all levels. In this chapter, the authors describe portfolio development at the graduate level providing information on the contents, evaluation, and challenges and concerns. Using their first hand experiences, the authors provide ideas for those using or wishing to use portfolio assessment in their M.Ed. programs.

Teacher education is undergoing a dramatic change as a consequence of the new vision of assessment that focuses on performance in addition to general knowledge attainment. The Maryland State Department of Education (MSDE) views "learning to teach as a developmental process in which there is continuous engagement with research, best practice, and expert opinion" (MSDE, 1993, p. ii). With this philosophy in mind, MSDE in collaboration with teacher educators throughout the state developed ten performance-based teacher education standards, the Essential Dimensions of Teaching. Each Essential lists performance indicators which are "intended to help programs develop and assess their curricula and their students' performance" (MSDE, 1993, p. 3). Emphasis on authentic assessment in recent years has caused some colleges to redesign their teacher education programs in response to state and national outcome-based standards.

Such standards necessitate that teacher interns demonstrate teaching proficiency as well as learning. How do we assess teaching proficiency and learning? According to Wiggins (1989) performance assessments more authentically and appropriately assess student learning than do standardized tests because they (a) resemble performance in the field; (b) provide greater attention to the teaching and learning of assessment criteria; (c) place emphasis on self assessment; and, (d) ensure mastery through student oral presentations (p. 45). Portfolio assessment is an important tool for measuring student performance.

Much has been written about portfolio assessment in a variety of contexts. One of the earliest uses of portfolio assessment documented in the literature is in writing instruction at all levels of education (Graves & Sunstein, 1992). There are reports of entire districts and states adopting portfolio assessment as a measure of achievement in content-specific disciplines (Marzano, 1994; Valencia & Place, 1994). Paulson, Paulson, and Meyer (1991) describe portfolios as providing "the opportunity to observe students in a broader context (than that which is possible through traditional methods of assessment): taking risks, developing creative solutions, and learning to make judgments about their own performances" (p. 176). Though Paulson et. al (1991) were referring to elementary school students, the same opportunities exist in postsecondary education.

Use of portfolios has been documented at the postsecondary level for a variety of purposes. Elbow and Belanoff (1986), for example, reported on the use of portfolios as a substitute for proficiency exams. Valeri-Gold, Olson, and Deming (1991-1992) described a portfolio model for college developmental learners. Stahle and Mitchell (1993) described the use of portfolios in preservice reading/language arts methods courses. The University of Dayton teacher education program provided a model of the exit portfolio (Geiger & Shugarman, 1988). Dayton students chose samples of work they judged demonstrative of growth in five domains: (a) professional responsibility; (b) command of subject matter; (c) content-specific pedagogy; (d) class organization and management; and, (e) student-specific pedagogy (Geiger & Shugarman, 1988, p. 32). Barton and Collins (1993) noted six reasons commonly cited in the literature to use portfolio assessment in teacher education. First, portfolios reflect student growth in a variety of areas, thus demonstrating the complexity of teaching. In addition, portfolio assessment enhances faculty advising and encourages opportunities for collaborative efforts between colleges, public schools, and students. Most importantly, portfolio assessment develops students' communication skills and facilitates student ownership of learning.

The purpose of this chapter is to describe how one small liberal arts college in Maryland applied the Essential Dimensions of Teaching through the use of portfolio assessment in its Masters of Education program in elementary education.

What is the M. Ed. Portfolio?

The M. Ed. Portfolio is a systematic collection of student work and serves as an on-going record of student class assignments, reflections, and growth. In effect, the M. Ed. Portfolio progresses through three distinct stages. First, it is a course portfolio; second, it is a "working" or developmental portfolio to which the student adds, modifies, and removes work samples; and third, it is a composite or "exit" portfolio which is formally presented to a Graduate Committee. As an assessment tool the course portfolio documents growth and levels of proficiency in each course. The "working" or developmental portfolio synthesizes student work from several courses providing even more evidence of growth and developing proficiency. The composite or "exit" portfolio takes the place of comprehensive examinations and a masters thesis as the end product of the M. Ed. program and as such it serves as a tool to assess student attainment of effective teacher competencies. The composite portfolio also serves as a window into the process of student learning throughout the entire program.

Over time students select work samples that represent "best work" as well as "works in progress." Works may include journal entries, lesson plans, thematic units, student-developed software, videotapes of teaching or presentations, letters of recognition, and other indicators of performance.

How Did the M. Ed. Portfolio Evolve?

In the summary of the Study of the Education of Educators, Goodlad (1990) outlined the need for program coherence in teacher preparation. Portfolio assessment as both a developmental and final product approach to assessment promotes program cohesion. Knowing that most of our students did not assemble portfolios as elementary or secondary students, we realized that to effectively convince them of the viability of this form of assessment, they would have to experience it themselves. Above and beyond that, we wanted to promote meaningful, reflective, and internalized learning that demonstrates a movement from theory to practice in our students.

A review of the literature on portfolio assessment distinguished multiple portfotio models and purposes. Of particular interest was the Aurora Public Schools model (1992). With its list of performance-based outcomes and indicators as high school graduate requirements, we began to think in terms of desired outcomes for M. Ed. program graduates. The literature on effective teachers describes educators who are complex problem solvers, effective communicators, users of pedagogy and content, and professional contributors. These characteristics became the four outcomes of the M. Ed. portfolio and provided the overall framework for the M. Ed. program.

At the same time that the college was developing its M. Ed. program the MSDE was collaborating state-wide on the Essential Dimensions of Teaching (See Appendix A). Faculty compared the list of ten essentials to the four M. Ed. program outcomes and realized that there was an overlap. Figure 1 shows the integration of the ten essentials into the M. Ed. schema of four outcomes.

1. An effective communicator

- Demonstrates an understanding that knowledge of the learner's physical, cognitive, emotional, and socio-cultural development is the basis of effective teaching.
- Incorporates a multicultural perspective which integrates culturally diverse resources, including those from the learner's family and community.
- Demonstrates a knowledge of strategies for integrating students with special needs into the regular classroom.
- Collaborates with the broad educational community including parents, businesses, and social service agencies.

2. A solver of complex problems

- Uses valid asssessment approaches, both formal and informal, which are age-appropriate and address a variety of developmental needs, conceptual abilities, curriculum outcomes and school goals.
- Organizes and manages a classroom using approaches supported by research, best practice, expert opinion, and student learning needs.
- Demonstrates an understanding that classrooms and schools are sites of ethical, social, and civic activity.

3. A user of pedagogy and content

- Demonstrates mastery of appropriate academic disciplines and a repertoire of teaching techniques.
- Use computer and computer-related technology to meet student and professional needs.

4. A professional contributor

- Engages in careful analysis, problem-solving, and reflection in all aspects of teaching.

Figure 1. Integration of M. Ed. outcomes and MSDE essentials.

How is the Portfolio Evaluated?

There are three stages of evaluation of the M. Ed. portfolio that concide with the three types of portfolios (course, developmental, and composite). An evaluation tool was designed to specifically evaluate student proficiency related to student outcomes. To do that faculty generated three to four indicators for each student outcome. Figure 2 identifies the M. Ed. student outcomes and indicators.

An Effective Communicator
- Demonstrates an understanding of human development and teaching models
- Demonstrates interactive communication
- Demonstrates consideration for individual differences

A Solver of Complex Problems
- Uses action research skills
- Applies research results to classroom setting
- Demonstrates competencies in measurement and assessment skills
- Uses a wide variety of strategies for managing complex issues

A User of Pedagogy and Content
- Demonstrates understanding of the factors which shape teaching and learning
- Demonstrates content knowledge in language arts, mathematics, science, and social studies
- Implements integrated instruction
- Utilizes educational technologies

A Professional Contributor
- Demonstrates knowledge about the teaching profession
- Takes a teacher leadership role
- Reflects on role as a professional

Figure 2. M.Ed. Student Outcomes and Indicators.

One rubric was formulated that was appropriate for the assessment of all four outcomes. "A scoring rubric consists of a fixed scale and characteristics describing performance for each point on the scale" (Marzano, 1994). Three points along a continuum of proficiency, "Beginning Level," ""Becoming Proficient," and "Proficient," became our scoring categories. Figure 3 presents the M. Ed. rubric.

Thus, we have one rubric applied to four outcomes and the same rubric is used by instructors, advisors, and the Graduate Committee to evaluate the M. Ed. portfolio at its various stages. Not surprisingly, the evaluation process fosters reflective thinking, program cohesion, and self assessment. In order to evaluate the portfolio one must consider the indicators for each outcome and determine students' level of proficiency based on the evidence collected. By the time students are ready to present their exit portfolios, it is expected that they will have evidence of their abilities in all four outcomes.

Beginning Level
- Sees issues as separate entities
- Has not begun to integrate critical issues into teaching or may have begun but rarely meets with success

Becoming Proficient
- Understands the major issues but does not see all of the implications
- Begins to integrate critical issues into teaching but does not always meet with success

Proficient
- Understands major issues and their implications
- Integrates critical issues into teaching with frequent success

Figure 3. M.Ed. Portfolio Rubric.

Who is Responsible for the M. Ed Portfolio?

Management of the portfolio becomes very important and the graduate student carries the greatest responsibility for the portfolio. Students truly own their portfolios: they maintain possession except when the portfolio is being academic advisors in conferences each semester. Furthermore, students (a) choose work samples (with consultation as necessary) to be included in the portfolio to fulfill course requirements; (b) select additional works to be included in the portfolio with an explanation of why the works are included; (c) reflect on the work samples and on their current level of proficiency and growth in each competency; (d) identify (with assistance as necessary) competencies on which they intend to focus; and (e) explain the purpose of the contents of the course and exit portfolios to the course instructor and Graduate Committee, respectively. However, portfolio responsibilities fall also to the course instructor, academic advisors, and the Graduate Committee.

The course instructor has the responsibility for developing the require-ments for the course portfolio. Instructors identify specific assignments and create rubrics to assess them. These are distributed as early as possible in the semester. Instructors are also responsible for reviewing the content of each student portfolio at the end of the semester as one method of student assessment. Additionally, instructors are expected to respond thoughtfully to student reflections about areas of growth and proficiency as well as areas of need.

Academic advisors play an important role in the on-going assembly and assessment of the developing portfolio. Each semester, graduate students meet with their advisors to review progress in all four competencies. Shulman

(1988) argues that portfolio development *should* involve interaction and mentoring in the same way that a doctoral dissertation reflects both the efforts of the candidate and the advice of the advisor (in Sheldin, 1991, p. 5). Together, advisors and students identify the growth made and proficiency level in each area. Additionally, advisors solicit students' perceived areas of need. At each advising session then, students identify concerns, discuss strategies, and develop a plan to meet their needs, given the courses currently taken and those yet to be taken.

A Graduate Committee, comprised of at least three members (academic advisor, college faculty member, and one Local Education Agency educator) evaluates composite portfolios. Members review portfolio contents prior to the student's oral multimedia presentation. Based on committee members' review of materials and student presentation, the Committee makes a recommendation regarding the conferral of the M. Ed degree.

A Scenario

The following scenario reflects an abbreviated version of the evaluation conference between the professor of EDUC 505 Teacher as Researcher and Chris, a student in the class. In this evaluation, the course professor used the rubric for the Effective Communicator outcome to guide Chris's assessment of her proficiency level.

P: What did you do in this class that would provide evidence that you are an effective communicator?

C: Well, I think I effectively communicated today when I presented my research proposal.

P: I agree. You did a wonderful job. What do you think made it effective?

C-   I think I was pretty organized . . .and I used overheads to point out important research.

P: I liked how you structured your literature review. You clearly touched on three areas: attitude formation, attitude change, and multiethnic literature. What other evidence do you have that you are an effective communicator?

C: (Pause) Hmm. I don't know.

P: Let's look at the rubric you have. (Pause) Is there anything that you did this semester that demonstrates your understanding of human development?

C: When I was planning my data collection I knew not to use a paper and pencil test because young children have short attention spans and might be limited by their writing abilities. That's why I decided to use a test that involved manipulatives and oral expression. I think that will keep their interest.

P: Good. That's a great example. Okay. Now let's look at the next indicator. Can you think of a time when you demonstrated interactive communication?

C: Well, that's about all we did in this class. (laughter) We participated in every class.

P: How? Can you be specific?

C: We talked about the readings, responded to each others' process papers, and conferenced with you. And today I answered everybody's questions about my proposal.

P: What about considerations for individual differences? Any evidence?

C: I think I accommodated a variety of learning styles in my presentation. I read aloud a multiethnic book, asked you to write about similarities between you and Eskimos, and like I already said, I used overheads as visual cues.

P: Now let's think about all this evidence you have. Based on your evidence, would you say you are at the beginning level, becoming proficient level, or proficient level as an effective communicator?

C: (Pause) Well, I guess I'd say I'm proficient since I got an A on both my presentation and written proposal.

P: What will you write on the rubric as evidence of proficiency? I think you'd probably want to write more than "I got an A on the research proposal and presentation."

C: Could I say this? "I researched prejudicial attitudes and multiethnic literature as a one way of developing positive attitudes in my classroom. I came up with a plan of action and was able to communicate it orally and in writing with success."

P: You can say that. Good. Be sure to say "in EDUC 505" because when you meet with your advisor you'll be adding evidence from other courses.

The professor and student proceeded through all of the outcomes during the portfolio evaluation conference in like manner. However, space limitations prohibit our sharing more.

What are Some Consequences of Portfolio Use?

There are instructional consequences resulting from the heavy reliance on portfolio assessment in the M. Ed. program. First, all instructors must endorse the concept of portfolio assessment, understand it, and use it. Instructors must, also, design their courses to incorporate the competencies as logical as possible, so it is important that instructors articulate how their courses do so to students. Third, all stakeholders must see that each course contributes to the composite portfolio.

There are also programmatic consequences worthy of mention. The M. Ed. program draws a diverse population of learners, representing varying degrees of experience and knowledge. Some of our graduate students are career changers and seek initial certification, some an M. Ed. degree, and some seek both. Because of the heavy reliance on portfolio assessment and self reflection, we are able to individualize students' programs of study based on current strengths and needs. In addition, portfolio assessment requires students to focus on their learning in all coursework, which in turn lends a cohesiveness to the program.

Finally, it is hoped that by modeling portfolio assessment, individualization, and student reflection, our graduate students will better understand the purposes for each component of teaching and transfer their experiences in the teacher education program to classroom teaching.

What are Some Challenges and Concerns?

There are some challenges and concerns that confront students and faculty of the M. Ed. program. Perhaps the primary challenge involves the time commitment involved on everyone's part. Over the course of the program students spend a great deal of time developing course, developmental, and composite portfolios. For instructors, it is initially very time consuming to develop the portfolio requirements and rubrics for each course. However, once completed, we expect they will need little modification. The time intensive portion of the instructors' work lies in the evaluation of course portfolios, which involves a thoughtful response providing insight and guidance. Some instructors respond in written form while others respond verbally during 30-minute end-of-semester conferences. As class size increases each year it is expected that response time will also increase. Even with limits on class size, twenty portfolios are burdensome for the thoughtful instructor.

The time intensive aspect also permeates the advisor-student relationship. Students meet with their advisors at least once each semester for a meeting that lasts approximately one hour, depending on the students' needs and progress in the program. When the advising conference is multiplied by fifteen graduate advisees and added to course evaluation conferences and undergraduate advising, portfolio assessment becomes formidable. While our faculty cherishes this time to work with advisees, it must be recognized that on most campuses, the time available for such advising meetings is very limited. Again, the continued growth of the M. Ed. program contributes to the challenge.

The challenge of time availability is directly related to the concern on everyone's part to carefully manage the development of the portfolio, keeping an eye toward the composite portfolio presentation. We suspect that, with experience, we will learn some short cuts and will also be better able to prioritize aspects of the portfolio and advising process, but we, too, are still learning. As we enter the third year of our M. Ed. program, we anticipate our first graduates and look forward to assessing with them not only their growth and proficiency, but ours as well.

References

Aurora Public Schools. (1992). *APS Graduation Portfolio Guidelines: Life long learner model.* Aurora, CO: Author

Barton, J., & Collins, A. (1993). Portfolios in teacher education. *Journal of Teacher Education, 44* (3), 200-210.

Black, L., Daiker, D. A., Sommers, J., & Stygall, G. (1994). *New directions in portfolio assessment: Reflective practice. critical theory and large-scale scoring.* New York: Heinemann.

Elbow, P., & Belanoff, P. (1986). Portfolios as a substitute for proficiency examination. *College Composition and Communication, 37,* 336-339.

Geiger, J. & Shugarman, S. (1988). Portfolios and case studies to evaluate teacher education students and programs. *Action in Teacher Education, 10* (3), 31-34.

Goodlad, J. I. (1990). Better teachers for our nation's schools. *Phi Delta Kappan,* 185-194.

Graves, D., & Sunstein, B. (Eds.) (1992). *Portfolio portraits.* Portsmouth, NH: Heinemann.

Maryland State Department of Education. (1993). *Essential dimensions of teaching.* Baltimore, MD: Author. MSDE, Division Section, 200 W. Baltimore St., Baltimore, MD

Marzano, R. J. (1994). Lessons from the field about outcome-based performance assessments. *Educational Leadership, 51* (6), 44-50.

Paulson, F. L., Paulson, P. R., & Meyer, C. A. (1991). What makes a portfolio a portfolio? *Educational Leadership. 48* (5), 60-63.

Seldin, P. (1991). *The teaching portfolio.* Bolton, MA: Anker Publishing.

Stahle, D. L, & Mitchell, J. P. (1993). Portfolio assessment in college methods courses: Practicing what we preach. *Journal of Reading, 36,* 538-542.

133

Valencia, S. W., & Place, N. (1994). Portfolios: A process for enhancing teaching and learning. The *Reading Teacher, 47*, 666-669.

Valeri-Gold, M., Olson, J. R., & Deming, M. P. (1991-1992). Portfolios: Collaborative authentic assessment opportunities for college developmental learners. *Journal of Reading, 35*, 298-305.

Wiggins, G. (1991). Standards, not standardization: Evoking quality student work. *Educational Leadership. 48* (5), 18-25.

Wiggins, G. (1989). Teaching to the (authentic) test. *Educational Leadership. 46* (7), 41-47.

Appendix

<u>Essential Dimensions of Teaching</u>

1. Demonstrate mastery of appropriate academic disciplines and a repertoire of teaching techniques.
2. Demonstrate an understanding that knowledge of the learner's physical, cognitive, emotional, and socio-cultural development is the basis of effective teaching.
3. Incorporate a multicultural perspective which integrates culturally diverse resources, including those from the learner's family and community.
4. Demonstrate a knowledge of strategies for integrating students with special needs into the regular classroom.
5. Use valid asssessment approaches, both formal and informal, which are age-appropriate and address a variety of developmental needs, conceptual abilities, curriculum outcomes and school goals.
6. Organize and manage a classroom using approaches supported by research, best practice, expert opinion, and student learning needs.
7. Use computer and computer-related technology to meet student and professional needs.
8. Demonstrate an understanding that classrooms and schools are sites of ethical, social, and civic activity.
9. Collaborate with the broad educational community including parents, businesses, and social service agencies.
10. Engage in careful analysis, problem-solving, and reflection in all aspects of teaching.

Authors' Note: The authors acknowledge the help of Dr. Lorraine Costella, Assistant State Superintendent for Instruction, in the development of the M. Ed. Portfolio outcomes and rubric.

Literacy Portfolios: The Myth and the Reality

Linda Irwin-DeVitis
Binghamton University

Educational innovations that attract great fanfare and then disappear without a trace have led to the cynical dismissal of the transitory "megatrends" in education. Portfolio assessment certainly qualifies as a current educational megatrend. It has been a hot topic among practitioners and researchers in literacy. The publication of books on portfolio assessment in literacy by Graves and Sunstein (1992) and Tierney, Carter and Desai (1991), the numerous articles and conference presentations on portfolios, and a new journal, *Portfolio,* attest to the incredible interest in this type of assessment. Unfortunately, many of those in assessment and evaluation who are examining the potential of literacy portfolios for assessment beyond the classroom and many teachers who are in districts where literacy portfolios have been mandated are already disenchanted. What is the future of portfolios in literacy assessment? The reality is that literacy portfolios can furnish opportunities for growth, collaboration and learning in informal, classroom contexts. The myth is that portfolios can also be a quick fix for legitimate concerns about the current state of large scale educational assessment.

Portfolios In the Literacy Classroom

Literacy portfolios are a welcome and powerful tool for informal assessment consistent with current theories in literacy and learning. Collections of work initiated and chosen by student authors with input and guidance from teachers, parents and peers are the very heart of portfolios. By nature, portfolios legitimize and celebrate the creative work of individual students. Who can forget Carol Avery's (1989) moving account of Laura, a first-grader whose parents, classmates, and teacher treasure her published work even after her tragic death? "Laura left a legacy. Part of that legacy is the six little published books and the five-inch-thick stack of paper that is her writing from our daily writing workshops. When we read her words, we hear again her voice and her laughter" (p. 274). Portfolios perform an archival function that is valued by the writer, peers, family and teachers who are personally involved.

Portfolios, used for informal, authentic individual assessment, also encourage the creativity that is too seldom nurtured in our schools. Kenny, a sixth grader, found his portfolio the perfect vehicle in which to develop a series of short stories, poems, and skits about Quarvo, a magical kingdom he created. He is currently working on a computer animation project set in Quarvo and based on one of his stories. The disk containing the animated story will also be a part of his literacy portfolio. As Elliot Eisner (1991) so eloquently states, "The imagination is, fundamentally, an important dimension of human consciousness and, at bottom, the engine of cultural and social progress" (p. 15). Literacy portfolios encourage students like Kenny to explore, to use their imaginations and to stretch the boundaries of their worlds. Because Kenny is the owner of his portfolio, he knows that it is his right and responsibility to include items that attest to the depth, breadth and creativity of his own literacy. While Kenny confers with his peers, seeks input from his teacher and his parents, ultimately he must decide what to include in his portfolio *and* he must be able to explain and justify his choices. In Kenny's classroom (and many other literacy classrooms where portfolios are valued for their individuality) the process of assembling a portfolio, deciding upon the content and organization, and reflecting upon the content is as important as the actual portfolio. Kenny and his teacher have examined his portfolio to identify his established strengths in writing (ability to use different genre, excellent use of dialogue, imaginative and fast-paced plots, thematic unity) as well as his emerging abilities (detailed and well-crafted description, rounded and well-developed characters, and sentence variety). The congruence between Kenny's self-selected reading preferences (his list of books read is 70% science fiction) and his writing was also clearly demonstrated in his portfolio. In the area of reading, Kenny's portfolio includes examples of his reader response entries from the beginning to the midpoint of the year. Early in the year his typical entry was two sentences without specific support. By December Kenny's typical log entry included detailed observations and evaluations on characters and plot structure and he frequently compared or contrasted his current reading with earlier reading or personal experiences. In one entry, Kenny himself pointed out the similarity between his use of dialogue and that of one of his favorite authors. Portfolios have added a new dimension and greater authenticity to literacy assessment in Kenny's classroom.

Individual literacy portfolios encourage learners and teachers to emphasize and recall process as well as product. Tam, an ESL student, chose to write prose and poetry based on her experiences as a "boat person" attempting to flee Viet Nam. Her pieces are powerful and poignant, a blend of two distinct cultural and linguistic traditions melded through the lens of her unique individual vision. Tam's drafts and revisions, the journal excerpts, and the finished pieces in her portfolio are evidence of Tam's development as a speaker and writer of English, an eloquent author and as a unique young woman. Tam chose to include Vietnamese as well as English versions of many of her pieces, and her non-English speaking parents value both the historical record that her portfolio represents and Tam's command of English. Tam's responses to her reading bring a divergent perspective. In her responses to literature, Tam frequently comments upon nuances to which students who are part of the dominant culture are oblivious. She was particularly struck by the differences between Vietnamese and American culture in the relationships of children and parents, students and teachers. Literacy portfolios like Tam's have the potential to provide an alternative and authentic evaluation of students' work.

Literacy Portfolios for Large Scale Assessment

However, the promise of literacy portfolios, though legitimate and exciting, is limited. As Maeroff (1991) states, " It may be that an alternative assessment that is a marvelous indicator of an individual child's academic progress will prove fairly useless for other purposes. Americans may have to decide whether comparisons are what they seek in alternative assessment or whether they prefer to use the approach for other more individualized purposes" (p. 276).

This paper is an attempt to clarify some of the issues surrounding portfolios and to caution that the legitimate uses and advantages of portfolios may be obscured if they are defined and implemented in ways that are inconsistent with their promise. The true potential of portfolios is realized in authentic, informal assessment that fosters diversity and creativity, is an integral part of instruction, and promotes the development of metacognitive strategies enabling the learner to move toward independence. Yet, there are states, districts, and educational experts who are heralding portfolios as the replacement for all traditional standardized assessment. That type of blind faith and unsubstantiated endorsement is dangerous. Worthen (1993) warns "...Educators should be as slow to accept claims that alternative assessment is the panacea for all of education's ills as they are to believe critics who portray the pimples of alternative assessment as terminal acne" (p. 454).

The Demand for Alternative Assessment in Literacy

Why is there a demand for alternative types of assessment in literacy? With the emergence of more constructivist, experiential and holistic approaches to learning and teaching that characterize the whole language movement in literacy, and the various thematic and interdisciplinary curricular approaches that have reappeared over the last decade, there has emerged a growing discontent with the traditional tools of assessment. Teachers and researchers note the chasm between the newer social-constructivist instructional frameworks and the theoretical and philosophical assumptions of traditional assessment (standardized and teacher-made tests that are typically reductionist and frequently de-contextualized). Many educators and researchers are calling for alternative types of assessment that are more authentic (Wiggins, 1989; Wolf, LeMahieu, & Eresh, 1992; Valencia, McGinley, & Pearson, 1990). These educators look to the portfolio, which has a long tradition in the arts, as one option. Artists, craft persons and writers, among others, have traditionally assembled representative pieces of their work in portfolios that define them as artists, show their creative depth and breadth and demonstrate the themes and nuances of their work. By definition, these types of portfolios are highly individual, include the artist's choice of representative pieces and cannot be reduced to a single grade, rank or category. Evaluation of these portfolios is a major factor in decisions about employment, commissions and grants, but the portfolio review process does not require ranking along a unitary construct. The artist may choose to include or omit various works depending upon the audience with whom the portfolio is to be shared. Thus, the portfolio represents a body of work and the artist's considered decisions about the exemplars chosen for inclusion. Portfolios celebrate diversity and the individual nature of the creative process. The artist's portfolio is certainly a prototype of authentic assessment that respects the differences among individuals. It is this authenticity and the compatibility with the pluralistic reality of public education that makes portfolio assessment so promising in educational settings.

An increasingly vocal group of literacy educators insists upon assessment that is not separate from instruction, and that represent real tasks relevant to the learner and are authentic in that they mirror the ways in which assessment counts in the real world beyond the classroom (Y. Goodman, 1989). In educational settings, literacy portfolios are certainly an alternative to traditional assessment, and they have the potential for a much greater degree of authenticity.

It is important to have clarity regarding the difference between **alternative** and **authentic** assessment. **Alternative assessment** is defined as any form of assessment that is other than traditional standardized tests, paper and pencil exercises and teacher-made examinations. The popularity of alternative forms of assessment is in large measure a result of the growing awareness of the inadequacy of traditional measures to furnish the kinds of evaluative information needed to make informed decisions about the educational strengths and weaknesses of individual students. Denny Taylor's (1991)

Learning Denied is one frightening example of the misuse of de-contextualized and reductionist assessment measures in evaluating an individual child. Literacy educators and policy-makers are interested in augmenting traditional assessment with more promising alternatives. Those who are seeking more authentic learning and teaching are also exploring alternative assessments congruent with their instructional philosophy and methodology.

Given current literacy theory that emphasizes process as well as product, real and relevant contexts, individual purposes and interests, educators are looking for **authentic assessments** that mirror the authenticity they strive for in literacy learning and teaching. Authentic assessment refers to assessment that is an integral part of instruction, is done for real purposes in specific contexts and includes student decision-making and self-evaluation, the metacognitive aspects of evaluation. Complex projects, integrated literacy experiences and the recursive nature of individual literacy learning demand authentic assessment. The process of compiling individual literacy portfolios nurtures the growing independence of the student, the development of his/her self-evaluative abilities as a reader and a writer, and the decision-making that allows personal values and preferences to be honored through feedback and collaboration in the process of meeting negotiated outcomes and individual goals. Unfortunately, in an attempt to promote the use of portfolios in literacy assessment, to stretch their utility by using them for comparison among students, educational policy-makers in many states and districts are advocating a different kind of portfolio, one that is mandated and standardized.

Standardized Literacy Portfolios

Many states, districts, and policy-makers view literacy portfolios as a large scale assessment tool that can effectively and efficiently replace traditional measures. In order to achieve objectivity, comparability, and efficiency in scoring, portfolios are "standardized," i.e., the content, form, and style is defined. "Standardized" literacy portfolios negate the promise and potential of portfolio assessment and fail to preserve its authenticity. Authentic assessment is shaped by context and reflects the individuality, metacognitve knowledge and decision-making of the learner in real and relevant situations; therefore, it **cannot** exist when the student/learner is left out of the decision-making process.

The following paragraphs describe situations in which portfolios are not authentic. A literacy portfolio is not authentic if it denies or subverts the ownership of the student. If a state, school district, or school require a "standard portfolio" defined by educational authorities in ways that prompt the student involvement in selection by defining the contents, the authenticity is lost.

In the case of a rural district in upstate New York, the literacy portfolio required by the district and defined by a committee of teachers and administrators have a mandated content that must include: an essay (or essays) on a standardized topic with all working papers, relevant test scores in reading and writing, a list of books read, book reports on several required books, examples of written work in three pre-determined genre, and a completed checklist designed to measure reading and writing skills and strategies. The ultimate decision as to which compositions are included is the responsibility of the teacher. Two of the book reports are based upon required readings, and the format is standardized. Input from parents and peers are not mentioned in the formal description of the portfolio assessment process.

Another case of the "standardized portfolio" that subverts authenticity occurs when the state, district, school or teacher assigns a unitary ranking based on preset criteria. As Tierney (1991) states, "The pursuit of simplification, standardization, and objectivity for portfolio evaluations seems contrary to actual portfolios that are by nature complex, individual, and subjective" (174). An authentic literacy portfolio cannot be reduced to a single score or ranking. The depth, breadth, creativity, and uniqueness of a portfolio defy reduction to a numerical abstraction similar to the single number or percentile produced in standardized testing. The rank, number, and percentile tell little about the individual's strengths and weaknesses, improvement and self-evaluative ability. When portfolios are reduced to this type of numerical abstraction, one hears administrators and teachers talk about the percentages of portfolios that are above the cut-off standard, the percentage of portfolio "passes" and the monotony of grading hundreds of essays and book reports on the same topics and books. The individual is reduced to a score to be compared to other scores.

Such "standardized portfolios" are also time-consuming and ponderous. While even standardized portfolios furnish information not available through standardized tests because they are a somewhat closer approximation of the real world, the time and effort involved in their assembly may not be worth the additional information. Teachers who have used standardized literacy portfolios often feel that little has been gained for the time and effort expended. As one teacher stated, "I have twenty-eight portfolios which are almost identical!" Parents, too, find little that is unique about these collections and students themselves rarely demonstrate pride and ownership.

In addition to sacrificing individuality and authenticity, standardized portfolios are costly in both time and money. Given the effort needed to standardize the components, the evaluation rubric, the inter-rater reliability of the evaluators, the standardized literacy portfolio is not a cost effective alternative to standardized assessment. As Maeroff (1991) states, "While it may be possible to be systematic about alternative assessment, there are ultimately no quick and easy ways to rate large numbers of performance-based tasks or portfolios" (p. 274). This is a particular concern when most educators agree that teachers need more time for collaboration, joint planning, and professional development. The notion of depriving classroom teachers of significant amounts of instructional or planning time in the name of large scale assessment is disturbing. The costs of planning, inservice education, and scoring (extra pay for teachers and/or substitute salaries) are substantial. The time, effort, and money required for large scale "standardized portfolio" assessment may not stand up well to cost-benefit analysis.

Ultimately, the information in standardized literacy portfolios may not even be helpful to the classroom teacher who has not been a part of the portfolio process. How feasible is it for a secondary teacher with over one hundred students to carefully examine each individual student's portfolio for the previous year? Is it more or less likely that teachers will take that time if the individual ownership and variety have been eliminated in search of objectivity, and/or quantitatively ranked comparisons? Even the elementary teacher may find the task of reviewing portfolios time-consuming and minimally beneficial if the student's choice of content, organization, and style, and the self-evaluative features are restricted or prohibited in the quest for standardization.

On the other hand, classroom teachers who use authentic literacy portfolios speak often of the added benefits of coming to know individual students not only as readers and writers, but also as unique people with specific needs and interests. For many teachers it is this personal quality that makes portfolios worth the time and effort. A seventh grade teacher remarked, "My incoming students' portfolios provided insights that otherwise would have taken weeks or months."

Parents and students also lose out when portfolios are standardized. One of the most meaningful experiences for students can be the presentation of portfolios to an audience that includes their parents. One teacher tells of a 95% attendance by parents when her fifth graders presented their portfolios. These fifth graders presented an array of portfolios including such disparate pieces as a poem on the aftermath of divorce, an essay on the life of a Little League coach, a comparison of youth slang in the 1960's and today, an annotated bibliography of books read which were ranked according to the Siskel and

Ebert "thumbs up, thumbs down" standard and one reading group's taped reading of Madeline L'Engle's *A Wrinkle in Time* complete with sound effects.

Portfolio presentation for parents makes little sense when the portfolio contents are standardized and mandated. "Standardized portfolio" assessment on a large scale sacrifices the personal nature and authenticity of individual literacy portfolios. What standardized portfolio will include the published picture book, *The Horse on the Carousel,* that a ninth grader wrote and illustrated for her kindergarten "reading buddy"? Will standardized portfolios showcase the wry humor of a high school junior who chose to develop a cartoon strip in which the characters, Mayhem (Hemingway), Thornehaw (Hawthorne) and Villemel (Melville) spoke in the cadence and style of the notable American author their names suggest? Will Carter's experimentation with rap, his analysis of its historical significance and its relationship to poetry be appropriate for a twelfth grade standardized portfolio? Will Maria's reading log entries as she and her teacher struggle to find books with characters and plots that will reflect and inform her life as the daughter of migrant workers who has never spent more that one year at any school fit into the carefully defined rubrics that generally accompany standardized portfolios?

The Promise of Individual Literacy Portfolios

For individualized literacy portfolios, imagination, reflection, diversity and individuality are not hindrances, but assets to be cherished and enjoyed. The conditions necessary for authentic portfolios include: first, the artifacts and pieces which are undertaken and selected for inclusion are the prerogative of the student (within but not restricted to the general framework of goals set by the teacher, school, state); second, the selection process, the choice of what is included in the portfolio, supports real and meaningful decision-making in which self-evaluation is critical and metacognitive strategies are developed and refined; third, individual opportunities for achieving goals through personally relevant activities and projects are an integral part of the portfolio process and reinforce the archival nature of the portfolio; fourth, parents and peers are actively involved in collaboration in the process of assembling the portfolio and are part of the audience for its presentation; and last, the evaluation of the portfolio occurs within an educational context in which the complexity of individual learning is not reduced to a standardized ranking or a competitive sorting.

As authentic and individual assessment, the portfolio has enormous promise. Individual literacy portfolios are a valid assessment process consistent with current learning theory. Rather than "time out" of the hectic day, portfolio assessment is integral. Literacy portfolios are a welcome addition to our battery of informal, context-specific assessment tools. However, portfolio assessment should not and cannot replace large scale, traditional measures of literacy learning.

Literacy portfolios, pioneered and developed by teachers, documented and celebrated by literacy researchers (Hansen, 1992; Seidel, 1989) as informal, authentic classroom assessment tools are now being appropriated for large scale standardized assessment by policy-makers at the district and state levels. Whatever the future for portfolio assessment in literacy, the impact upon students and the needs and wishes of teachers must be a part of the debate. Literacy researchers and educators must be vocal advocates of portfolio assessment that is congruent with literacy theory and instruction. The future of portfolio assessment must be informed by those who are most directly involved. Educators and policy-makers must actively resist the temptation to reduce the authentic to algorithm, and, in so doing, to homogenize the invigorating diversity of our students and their work. The true power of literacy portfolios is to document, celebrate and foster the unique and idiosyncratic nature of individual literacy development.

References

Avery, C. (1989). Afterword: Laura's legacy. In K.S. Goodman, Y. M. Goodman, & W. J. Hood, (Eds.) *The whole language evaluation book* (pp. 273-274). Portsmouth, NH: Heinemann.

ILEA/Centre for Language in Primary Education. (1988). *The primary language record handbook for teachers.* Portsmouth, NH: Heinemann.

Eisner, E. W. (1991). What really counts in schools. *Educational Leadership, 48*, (5), 10-17.

Goodman, Y. M. (1989). Evaluation of students: Evaluation of teachers. In K.S. Goodman, Y. M. Goodman, & W. J. Hood, (Eds.), *The whole language evaluation book.* (pp. 3-14). Portsmouth, NH: Heinemann.

Graves, D. H. & Sunstein, B. S. (1992). *Portfolio Portraits.* Portsmouth, NH: Heinemann.

Hansen, J. (1992). Literacy portfolios emerge. *The Reading Teacher, 45,* 604-607.

Maeroff, G. I. (1991). Assessing alternative assessment. *Phi Delta Kappan, 73,* (4), 272-281.

Seidel, S. (1989). Even before portfolios: The activities and atmosphere of a portfolio classroom. *Portfolio,* (Nov.) 6-9.

Simons, J. (1992). Portfolios for large scale assessment. In D. Graves & B. Sunstein (Eds.) *Portfolio portraits.* (pp. 96-113). Portsmouth, NH: Heinemann.

Taylor, D. (1991). *Learning Denied.* Portsmouth, NH: Heinemann.

Tierney, R. J., Carter, M.A. & Desai, L. E. (1991). *Portfolio assessment in the reading writing classroom.* Norwood, MA: Christopher-Gordon.

144

Valencia, S. W., McGinley, W., & Pearson, P.D. (1990). Assessing reading and writing. In G. Duffy (Ed.), *Reading in the middle school,* (pp. 124-153). Newark, DE: International Reading Association.

Wiggins, G. (1989). A true test: Toward more authentic and equitable assessment. *Phi Delta Kappan, 70,* 703-713.

Wolf, D. P., LeMahieu, P.G. & Eresh, J. (1992). Good measure: Assessment as a tool for educational reform. *Educational Leadership, 49* (8), 8-13.

Worthen, B. R. (1993). Critical issues that will determine the future of alternative assessment. *Kappan, 74,* 444-454.

Pre and Post Course Literacy Self-Assessment: Its Positive Impact on Preservice Teachers

Jane Brady Matanzo
Florida Atlantic University

Use of portfolio assessment in higher education has received much attention. By encouraging experiences with the portfolio in preservice classes, we can model an assessment instrument appropriate for use in pre-K through 12 teaching. This study describes the use of portfolios with preservice teachers and their reflections on the experiences.

Literacy assessment is currently receiving extensive attention. Focus is upon the inclusion of portfolios, student self-assessment checklists, student-teacher conferences, and other forms of assessment that actively empower students to offer individual input and self-evaluate their progress (Au, Sheu, Kawakami, & Herman, 1990; Cambourne & Turbill, 1990; Herman, Aschbacher, & Winters, 1992; Johnston, 1992; Paris, Calfee, et al., 1992; Routman, 1991; Valencia, 1990; Valencia, Hiebert, & Afflerbach, 1994; Winograd, Paris, & Bridge, 1991). Although much of this emphasis is on employing such procedures in school settings, pre-K through grade 12, it seems that like emphasis should be experienced by preservice teachers in their university classes. A reason for this is that if preservice teachers positively experience a skill, activity, or practice which may be conducive to the success of students they will teach, they may be more likely to transmit that skill, activity, or practice to their own students once they become teachers.

This university to school-based transfer has been effective for university students who experienced portfolio assessments during their training and replicated this practice with their students during pre and post student teaching (Rousculp & Maring, 1992; Wagner, Brock, & Agnew, 1994). In the first study, follow-up during student teaching cited that several students implemented portfolios as one assessment tool in their placement classrooms. The latter study required students to write summative post assessment statements after experiencing portfolio assessment in a language arts methods course. A professional goal expressed by various students was to continue to expand their personal portfolios and to implement portfolios with students they would be teaching. An additional study, which helped pre and inservice teachers become teacher researchers in assessment and other self-selected research areas, found that the far majority of those students continued "kidwatching", read more professional research articles, initiated additional research projects, and felt more empowered as decision-makers (Gray-Schlegel & Matanzo, 1993). All three studies provided students with reflection time and opportunities to share with peers and their instructors how they felt about the portfolio or research experience and opportunities to envision ways the practice they experienced could be applied to their future classroom teaching experiences.

In light of this emphasis on the implementation of student involved assessments and through personal observation that practices preservice teachers successfully experience prior to teaching appear more likely to transfer to actual teaching situations, this author implemented an assessment practice in two different elementary methodology courses. In planning this assessment, it seemed important to include components stressed in the literature: a) a pre and post course evaluation connected to course objectives so growth could be realized in more concrete ways (Herrmann, 1990; Platt & Williams, 1988; Wiggins, 1992); b) a vehicle for self-assessment and reflection (Anthony, Johnson, Mickelson ,& Preece, 1991; Gipe & Richards, 1990; Johnston, 1992; Rumelhart, 1981; Valencia, Hiebert, & Afflerbach, 1994); and 3) a means to determine if transfer to teaching experiences is intended and/or has occurred (Rousculp & Maring, 1992).

Method

Subjects

The population for this study consisted of 112 sophomore, junior, and senior undergraduate students enrolled in four different sections of The Teaching of Children's Literature and 138 junior and senior elementary and special education undergraduate students enrolled in five different sections of The Diagnostic Teaching of Reading. A total of 250 students participated. The various course sections were scheduled respectively during a two year period. All courses were taught by the same instructor.

Assessment Materials

Cognitive, application, and affective goals and objectives were scrutinized for each course by the course instructor. Based upon this examination, pre and post assessment forms were developed which featured a sampling of each of the goals and objectives. Anticipated cognitive, skill, and affective behaviors were included. It seemed important to keep the forms simple, short, and open-ended in order to facilitate completion and self-expression. The assessment design elicited responses that could be given in degrees so that responses could reflect the prior knowledge and perceived gains of each student. The length of each pre-assessment was limited to the front and back of one standard-sized page.

The post assessment replicated the pre-assessment as well as one additional page which encouraged reflection about the course in its entirety and requested input regarding the use of this practice in their future teaching situations. Students were encouraged to relate this reflection in creative ways such as letter form, cassette tapes, play dialogues, and artistic presentations. If students elected to summarize their reflective thinking in traditional written form, they could attach additional pages as needed. (see Appendices A, B, and C for examples of the assessments.)

Procedures

The pre-assessment was administered at the beginning of the first class meeting for each course *prior* to distribution of the syllabus, statements about course expectations, or instruction. Students were asked to note on the Pre-Course Self-Assessment form what they knew or felt about any of the listed items. Upon turning in the completed pre-assessment, students were informed they had just finished a part of their final examination!

Two weeks before the last course session, completed pre-course assessments were returned to students along with the post course assessment forms. Students were given a two week period to reflect personally on their course accomplishments. The forms were due, discussed, and collected at the last course session. The completion of the assessment forms and whole class discussion and reflection were in lieu of a more formal final course examination. If students completed the assessments before and after the course and participated in peer discussions, they received 25 points toward the final course grade for the effort. The pre and post assessments were not assigned letter grades.

Pre and post responses were read, analyzed, and categorized into one of four categories by three trained coders. The reflective responses were categorized and tallied in terms of the frequency of given response patterns.

Pre-assessment forms were used by the instructor to ascertain more fully the prior knowledge, skills, and attitudes of students and to plan course sessions accordingly. Attention to pre-assessment responses often resulted in modifications to the instructor's initial plans to meet more fully the needs of the population of each course section. Post-assessment findings, likewise, were examined fully by the instructor and impacted the teaching of future methodology course sections.

Findings

Pre-and post-assessment findings for each of the two methodology courses were analyzed and categorized as follows:

+ =   Thorough, elaborated, and/or exampled response beyond response requested;

Adequate (Adeq)=   Acceptable for type of response requested;

Partial (Part)=   Some response given but not acceptable/ complete in terms of request;

No Response (NR) =   No response conveyed for given item.

In analysis, a composite percentage for both courses on the *pre-assessment* responses showed an average of 11% of the responses as adequate; 28% as *partial*; and 61% as having *no response*. None of the pre-assessment responses merited the + category. It should be noted that partial credit was given if the course was called "kiddie lit", not children's literature. Also, if students responded negatively to "feeling" types of items such as "I have always hated to read", the response was considered partial.

A composite percentage for both courses on the *post-assessment* responses showed 66% as exceeding expectations which was assigned to the + category. Thirty-four of the responses were considered *adequate*. No post assessment responses were placed in either the partial or no response categories.

For the post-assessment, 165 or 66% of the students elaborated on answers compared to none of the 250 students in the pre-assessment. For the pre-assessment, all 250 students gave no response to one or more items compared to no students leaving a response blank for the post-assessment. There also were no post-assessment responses categorized as partial. See Tables 1 and 2 for the percentage of pre-and post-assessment responses for the specific items of each course.

When asked if the pre-and post-assessment technique helped them realize any gains made in either of the courses, 88% of the students responded yes; 12% responded *somewhat*; and 0% responded *no*. Therefore, all students were aware they had progressed. Sample comments to support this awareness included, "I now can answer everything and **more** from my head. I left a lot of blanks on the first form. It's easy and makes sense now!; "I now can add

Table 1.
The Teaching of Children's Literature: Pre and Post Assessment Findings

Items	+	Pre Adeq.	Part.	NR	+	Post Adeq.	Part	NR
1. Course name*	-	65%	35%	-	-	100%	-	-
2. Reading/lit. att.	-	54%	46%	-	93%	7%	-	-
3. Ch. lit def.	-	48%	52%	-	22%	78%	-	-
4. Genre'	-	-	8%	92%	22%	78%	-	-
5. Pic. bk. titles, etc.	-	15%	52%	33%	42%	58%	-	-
6. Illustrators	-	-	2%	98%	47%	53%	-	-
7. Trad. lit. def.	-	-	15%	85%	56%	44%	-	-
8. Trad. titles, etc.	-	8%	11%	81%	34%	66%	-	-
9. Poets	-	-	22%	78%	87%	13%	-	-
10. Fantasy	-	27%	30%	57%	92%	8%	-	-
11. Lit. elements	-	-	44%	56%	83%	17%	-	-
12. Non-fic. authors	-	-	-	100%	12%	88%	-	-
13. Realistic fic., etc.	-	7%	72%	21%	85%	15%	-	-
14. Awards	-	-	12%	88%	-	100%	-	-
15. Issues	-	-	54%	46%	91%	9%	-	-
16. Motivate/involve	-	9%	73%	18%	97%	3%	-	-
17. Importance of lit.	-	7%	91%	2%	82%	18%	-	-
18. Additional info.	-	8%	-	92%	See reflective comments			

* Items abbreviated here; see Form 1 in the Appendix for full statement of item.

to or correct things I thought were right in the beginning that I wrote down.";
or "This is the first class where I could tell what I knew about some things at
the beginning of the class and then be able to compare it to what I knew at the
end. The pre-assessment gave me a condensed overview of what was going to
be covered in the course. I'm amazed in seeing what I learned and what I can
do now!" All students wrote some supportive statement in their post
assessment to substantiate their perceived progress.

In responding to the post assessment item, "Would you use a pre-and post-
assessment with students you might teach?", 73% of the students said yes;
23%, *maybe*; and four percent, *no*. Those who responded *yes* supported their
answer by claiming this type of assessment helps one see what one has learned

Table 2.

The Diagnostic Teaching of Reading: Pre and Post Assessment Findings

Items	+	Pre Adeq.	Part.	NR	+	Post Adeq.	Part	NR
1. Reading model	-	10%	32%	58%	83%	17%	-	-
2. Decision Cycle	-	-	-	100%	91%	9%	-	-
3. Reader differences	-	-	26%	74%	96%	4%	-	-
4. Metacognition def.	-	38%	43%	19%	62%	38%	-	-
5. Schema def.	-	42%	45%	87%	4%	96%	-	-
6. IRI description	-	-	18%	72%	68%	32%	-	-
7. Ident. reading assess.	-	-	22%	88%	33%	66%	-	-
8. Instr. rdg. strategies	-	-	16%	84%	97%	3%	-	-
9. Before rdg. practices	-	6%	20%	74%	96%	4%	-	-
10. During rdg. practices	-	5%	20%	75%	96%	4%	-	-
11. After rdg. practices	-	5%	23%	72%	96%	4%	-	-
12. Reads haltingly	-	-	9%	91%	82%	18%	-	-
13. Substitutes words	-	-	9%	91%	93%	7%	-	-
14. Omits words	-	-	9%	91%	90%	10%	-	-
15. Phonics knowledge	-	-	7%	93%	86%	14%	-	-
16. Less able rdrs. attit.	-	10%	86%	4%	45%	55%	-	-
17. Tchg. rdg. feelings	-	8%	92%	-	91%	9%	-	-
18. Additional info.	-	15%	-	85%	See reflective comments			

*Items abbreviated here; see Form 2 in the Appendix for full statement of item.

or can do after being taught. They commented that it also opened one more way they could use to assess students and to encourage and engage students to be active analyzers of their own learning. Students who responded *maybe* said their use of the pre-and post-assessment process depended upon their cooperating teacher's willingness for them to use it or upon the types of assessments the school practiced. Students who responded n*o* offered few reasons other than they didn't like this technique, they felt students already seemed to be satisfied with more traditional assessment means, or it seemed like too much work to keep pre-assessments and compare them with post findings.

Thirty-seven students, including those doing their student teaching experience simultaneously with the courses, were willing to be interviewed during their field experiences. At the time of interview, 64% of the volunteers had used the pre and post assessment technique during student teaching; 52% used it on a regular basis in rather informal ways before and after they taught a lesson. They felt the technique helped them more fully realize what their students knew before and after instruction, plan appropriate instruction, and provide proof to their students as to what each had learned. Those who did not use the pre and post assessment said it was not used by their cooperating teachers or they had not had time to implement it yet in their teaching experiences.

The post-assessment reflective statements also were analyzed for patterns of statements. Three major patterns of statements made by students enrolled in The Teaching of Children's Literature as major gains they perceived were a) an increased confidence in knowing, choosing, and using children's literature; b) more enthusiasm for the subject; and c) an increased desire to read children's literature. Three major patterns of statements made by students enrolled in The Teaching of Diagnostic Reading referred to a) increased confidence in teaching reading; b) extensive instructional strategy knowledge; and c) a greater skill in diagnosing and making a plan for problem readers. Reflective statements varied from one to five pages with many students giving extensive support for aforementioned patterns.

Representative *excerpts* from the reflective statements included the following:

This is one class that I have taken that I have learned much more than I thought I would. I cannot believe how much I know about children's literature now. When I took the pre-course assessment, I could not even name five picture books, much less the authors to go along with them. It feels very good to have gained this much knowledge in such a short time. I feel that I have a better understanding for how much hard work and effort goes into writing for children. It is tough enough to write a book but it goes even further if the book is considered a quality book.... I think that this class has given me an overall appreciation of children's literature. Now when I go to a book store, I stay in there for a couple of hours. I used to walk in, get what I needed, and then leave. It feels terrific to recognize so many of the authors and illustrators as I walk by the bookshelves. In the beginning of his course, I really didn't believe that I could learn as much as I have... One last thing, I started writing my own children's book...

Ali, The Teaching of Children's Literature

Before I had this class, I would look at a book and see nothing but a book. I never took notice of authors, illustrators, or the illustrations. If I chose to read the book, I finished it and thought no farther than "I liked it." or "I didn't like it." Now when I look at a book, I'm more interested in who it's by and what type of book it is. Since my goal is to become a teacher, I also look at how the book could be used in the classroom and whether or not there is anything outstanding about it that might be useful in the future. Through taking this class, I have developed a genuine appreciation and respect for quality literature. This, I feel, is a great outcome since I went into the class hating to read. I learned to enjoy literature and know quite a bit.

Jason, The Teaching of Children's Literature

It really amazes me when I look at the pre-course self-assessment to see that I only answered seven of the eighteen questions and I should mention that not all seven were correct answers. Now I can answer all of the questions correctly, without even opening a book. I sat down and read each individual question and the answers seemed to come naturally. It feels as if diagnostic reading is second nature to me. The drastic progress is seen just as a student sees her progress in a portfolio. This post course assessment is a great idea because it really makes you feel good about your advancement and achievement.....I feel proud about my accomplishments and actually feel confident as a reading diagnostician.

Jill, The Diagnostic Teaching of Reading

As I looked over my pre-course self-assessment, my first reaction was one of embarrassment. I was ashamed that I was that ignorant of such important information about reading. But then it dawned on me that the purpose of this class was to teach me all the objectives (and more) on the assessment sheet. If I knew all the answers at the beginning of the semester, the course would have been redundant...When I think back to the beginning of the semester, when I didn't even know the meaning of the words, diagnostic reading, to the end of the semester, I realize that I have come a long way. But what I care about the most is that, unlike almost all my other classes, what I have learned and the way I have learned it, will enable me to retain it for a lifetime.

Jennifer, The Diagnostic Teaching of Reading

First of all, I would like to say I can not believe how much I did NOT know coming into this class! I actually thought the pre-assessment was quite difficult! Now, looking back, I see that these questions are "the basics" one should know about diagnostic teaching and reading...There is so much I could go on about that I got out of this class, which I must admit comes as a surprise to me. Usually I think that the classes I have gotten a lot out of are very difficult, and not at all interesting! I did work hard in this class but the class has actually been enjoyable which I think has a lot to do with the many different teaching techniques used in class. This post-course assessment is a great idea for showing all of us how much more we now know about being not only teachers; but, better yet, what we now know about being DIAGNOSTIC TEACHERS!

Karen, The Diagnostic Teaching of Reading

The selected excerpts are from individual reflection statements which averaged a length of three pages. The statements are representative of many of the statements made. It should be noted that students frequently offered specific examples of content, skills, and attitudes gained to support their reflections. During the final course session, students referred to both the pre and post assessments as they discussed and compared what was gained from the course. Discussions were focused with students realizing that many of them had started the course with different degrees of knowledge and were completing the course with varied degrees of growth. They conversed about content and skills that were gained, questioned each other about attitudes and opinions toward issues and diagnostic practices, shared strategies they preferred, and offered constructive input for the course.

The majority of post-assessment reflective statements given the instructor were presented in traditional written prose form. However, three students reflected in letter format, four students submitted audio tapes, one student developed a play sharing her reflections through dialogue between a pre-asaurus and a post-asaurus, and one student created a three-dimensional knapsack which bulged with support for what was gained in the course.

The primary course suggestion given by the majority of students was a need for more time for given course activities. Children's literature students wanted more time for book browsing and peer sharing. Diagnostic reading students noted a need for more time to do additional case studies and to learn and practice more instructional strategies.

154

Conclusions and Recommendations

The pre-and post-assessment technique provided an opportunity for preservice students in two education methodology courses to respond to a sampling of course content and skills stimuli prior to course instruction. Students presented, in writing, relevant knowledge they already possessed. This can be a valuable tool also for the instructor who can delete, modify, or add to course instruction dependent on at least a part of students' expressed prior knowledge.

The extreme differences between the degree of student responses on the pre- and post-assessments were anticipated with all the responses on the post assessments completed adequately or exceeding adequacy. In analyzing the pre-assessments, only 11% of the responses were considered adequate and none exceeded adequacy. It is hoped that students ordinarily would make such course gains through effective and appropriate instruction. However, it is not a usual practice, at least for the subjects of this study, that preservice students are encouraged to compare written records of their pre and post expressed knowledge and skills other than to see differences in various test score results. It should be noted that a difference between the way the pre-assessment responses and the post-assessment responses were collected may account partially for the sizeable categorical differences of the responses. Pre-assessment responses were completed solely on the basis of each individual student's prior knowledge recall during an approximate time of 40 minutes in the setting of a university classroom before any course instruction. In contrast, the same students were given a two week period near the conclusion of course instruction to review the pre-assessment and ascertain if any changes had occurred. Resource materials including the textbook, course notes, and course handouts could be referenced as students reflected on their individual gains and the course as a whole.

One result of this type of pre-and post-assessment technique was to minimize the forced memorization of facts and their regurgitation as traditional whole class final examinations often require. This practice was replaced with a technique that encouraged students to review and compare individually what they knew based on their prior knowledge at the beginning of the course and to use information gained through instruction and their ability to employ course resources to demonstrate what they knew and could do by the end of the course. By using the course materials to summarize, recheck, and reinforce ideas, students reviewed and expressed post-course knowledge to a greater depth than is usually experienced on traditional assessments. In analyzing post assessments, students perceived their course achievement as being both considerable and personal. No two pre-and post-assessments were identical for any of the 250 preservice students. Since using this pre-and post-assessment technique, this instructor has observed that students do comprehend and can discuss well beyond the base knowledge. Students often affirmed in their reflective statements that they completed the post assessment content forms "from their heads" and that they really felt they knew well the information and skills imparted during the course. This growth was substantiated through both content and reflective responses which were elaborative and well-articulated. However, a unique difference in using this type of pre-and post-assessment is that response patterns further indicated that the vast majority of students felt they had gained increased self-confidence in their abilities and knowledge to work effectively with students in the teaching of reading and/or children's literature. It also was seen that more than half of the preservice students monitored during their student teaching felt that the pre-and post-assessment technique helped them know more about their students before teaching them something and aided those they taught to better visualize the degree of their own progress.

In regard to student's perceived growth in using the pre and post assessment technique, it is recommended that:

1. Preservice students have an opportunity to self-compare pre-course knowledge and skills possessed with post-course knowledge and skills gained;

2. Preservice students be given a means and time to reflect on the totality of a course and to express that reflection in a non-evaluated, creative way(s) to their peers and instructor;

3. Preservice students be introduced to types of assessments that will encourage students they eventually will teach to monitor and evaluate progress between pre- and post- instructional experiences; and

4. University instructors consider using a pre and post assessment technique in order to model such a technique for preservice students as well as refine their own teaching and course practices, based partly on pre-assessment information, to meet appropriately the ascertained needs and strengths of students in *their* classes.

Since using the pre-and post-assessment technique, this instructor has approached each new section of these two courses differently depending on the pre-assessment findings. As this assessment technique is modeled and as students realize parts of the course may be modified to meet more fully their individual needs, it is hoped that preservice students will realize the value of this technique and apply it in their own teaching. This concept of implementation transfer is best summarized through the words of one preservice student who wrote:

> You (the instructor) modeled many things for us. It really made me feel good that you paid attention to what I knew at the beginning of the course and let me think about and compare it to what I knew at the end of the course. I feel really competent. I hope the students I teach will feel the same way!

References

Anthony, R. J., Johnson, T. D., Mickelson, N. I., & Preece, A. (1991). *Evaluating literacy: A perspective for change.* Portsmouth, NH: Heinemann.

Au, K. H., Scheu, J. A., Kawakami, A. J., & Herman, P. A. (1990). Assessment and accountability in a whole literacy curriculum. *The Reading Teacher, 43,* 574-578.

Cambourne, B., & Turbill, J. (1990). Assessment in whole language classrooms: Theory into practice. *Elementary School Journal, 90,* 337-349.

Gipe, J. P. & Richards, J. C. (1990). Promoting reflection about reading instruction through journaling. *Journal of Reading Education, 15,* 6-13.

Gray-Schlegel, M. A., & Matanzo, J. B. (1993). Action research: Classroom teachers' perceptions of its impact on the teaching of reading. In T. V. Rasinski & N. D. Padak (Eds.), *Inquiries in literacy learning and instruction* (pp. 135-142). Pittsburg, KS: College Reading Association.

Herman, J. L., Aschbacher, P. R, & Winters, L. (1992). *A practical guide to alternative assessment.* Alexandria, VA: Association for Supervision and Curriculum Development.

Herrmann, B. A. (1990). A longitudinal study of preservice teachers' knowledge structures. In J. Zutell & S. McCormick (Eds.), *Literacy theory and research: Analyses from multiple paradigms* (pp. 145-152). Chicago, IL: National Reading Conference.

Johnston, P. H. (1992). *Constructive evaluation of literate activity.* White Plains, NY: Longman Publishing Group.

Paris, S., Calfee, R., Filby, N., Hiebert, E. H., Pearson, P. D., Valencia, S. W., & Wolf, K. (1992). A framework for authentic literacy assessment. *The Reading Teacher. 46,* 88-98.

Platt, J. M., & Williams, K. (1988). Preservice and inservice teachers' reading comprehension skills and their metacognitive awareness of processing of text. In D. Lumpkin, M. Harshbarger, P. Ransom, & J. Williams (Eds.), *The dilemmas of teaching reading* (pp. 77-80). Muncie, IN: Ball State University.

Rousculp, E. E. , & Maring, G. H. (1992). Portfolios for a community of learners. *Journal of Reading, 35*, 378-385.

Routman, R. (1991). *Invitations: Changing as teachers and learners, K-12.* Portsmouth, NH: Heinemann.

Rumelhart, D. E. (1981). Schemata: The building blocks of cognition. In J. T. Guthrie (Ed.), *Comprehension and teaching: Research reviews.* (pp. 26-27). Newark, DE: International Reading Association.

Valencia, S. W. (1990). A portfolio approach to classroom reading assessment: The whys, whats, and hows. *The Reading Teacher, 43*, 338-340.

Valencia, S. W., Hiebert, E. H., & Afflerbach, P. P. (1994). *Authentic reading assessment: Practices and possibilities.* Newark, DE: International Reading Association.

Wagner, C. L., Brock, D. R., & Agnew, A. T. (1994). Developing literacy portfolios in teacher education courses. *Journal of Reading, 37*, 668-674.

Wiggins, G. (1992). Creating tests worth taking. *Educational Leadership, 49*, 26-33.

Winograd, P., Paris, S., & Bridge, C. (1991). Improving the assessment of literacy. *The Reading Teacher, 45*, 108-116.

Appendix A

Pre and Post Self-Assessment Forms 1, 2, 3

Form 1: The Teaching of Children's Literature: PreCourse Self-Assessment

Name _____Date_____Section_____

Directions: Complete the following items as best you can in terms of what you NOW know.

1. When I speak about this course to friends, I call it *(name you give course)*:*
2. Ways I feel about any of my experiences with reading and children's literature are:
3. Children's literature is:
4. The genre' of children's literature are:
5. Five or more picture book titles and their authors and/or illustrators are:
6. Two or more highly respected children's literature illustrators are:
7. Traditional literature is:
8. Three or more traditional literature titles and collectors are:
9. Leading poets whose work(s) children enjoy reading include:
10. Three or more fantasy characters are:
11. When critiquing children's literature, elements to consider are:
12. Leading non-fiction authors enjoyed by children include:
13. Three or more titles and authors of realistic fiction are:
14. The Caldecott, Newbery, and Orbis Pictus Awards are:
15. Issues in children's literature include:
16. Ways to motivate and actively involve children in children's literature include:
17. My feelings toward the importance and use of children's literature in teaching are:
18. Additional information to demonstrate my knowledge, experiences, and/or attitudes toward children's literature includes:

This and other assessment forms normally would be on the front and back side of one page allowing more sufficient space for response. Additional pages could be attached if needed.

Appendix B

Form 2: The Diagnostic Teaching of Reading: Pre-Course Self-Assessment

Name _____Date_____Section_____

Directions: Complete the following items as best you can in terms of what you NOW know.

1. Describe a model of reading you believe is effective:
2. The Decision-making Cycle of Diagnostic Teaching includes:
3. Major differences between able readers and less able readers are:
4. Metacognition is:
5. Schema is:
6. An IRI is:
7. Examples of effective reading assessments are:
8. Effective instructional reading strategies include:
9. Before reading a selection, a student could
10. During reading, a student could
11. After reading, a student could
12. When a student reads haltingly but seems to know all the words, the teacher might
13. When a student regularly substitutes other words for printed words, the teacher might
14. When a student frequently omits words while reading orally, the teacher might
15. If a student cannot apply phonics knowledge, the teacher might
16. My feelings about working with less able readers are:
17. The way I feel about teaching reading is:
18. Additional information to demonstrate my knowledge, experiences, and/or attitudes:

Appendix C

Form 3:   Post Course Self-Assessment

Directions: Complete the following items as best you can in terms of what you NOW know.

> *(The first page, front and back side, of the post-assessment is identical to the pre-assessment, Form 1; so, that page is not reproduced here. However, a second page as noted below was included in the post-assessment also. As the additional page for either of the two courses is the same, only one generic example is given).*

Name_____**Date**_____**Section**____

19.   Do you feel this type of assessment helped you realize any gains you made in this course?   YES   NO
Support why or why not.

20.   Would you use a pre-and post-assessment technique with students you might teach?   YES   NO
Support why or why not.

21.   During student teaching and/or teaching, would you be willing to be contacted by this professor to share some of the strategies you have tried in your classroom?   YES   NO

If yes, when do plan to do student teaching?

22.   Summarize major knowledge, attitudes, and appreciations gained.

Note also parts of the course you would modify, make additions, and/or delete. Your comments should **reflect** what **you gained** in this course from **your point of view**. You are encouraged to be creative in the presentation of your ideas. You may select alternate forms to express yourself. If you choose to write, additional pages may be attached as needed. Please return the pre-assessment with your post-assessment. Be prepared to discuss your knowledge and reflections at the final course session.

Rethinking the Role and Practice of Assessment in Teacher Education: Learning to Assess Authentically on Multiple Levels

N. Suzanne Standerford
Northern Michigan University

This chapter describes a teacher education course focusing on literacy assessment and instruction which undergraduates take just before student teaching. Using an integrated language arts in the elementary school course that is based on whole language philosophy, students assess the learning needs of children and determine procedures that best provide for those needs within the context of the classroom and community.

In the last decade, assessment in elementary school literacy programs has been moving toward "authentic assessment" where teachers assess students as they perform the types of tasks which "go to the heart of essential learnings, i.e., they ask for exhibitions of understandings and abilities that matter" (Parker, 1991, p. 88). As elementary students engage in authentic, meaningful tasks, they learn the concepts and develop the abilities and skills they need for success in school and beyond (Caine & Caine, 1991; Gardner, 1991; Perkins, 1992). Such assessment of student progress in authentic situations requires that teachers observe their students closely and use information gathered through observation and interaction to guide instruction, i.e., "kidwatching" (Goodman, 1989). This movement in K-12 literacy education, one component of what is popularly termed "whole language," requires teachers who know how to assess through observation of and interaction with their students (Ibid.) and are confident enough in their own kidwatching skills to use that knowledge in planning instruction (Johnston, 1992a). In addition, whole language philosophy stresses that learners be more in control of their own learning, which can make assessment of their progress more difficult for the teacher (Eisner, 1991). It also requires that learners become partners in assessment by practicing self-assessment and providing relevant assessment information to aid teachers in instructional planning.

This notion of assessment differs from traditional forms of assessment found in elementary literacy instruction. Traditionally, teachers have used formal and informal instruments prepared by others, trusted those instruments to measure student achievement and progress, and depended on commercial materials to guide their instructional planning (Hanson, 1989). Teacher education programs have most often provided superficial attention to on-going formative assessment. As a result, they have left teachers without the necessary confidence to move beyond this reliance on "experts" to assessing their students' progress during authentic learning tasks and using that information to design appropriate instruction (Hiebert & Calfee, 1989). As whole language beliefs take hold in classrooms across the nation, assessment is beginning to move toward authentic, performance-based assessment, i.e., careful observation of students during learning tasks, reflection upon those observations, and instructional decision-making based on the reflections. Teacher education programs must meet this challenge by rethinking how assessment is taught in university courses.

Assessment and instruction in whole language classrooms require that teachers use reflective thinking about their knowledge and practice as an on-going form of professional development and learning (Goodman, 1989). Reflection is defined as "the practice or act of analyzing our actions, decisions, or products by focusing on our process of achieving them" (Killion & Todnem, 1991, p. 15). Expanding on the work of Schon (1973), who identified two kinds of reflection (i.e., reflection in action and reflection on action), Killion and Todnem add "reflection *for* action" that is using reflection to guide future actions and to give insight into future decisions (p. 15). Thus, reflection can be both a means of assessing one's own learning and a means of improving one's practice through more informed future decisions. Reflection also allows teachers to develop a sense of voice, i.e., to say what they think rather than to say what they are expected to say, and leads to insights about oneself that bring positive changes in self-concept and confidence as a teacher (Bradley, 1994; Canning, 1991).

Authentic assessment can play a key role in helping teacher candidates develop a strong knowledge base, a commitment to reflective practice, and a sense of empowerment and confidence. However, most teacher candidates have few opportunities to experience authentic assessment and reflective practice from the learner's or the teacher's perspective in their teacher education programs. For instance, assessment courses for preservice teachers typically provide teacher candidates with background information about commercial testing materials such as textbook exams, standardized tests, and informal reading inventories. Such a focus upon "how to use" materials prepared by others to assess the literacy needs of one's students does not align with current trends toward a "whole language" philosophy of assessment and instruction. Such practices perpetuate the view that absent "experts" can better identify students' learning needs than can classroom teachers.

Assessment practices in the university most often involve testing and grading which are summative and evaluative, i.e., they provide gatekeeping functions rather than guiding student learning (Farr, 1992; Rhodes & Shanklin, 1993). Such practices continue to support by demonstration the idea that assessment is the domain of the experts and is done mainly to assign a grade. In addition, written tests usually fail to assess the student mastery of critical behaviors such as observing closely what students can do before deciding what to teach, presenting content knowledge in ways which students can understand, or providing a context for maximum student engagement and learning (Wiggins, 1993). Therefore, even if students achieve high scores on many traditional university assessments, these scores tell little about their abilities to put those ideas into practice. Goodlad (1991) suggests that preservice teachers can best connect theory and practice through university courses that include integrated field experiences. Such courses allow teacher candidates to discuss and analyze their own practice and that of their peers, thereby firmly fitting theory into practice. Teacher educators must face the challenges of preparing teachers for assessment and instruction in whole language classrooms by rethinking both how we assess preservice teachers and how we help them learn to assess their students.

Changing the Role of Assessment in Teacher Education

For the last two years, I have been working to redefine both how one teaches preservice teachers to assess elementary students' literacy development and to explore how teacher candidates can use reflection as a tool for self-assessment and improvement of their own teaching practice. Principles which guide this work include: 1) assessment should be formative both contributing to and guiding learning and teaching (Rhodes & Shanklin, 1993); 2) assessment should identify students' strengths and areas for improvement in *authentic* situations (Wiggins, 1993); 3) assessment should aid the teacher in refining and improving instructional practice (Rhodes & Shanklin, 1993; Goodman, 1989); 4) assessment should develop teachers' ability to use good judgment in teaching practice (Wiggins, 1993); and 5) assessment should ultimately teach students to take responsibility for assessing their own learning and learning needs through reflection about their work (Johnston, 1992).

This paper describes a teacher education course focusing on literacy assessment and instruction which undergraduates take just before student teaching. The course follows an intensive (ten hour per week) integrated course on teaching the language arts in the elementary school. Both courses are grounded in a whole language philosophy based on the following principles: 1) the purpose of language is communication; 2) meaning is constructed during each of the language processes (i.e., speaking, listening, reading, and writing); 3) children become literate by using language in authentic, meaningful ways; 4) individuals seek to see connections between what they know and what they are to learn; 5) there is no preset sequence of skills through which all children must proceed as they become literate; and 6) teachers are the most important resource in helping children become literate. As such, they must be allowed to assess students' learning needs and decide how to best provide for those needs within the context of their own classrooms and communities (for a more thorough explanation of whole language beliefs on assessment see Cooper, 1993; Goodman, 1989; Pike, Compain, & Mumper, 1994).

The assessment class meets one morning per week in a local elementary school. The preservice teachers meet weekly for 2 hours of class and spend 50 minutes working with the elementary students. The purpose of the field experience is for teacher candidates to learn both 1) how to assess student needs through a variety of means including "kidwatching" and 2) how to reflect upon their own practice and professional development through self-assessment and collegial exchanges. Assessment of the elementary students' progress takes place during authentic learning situations, and the information gathered is the basis for subsequent instruction. To support the students in learning to do this, we use a course text which provides guidance in learning to "kidwatch" (see Rhodes & Shanklin, 1993). Reflection and collegial discussions occur immediately after working with the elementary students and are focused on the preservice teachers' instructional practice. Course assignments center on the field experiences and require reflection and analysis of both the teacher candidate's development and the elementary student's needs.

Learning to Assess Student Needs: Kidwatching in Action

The university students are paired with one or two elementary students for the entire semester. During this time, the preservice teachers are responsible for assessing the strengths, needs, and interests of their students and for using that information in planning weekly literacy instruction. They learn to use a wide range of assessment approaches such as 1) analyzing students' writing samples for both development of spelling and grammar skills and for comprehension and communication development; 2) analyzing oral reading errors through both running records (Clay, 1979) and miscue analysis (Rhodes & Shanklin, 1993) to get a sense of which cueing systems students are using fluently and which need strengthening; 3) interviewing and surveying students to identify interests and attitudes for themes and topics of study; 4) using story grammar as a framework for comprehension responses to narrative text; and 5) developing a variety of projects that assess and develop comprehension of expository text. The teacher candidates receive support and feedback throughout the experience from themselves (through reflective assignments), from peers (through class discussions), from both the classroom teacher (through weekly notes), and from the course instructor (through comments in dialogue journals and on papers). These opportunities to use authentic assessment with real students and to analyze and improve their own practice help them to see the connections between theory and practice and are essential to their professional development (Goodlad, 1991).

Each week half of the students meet in the elementary classroom assigned to the university class and the other half meet in the elementary students' classroom. They switch locations every other week. In this way, the classroom teacher and the instructor can closely observe the students and interact with them on a regular basis. As the pairs work, lesson plans for the day rest on the table so that the "supervisor" can see what the goals are and how the student plans to reach those goals. The elementary teacher provides weekly written feedback from the perspective of what she knows about the elementary students' needs; I provide feedback from what I know about the teacher candidates' development (post-it notes make management easy). In essence, we both model kidwatching as well as provide two different perspectives on their work. Sample comments from the classroom teachers include:

> I am glad you are giving Sara a chance to talk about her weekend. She needs someone to listen so she can develop her speaking abilities.

> Chuck finds writing so difficult. I am glad to see you encourage him to share his ideas orally before writing.

Comments from the university instructor:

> I see that you are using the child's interest in hunting to make the hunting catalog. Starting with the child's interests is an important principle in teaching.

> The passports and map of your adventure through the story were a novel way to both increase students' interest and to integrate social studies skills into your lesson. Great idea!

Although we both try to provide positive feedback during this time, it is also necessary to make suggestions to help the teacher candidates.

> I see that your plans are a bit sketchy. More thorough lesson plans will help you focus more clearly and will avoid lapses when you are unsure what to do next.

> I see that you are not jotting any notes down during instruction. Remember that these notes will help you remember important assessment information that will escape your memory otherwise.

The weekly notes allow me to make connections between theoretical knowledge and teacher candidates' instructional practice more explicit in an ongoing way, something novice teachers have difficulty doing for themselves (Berliner, 1986).

The university students were eager to read their "post-it" notes after the session and sometimes stayed after class to discuss or explain their ideas further. For instance, after I commented on the passport and mapping activity, Judy stayed after class to show me the finished product, to tell me how she came up with the idea, and to show me what type of assessment information she had gathered from the lesson. Such personal interchanges allow the preservice teachers a chance to have their work noted and to discuss their ideas with an interested colleague, something missing from the lives of most teachers. When lesson plans are turned in later in the semester for further comments, the notes are always attached which further indicates that the students do value these personal remarks concerning their work. Both the elementary teacher and I were able to build on students' strengths by supporting and encouraging them. In addition, we modeled the use of observation and interaction as assessment tools in much the same way we expected them to assess and instruct their elementary students.

The opportunity to watch my students closely as they applied what they had been learning in their teacher education program also gave me a different slant on the strengths of each candidate as the following entry from my journal indicates.

> I am loving the work. I can see the students in roles that are real and I can offer advice that is pertinent and helpful. I was so glad to see

Trudy doing a great job with her student. She is not terribly strong academically, but I think she has so many other qualities which we would miss in a university classroom (Reflective journal, 10/23/93). Of course, these novice educators occasionally make mistakes in their assessments and sometimes turn down unproductive paths as they learn. However, most take their responsibility to the students so seriously that they ask either the teacher of me to look at their plans when they feel any doubts. Overall, there have been no serious negative results for either the preservice or the elementary students.

Learning to Assess Student Needs: Collegial Exchange and Support

Immediately following each session with the children, the university students spend forty-five minutes discussing their experiences in both small groups and as a whole class. This time is used for students to celebrate joyful experiences when they begin to feel like "real teachers," and to share disappointing or confusing experiences when they feel they need extra support or advice. The discussions allow the students to explore important issues and raise questions to be analyzed and examined considering theoretical knowledge gained from their courses. Preservice teachers need opportunities to translate theories into practice in supportive climates where reflection on one's work is the rule. Reflection allows them to grasp the implications of their experiences, and with frequent practice, reflective thinking can become habitual (Caine & Caine, 1991). Developing a climate of collegiality with all focused on high standards of cooperation and practice has profound effects on the success of individuals (Berger, 1991, p. 33). Thus, the collegial atmosphere, support, and collective reflection and problem-solving aid each teacher candidate in learning the most from the field experiences.

The discussions also allow the instructor to help students see connections, to make their learning more explicit, and to broaden their views from the specific instances to more general situations similar to using case studies (Shulman, 1986). I have also had to learn how to facilitate their growth without providing pat answers for all their questions. The first semester a very wise student suggested that I (the professor) "sometimes answered questions that we could have answered for each other," and so I continue learning to let them explore their own questions. However, novice and experienced teachers do see classroom events differently (Berliner, 1986), and so I join the conversation when I sense their views can be expanded with my input.

Allowing them to analyze their individual and collective questions collaboratively enable them to develop both their understandings of assessment and instruction and their confidence in their own capabilities to do both (Bradley, 1994). Collegial sharing is crucial to sustaining teachers who are trying to make change in the face of obstacles, i.e., providing a sense of efficacy and confidence to persevere in the face of uncertainty (Ashton & Webb, 1986; Midgley & Wood, 1993). Teachers who hope to teach from a whole language perspective need confidence in themselves and collegial support.

The students found the discussions a valuable time to wrestle with important issues and to search for explanations and ideas to address their collective teaching dilemmas. They also saw the school setting as conducive to better discussions as illustrated by their comments.

> Being in the school was important because after each session we had a discussion time and that was great. If we had to go back to campus, we would forget our questions by the time we got there, but we do it right away, right here. That is better. We really helped each other as peers. We could ask for help and share ideas. That was wonderful and really helped me (Fieldnotes, 12/8/93).

The class discussion time also allowed the instructor time to assess. As I listened to the students' celebrations, questions, concerns, and advice, I noted individual and collective strengths and needs. These notes were then recorded in my reflective journal and helped guide my planning for future class sessions. Early one semester the students voiced much frustration that I would not tell them what books a second grader should be reading. As I struggled for a response, Betty responded to her peers' doubts with insight and maturity:

> I am trying not to get caught up in knowing just what level is right yet. I figure this semester is for learning, and I will learn how to do that as I go, but it is very uncomfortable not knowing (Fieldnotes, 1/25/94).

Betty was able to clarify for everyone the purpose of the course and the need for living with uncertainty as we learn. As I listened, I was able to assess which students were constructing a sense of what they learning and which were still hoping for easy, prescriptive approaches to teaching and learning. I later did a short lesson on the limitations of readability formulas and the importance of student interest and prior knowledge to book selection.

This collegial sharing portion of class provides teacher candidates with learning communities and collegial support, two critical forms of support for teacher learning. (Ashton & Webb, 1986; Midgley & Wood, 1993). One adjustment that I made after the first semester was to have fifteen minutes of small group sharing (to allow more students to participate fully) followed by a half hour of class sharing. This change has been supported by unanimous positive feedback from students.

Learning to Assess Student Needs: Reflective Journals

The last component of the field experience that enabled students to construct a better understanding of how to conduct on-going literacy assessments was the weekly journal. Each student kept a journal that had three parts: weekly lesson plans, a summary of what actually happened during the instruction, and a reflection on what they had learned during that day about their students, about assessment, and about themselves as teachers. Periodically, the teacher candidates were asked to "step back" from the experience, reread and reflect upon their journals, and write short papers discussing what they were learning. Such on-going reflection and assessment of one's own work with educated feedback from supervisors and colleagues enables preservice teachers to improve their practice and to learn about assessment from both the learner's and the teacher's perspective (Bradley, 1994). These few excerpts give a sense of the poignancy with which students wrote about their own learning and development.

> Teaching reading is something I've always been scared of. I've said that I want to teach older children who already know how to read and write. From this class and practicum I have realized a couple of things. First, no matter what grade I teach, I will have students who can't read, or at least not at the level they should be. And second, that teaching reading isn't as hard as I thought it would be—I really can do it. I have learned to encourage the student to try on his/her own rather than depend on the teacher's help. For example, after writing my needs analysis paper I was very careful not to tell Lucy the word she was stumped on. Instead, I would say, "Try it—you can do it." When Lucy read Dizzy the Pony I really spent time concentrating on, "What could it be? Think about what is happening. Does the story make sense without the word? If so, we can come back to it later." (Student paper, 12/1/93).

I believe the reflection part of the journal is one of the most important things in record keeping. By actually writing a reflection on your lesson, you are allowed to critically think about and analyze the successes or failures of each task. This way, what worked or did not work with your student is clearly thought out and written down on paper for future use. What have I learned from keeping a journal in this class? After looking back and thinking about what I had written in my journal, I realized that Dave learns better with a concrete lesson than a more abstract or open idea. Things have to be narrowed down so he can concentrate on only one idea at a time. He panics when I ask him to use his imagination or try to link several ideas together. For example, he did much better at the tasks of making a mobile based on a particular book and reading a specific book aloud to me than listing things he knows about or making up a title for a picture. I just do not think he has enough confidence in his abilities yet to be a risk-taker. I hope he will learn. (Student paper, 12/1/93).

Reading and responding to the students' journals and papers allowed me to hold private conversations with each student about their learning and about their assessment of the elementary students. It enabled me to identify and encourage students who were able to synthesize concepts and translate theory into practice. It also allowed me to identify and support those students who seemed unable or unwilling to truly reflect in their journals. The journal entries helped me see what types of behaviors they were tuning into and what rich data they were missing. These observations and interactions signaled to me the types of lessons I needed to provide during the weekly class sessions, i.e., they guided my instructional planning. For instance, about midterm in the semester, I realized that many students were writing about their frustration that the elementary students had not shown significant improvement in their reading behaviors. I decided to spend some time the following week discussing the short time they had actually been with their students and the unrealistic demands they were placing on themselves. Following this mini-lesson, the sighs of relief were audible as well as noticeable. Moreover, the students' attitudes toward their work became noticeably more positive. For example, one student frequently wrote that her student was so inconsistent in her literacy behaviors that assessment seemed impossible. I sat with this candidate, went back through her observation notes, and helped her begin to spot the consistent errors that had previously been invisible to her.

Field Experience: Authentic Assessment in Action

Overall, incorporating the field experience into the class sessions as an integral part of learning about assessing students' literacy development and asking students to search within themselves for questions and answers provides a very successful way to help these preservice teachers develop both their knowledge base and their confidence. Providing opportunities for learners to reflect on their own actions during their experiences as well as afterwards is the most powerful form of assessment: self-assessment (Watson, 1994). Comments from the students illustrate the variety of ways they saw the experience helped them develop as teachers. Kim points out how observing a colleague in action spurred her on to improving her own work.

> This day was spent observing Pam (Kim's elementary student was absent). It proved to be a very good opportunity to observe the skills and style of a colleague. It also provided reflection time for me to consider my own lesson plan. Seeing what Pam had so meticulously planned proved to be an incentive for me to take a closer look at my own plans. I think I put off closely scrutinizing my lesson because I was afraid I wouldn't like what I had planned and I did not want to face up to my fear of failure. Overall, I don't think I could have learned a better lesson than the one this day provided. I altered my lesson and did better because of it. I also believe that the importance of self-examination and learning from peers really became a part of me after this day. (Student paper, 2/23/94).

Deb learned from her student that assessment information must be continuously reconsidered and refined and that learning difficulties are not always within the student.

> One of the biggest things I have learned is how important assessment is and yet how difficult it can be at times. When you are assessing a student by looking at his work and his ways of getting the work done, you come up with an assumption of what you think the child is doing. Just when you feel comfortable with this assumption something will happen that throws that idea out the window. I also found that assessment of my teaching methods was needed. I think it is very important for teachers to look not only at the students, but at them-

selves and their teaching methods when problems arise. The problem does not always lie with the child. At times the way the teacher is giving information to the students is causing road blocks in their learning. (Student paper, 2/23/94).

Jessi learned that teaching is uncertain (Lortie, 1975; Jackson, 1976), that deciding what a student needs is not as simple as administering a test and focusing on a specific skill.

Working with Jeff has been an eye-opening experience for me. Teaching is not at all what I thought it to be! For a long time, I had believed it to be a cut and dry profession, but from trying to help Jeff, I have learned that it is not. Using only one method, one strategy, rarely solves the child's problem...many times teaching isn't something that you get right on the first try. I've found through trying to find strategies to help Jeff that it can be a process of trial and error. (Student paper, 3/1/94).

The field experiences provide opportunities for these preservice teachers to develop good judgment, competence, and a habit of seeing assessment as a means to "thoughtful and effective understanding" (Wiggins, 1993, p. 204) rather than as a pat answer found on a commercial test. They begin to realize that teachers must be careful observers and deep thinkers. Wiggins suggests that to become a true thinker one must "acquire the habit of inquiring and engaging in discourse with care and thoroughness" (p. 204), something the students are learning to do in their weekly discussions and journals. He goes on to suggest that assessment can be a powerful means to helping students develop

a thoughtful control over performance (which) depends not so much on learning and employing 'knowledge and skills' but on having our judgment awakened and empowered through problems that demand judgment (Ibid., p. 204).

This field experience allows teacher candidates to develop their judgment in a supportive, collegial environment and enables them to construct more thorough understandings of assessment and its role in teaching. Actually using authentic assessment while receiving support and advice from colleagues helps them develop the knowledge and confidence they will need to use authentic, performance-based assessment in the future.

Assessing Oneself: The Ultimate Goal of Assessment

Students in this course learn to move from formative assessment to summative evaluation by assessing their own work throughout the semester and assigning their own grades. Although this practice is sticky and not yet entirely comfortable for any of us, approaching self-assessment in this way confronts three major issues with which most whole language teachers struggle.

The first issue is recognizing the difference between assessment and evaluation and trying to move from a focus on evaluation to a focus on assessment.

> ...*evaluation* connotes making judgments about students' products that result in a mark, score, or grade, judgments that often have little connection with the teacher's instructional plans. In contrast, the term *assessment* implies the process of carefully collecting or recording and analyzing students' literacy products and processes in a way that establishes a strong connection between the assessment data and the teacher's instructional plans (Rhodes & Shanklin, 1993).

Evaluation within our schools most often requires that students' achievement be reported in the form of a letter or numerical score, a simplistic view of students' complex layers of achievement. Assessment, on the other hand, allows a focus on their individual and collective strengths, needs, and growth. Anecdotal notes build a more accurate and full-bodied sense of students' strengths and needs, assessment information that then guides instruction. The students must learn how to use assessment to guide their instruction, but they must learn to evaluate as well to meet systemic expectations of teachers to give grades on student work.

A second issue is the belief that all students must learn one right answer or one right way to do something for a grade. If students were asked to memorize theories of assessment and to recognize those theories on multiple choice exams, it would be fairly easy to assign "fair, accurate" grades. However, such an approach would not allow students to truly internalize those ideas nor to move beyond knowledge *about* assessment to understanding how to apply the ideas in practice. Teaching is not a simple transfer of factual information into practice; it is a messy, uncertain endeavor with no "best" approach for every student in every situation (Lortie, 1975; Jackson, 1976). Using the students' teaching practice as the basis of course assessment means assessing understandings and abilities that matter (Parker, 1991); yet, it brings many troubling dilemmas (dilemmas which parallel issues of accountability for inservice teachers). Some of the preservice teachers are assigned one student and some are assigned two. Some of the elementary students are strong readers and some are struggling. Some of the youngsters are labeled with a variety of special needs and others are eager and able to do whatever is planned for them. The context of each teacher candidate's assignment is different depending on the student with whom they work, and thus, each of them is constructing varied understandings of course concepts. Grading students solely on their lesson plans and instructional actions would not be fair. Resorting to paper/pencil exams would not provide the clear picture of students' learning which I seek. Wiggins (1993) addresses this dilemma by questioning the nature of education.

> Is schooling meant to yield common knowledge? If so, then it makes perfect sense to think of tests as properly focusing on what students hold in common. But what if education is seen to be a personal, idiosyncratic affair, where the meaning and personal effectiveness that I derive from coursework is more important than what knowledge we all hold in common? In that case, any kind of standardized, indirect test would make no sense. What could we possibly mean by a standardized test of meaning of educational experience?...achievement should be validated by a person's demonstrated ability to use knowledge in the field (p. 213).

Recognizing that education is "personal and idiosyncratic" is one thing, but acting on that belief in current educational systems is quite another. I continue to struggle with ways to make the students' grades accurately reflect their learning and performance.

The third issue is that practice requires one to act from one set of beliefs while living within a system that continues to operate on a different and opposing set of beliefs. Much of the literature in education today supports the necessity of having self-assessment as the ultimate goal of all assessment (see for example Rhodes & Shanklin, 1993; Johnston, 1992; Wiggins, 1993; Costa, 1989; Perrone, 1991). Yet, at all levels of the educational system, teachers are expected to assign letter or numerical grades to communicate student achievement with little input from the students on how that grade is assigned. Even though there is widespread movement in education toward the use of portfolios, faith in grades and test scores is not disappearing. Entrance requirements for the teacher education program at our institution are stringent and primarily based on grade point averages and standardized test scores. To continue in the program, students must maintain above average grades and must pass an additional set of state mandated standardized tests. The importance of grades and of knowing the correct information cannot be disregarded; students are under tremendous pressure.

Not often, but at times students assign inaccurate grades to their work. This usually happens when the standards are not well understood. Because assigning their own grades is meant to both teach them about assessment and to develop their confidence within as teachers, taking the responsibility for grade assignment away from them would be counterproductive. However, to fulfill my responsibility to the university for honest grades, I do at times provide feedback to students and ask them to reconsider their grades by either revising their work or assigning a new grade. The choice remains theirs; revised work is accepted without penalty. In every instance, the students have chosen to revise their work, thus, learning much more than if the lower quality work had been the end product. Future teachers need to believe that work is not done until it is done right (Wiggins, 1991).

Self-Assessment in Practice

Each student assignment is accompanied by a cover sheet answering the following five questions:

1. What are the strengths of this assignment?
2. What type of effort was put into completing the assignment?
3. What did I learn by doing this assignment?
4. If I could start over now, what changes would I make in the product?
5. What grade would I assign to the product and why?

These same questions are used when students assign a grade for the course (substituting "course" for "assignment or product"). In the beginning of the term, students often write that the assignment is worth the maximum points possible because it "meets the requirements on the syllabus." I continue pushing them to look beyond the "requirement" and truly reflect on their work, and gradually, these type statements disappear. As the students write their self-assessments, they make explicit to themselves and to me the types of learning which are occurring. I am able to assess their progress as I see what criteria and standards they use in assessing their own work, what processes they use to complete assignments, and how they are growing in their confidence and understanding of how to assess their students' work.

As the students wrote about their learning and then reflected upon those papers for the self-assessment, their comments showed maturity and a critical ability to examine their own work. Kennedy (1991) states that many novice teachers have not learned to critically examine their own practice; yet, successful teachers must learn to observe, think through, and deeply understand their own practice (Evans, 1991). Answering the five questions provides an opportunity for students to critically examine their work.

> I believe my strength in this assignment was that I really stopped and took a hard look at what I was doing. I didn't try to paint a flowery picture so that it looked good on paper, although at times this is what I wanted to do. I looked at what I was doing with Roberta and asked "Am I doing all that I can do?" It's hard to critique your own work, but I feel that I was fair and realistic.

> My grammar and spelling is always a concern as it is my weak point. I continue to struggle and work on improving this part of my writing. I question myself, use dictionaries, read, and re-read for clarity and accuracy.

Many students comment that self-assessment makes their own learning more explicit to them, and they find that assessing the work themselves often requires that they produce stronger work than when someone else assesses it for them.

> Always, I am learning. This assignment made me reflect upon my experience. As I was writing this short paper, I was constantly realizing my new knowledge—the knowledge I would otherwise overlook. I know I am learning what questions to ask and what kind of samples to obtain when I analyze a student, but I don't realize I am also learning such things like "I'm a teacher now."

> I really enjoy evaluating my own papers because it really helps me to take ownership in my own learning. It's easy to just do a paper, turn it in and pray the professor likes it, but when you have to like it

yourself and do a good job for yourself—that's when it becomes difficult. It has really helped me to become more responsible for my own learning and has also helped me to become more critical of myself.

Well, here we go again with one of the more humbling things I've had to experience in my life, the self-grading process. It, however, has had an interesting effect on my work in that it makes my work of better quality at least in my opinion. Knowing that I have to do this after I've written my paper makes me bear down a little harder while I'm actually writing it. I want to give myself a good grade, but I know that I can't unless my work substantiates such a mark.

Since the course is designed to help teacher candidates learn as much about assessment and instruction as possible, I pay particular attention to comments such as the following that illustrate what the students are learning about assessment.

I learned a lot this time regarding my personal interpretation of assessment and how important this really is. I learned that this makes a big difference in how you teach a child and if you meet that child's needs. Assessment is an ongoing process and teachers must constantly interpret the results in order to best meet that child's needs. I learned personally the gains that can be made when this happens.

I've learned that I make a lot of judgments based on my assessment procedures. This made me realize how closely assessment and teaching are related.

The self-assessment cover sheets also allow me to discuss students' understandings of assessment with them and to help them broaden their perspectives. Bob was quite amused in the beginning of the course that I wanted him to assess himself. After writing his paper assessing the students' needs, he wrote to me "I find it quite ironic that this time we are being asked to assess ourselves on an assessment paper. This is ironic to the point of almost being comical." I explained to Bob privately that teaching requires constant reflection on one's assessment of students' needs as those needs are ever-changing and often difficult to accurately identify. I also based a mini-lesson for the whole class around this concept. Over time, Bob became more willing to assess his own work: "Yes, maybe I am finally getting more comfortable in grading myself. I'm just not that used to 'tooting my own horn' so to speak, but at least it·has become bearable." My goal is that by helping Bob use reflection for self-assessment and become more comfortable with "tooting his own horn," I am also helping him develop a sense of voice and confidence in himself as a teacher.

Enabling students to grow in their confidence and their sense of themselves as teachers are very important goals in this course. The most frequent comment I hear from supervisors of student teachers is that preservice teachers lack confidence in themselves, leading to a variety of problems as they assume the role of teacher. Although confidence often comes with experience and success, I believe that the changes made in this pre-student teaching course will add to the process of building teacher candidates' confidence. The following comments from students suggest that they are beginning to make the shift in their thinking from student to teacher.

> I learned that I am beginning to put things together and starting to think like a teacher. This semester has been a catharsis for me. I have for the first time started thinking as a teacher and I look at things like a teacher. I can't wait to have my own class.

> I am learning to analyze situations with closer detail. I am learning to appreciate my own accomplishments. This is something that I have never been able to do before. Through working on Diane's confidence, I have been able to trust myself and my own instincts.

At the end of the course, I have the students write anonymous evaluations of the course for me to use in planning for the next semester. One thing that is most frequently mentioned is the value of self-assessment. Students overwhelmingly feel that it is a very positive learning experience for them.

> The self-evaluation process was hard at first only because I wasn't used to it. But, as the semester rolled on, I realized how important it was and how closely you have to observe things so after I did that it became easier. As long as you set certain standards for yourself, you will be satisfied each time you evalute yourself as long as you live up to and meet those standards. I learned a lot from this even though it was so humbling.

I was really leery of self-assessment, but I found that it really helped me to take a serious look at myself and my work; something I've never really done before.

The ideas of assessing the student and myself relate to one another well. It's beneficial to assess yourself because it makes you aware of what assignments need, what to look for when assessing, and how to grade students based on assessment. I have not yet found a way to make self-evaluation work well for all students. A few stated that they did not feel the self-evaluations were helpful to them.

In all honesty, though, it is very hard for me to gain something from self-evaluation. I have not put much effort into it. If I had, maybe I would have gotten more from it.

The only part I didn't feel comfortable with was the actual grading because I get caught between wanting a good grade and being very hard on myself. Overall, self-evaluation is a good tool. It prepares us for teaching by evaluating ourselves.

I don't feel that evaluating myself was very useful because I think that we always do our best work so in that way feel we deserve the full points. However, had you graded the papers, I'm sure you wouldn't have given me all the points. I don't know where points would have been taken away, but I'm sure they would have been.

These last comments show that not all students see the value in reflection and self-assessment. Some are so used to living in the traditional role of student that they refuse to take this new role seriously. Some struggle with the need to achieve high grades to continue in the program. Some believe that my assessment, though mysterious to them, is still more valid than their own; trusting the experts has been ingrained deeply into them. We have a way to go in figuring out how to develop all preservice teachers into truly reflective practitioners.

Table 1.
<u>Learning to Assess Authentically</u>

	Preservice Teachers	University Professor
Self-Evaluation	• On course assignments • Of assesment/instruction practice	• From student self and course evaluations
Reflective Papers	• Reflection on own develop ment as a teacher	• Opportunity to assess what student sees as significant and to conference individually
Dialogue Journals	• Weekly analysis of practice related to course readings	• Personal dialogue with and assessment of each student's progress
Collegial Sharing	• Weekly discussions of their teaching practice	• Observation to assess individual and collective development through their questions, answers, and comments
Kidwatching	• Weekly assessment/ instruction sessions with elementary students	• Weekly observations of preservice teachers in teaching role

Conclusion

Often we hear that the pendulum swings frequently in education and if one waits long enough, all innovations will disappear as we revert back to former ways of teaching. Preparing future teachers to have the knowledge and the confidence to teach from a whole language perspective is one way of stopping the pendulum. Reconceiving the way we assess teacher candidates as well as how we teach them to assess their own students is critical. Wiggins (1993) suggests removing the focus of education from "accretion of knowledge" and instead allowing learners to move from "a *crude* grasp of the whole to a *sophisticated* grasp of the whole" (p. 202) through actually performing the practice we are preparing them to perform. In this teacher education literacy course, the desired performance is assessing and teaching elementary students. Preservice teachers who learn how to assess elementary students' needs, provide instruction to meet those needs, and assess and reflect upon their own work are learning how to "perform with knowledge by practicing the criterion performance" (Ibid., p. 205). As a teacher of teachers, "walking the walk" of a whole language teacher and learning to assess my students in authentic ways provides both a model of such practice for my students and allows each teacher candidate to construct a personal sense of what it means to be a teacher as well as the confidence to carry out that vision.

References

Ashton, P. T., & Webb, R. B. (1986). *Making a difference: Teachers' sense of efficacy and student achievement.* (Research on Teaching Monograph Series). New York: Longman.

Berger, R. (1991). Building a school culture of high standards: A teacher's perspective. In V. Perrone (Ed.), *Expanding Student Assessment* (pp. 32-39), Alexandria, VA: Association for Supervision and Curriculum Development.

Berliner, D. (1986, Aug./Sept.). In pursuit of the expert pedagogue. *Educational Researcher,* 5-13.

Bradley, A. (1994, May 11). Practice what you teach. *Education Week,* 13(33), 26-28.

Caine, R.N., & Caine, G. (1991). *Making connections: Teaching and the human brain.* Alexandria, VA: Association for Supervision and Curriculum Development.

Canning, C. (1991, March). What teachers say about reflection. *Educational Leadership, 48* (6), 18-21.

Clay, M. (1979). *The early detection of reading difficulties, Third edition.* Portsmouth, NH: Heinemann.

Cooper, J. D. (1993). *Literacy: Helping children construct meaning.* Boston: Houghton Mifflin Co.

Costa, A. L. (1989, April). Re-assessing assessment. *Educational Leadership, 46* (7), 2.

Eisner, E. W. (1991). What really counts in schools. *Educational Leadership, 48* (5), 10-17.

Evans, C. (1991). Support for teachers studying their own work. *Educational Leadership, 48* (6), 11-13.

Farr, R. (1992). Putting it all together: Solving the reading assessment puzzle. *The Reading Teacher, 46* (1), 26-37.

Gardner, H. (1991). *The unschooled mind: How children think and how schools should teach.* New York: HarperCollins Publishers (Basic Books).

Goodlad, J. I. (1991). Why we need a complete redesign of teacher education. *Educational Leadership, 49* (3), 4-10.

182

Goodman, Y. M. (1989). Evaluation of students. In K. Goodman, Y.M. Goodman, & W.J. Hood (Eds.), *The whole language evaluation book*, (pp. 3-14). Portsmouth, NH: Heinemann.

Hanson, G. R. (1989). Whole language, whole teaching, whole being: The need for reflection in the teaching process. In K. S. Goodman, Y. M. Goodman, W.J. Hood (Eds.), *The whole language evaluation book*, (pp. 263-272). Portsmouth, NH: Heinemann.

Hiebert, E. H., & Calfee, R. C. (1989). Advancing academic literacy through teachers' assessments. *Educational Leadership, 46* (7), 50-52.

Jackson, P. (1976). *The practice of teaching*. New York: Teachers College Press.

Johnston, P. H. (1992). Nontechnical assessment. *The Reading Teacher, 46* (1), 10-62.

Johnston, P. H. (1992). *Constructive evaluation of literate activity*. New York: Longman.

Kennedy, M. M. (1991). Some surprising findings on how teachers learn to teach. *Educational Leadership, 49* (3), 14-17.

Killion, J. P., & Todnem, G. R. (1991). A process for personal theory building. *Educational Leadership, 48* (6), 14-16.

Leslie, L., & Caldwell, J. (1990). *Qualitative reading inventory*. New York: HarperCollins Publishers.

Lortie, D. C. (1975). *Schoolteacher*. Chicago: The University of Chicago Press.

Midgley, C., & Wood, S. (1993). Beyond site-based management: Empowering teachers to reform schools. *Phi Delta Kappan, 75* (3), 245-252.

Parker, W. C. (1991). *Renewing the social studies curriculum*. Alexandria, VA: Association for Supervision and Curriculum Development.

Perkins, D. (1992). *Smart schools: From training memories to educating minds*. New York: The Free Press, A Division of Macmillan Publishers.

Perrone, V. (1991). Moving toward more powerful assessment. In V. Perrone (Ed.), *Expanding Student Assessment* (pp. 164-166.) Alexandriz, VA: Association for Supervision and Curriculum Development.

Pike, K., Compain, R. & Mumper, J. (1994). *New connections: An integrated approach to literacy*. New York: HarperCollins Publishers.

Rhodes, L. K., & Shanklin, N. (1993). *Windows into literacy: Assessing learners K-8*. Portsmouth, NH: Heinemann.

Rich, S. J. (1989). Restoring power to teachers: The impact of "whole language." In G. Manning and M.M. Manning (Eds.), *Whole language: Beliefs and practices, K-8*. (pp.220-228). Washington, D.C.: National Education Association.

Schon, D. (1973). *The reflective practitioner*. New York: Basic Books.

Shulman, L. (1986). Those who understand: Knowledge growth in teaching. *Educational Researcher*, 4-14.

Watson, D. J. (1994). Whole language: Why bother? *The Reading Teacher,* *47* (8), 600-607.

Wiggns, G. (1993). Assessment: Authenticity, context, and validity. *Phi Delta Kappan, 75* (3), 200-214.

Wiggins, G. (1991). Standards, not standardization: Evoking quality student work. *Educational Leadership, 48* (5), 18-25.

Portfolio Assessment in Adult Education Programs

Linda Thistlethwaite

Western Illinois University

Portfolio assessment is authentic assessment that is on-going and multi-dimensional. This type of assessment is based on a collection of the student's work samples as well as observational data that both the student and the teacher have collected in the form of checklists, rating scales, and comments. Part I of this chapter focuses on establishing a rationale for using portfolios in adult education, first discussing dissatisfaction with standardized tests, and then looking at the compatibility of portfolio assessment with tenets of adult education. As part of the rationale, six facets of current learning theory are applied to portfolio assessment. Finally, student/teacher mobility and present retention rates in adult education programs are suggested as reasons for considering portfolio assessment. Part II delineates the key steps to consider in implementing portfolio assessment, including how five adult education programs began this process.

Two adult educators participating in an adult education workshop on portfolio assessment have volunteered to participate in an activity to introduce the workshop and are sitting at two small tables slightly facing away from one another. Each has been given an envelope containing an identical set of 12 puzzle pieces but different directions for putting them together. After a minute of work, time is called. Volunteer A has successfully put together her puzzle while Volunteer B has barely begun. When asked to share with the group their strategies for putting their puzzles together, Volunteer A said that she simply followed the directions which stated that she put together the numbered pieces in the manner shown at the bottom of the page, with puzzle pieces in order from 1-12, left to right and top to bottom. Volunteer B said that his directions reminded him to remember how he used to get started when putting jigsaw puzzles together as a child and to work as quickly as possible. None of his pieces were numbered.He began by locating the four corner pieces and was almost finished locating the edge pieces when time was called. Together these two volunteers have demonstrated two important concepts to consider when implementing portfolio assessment: first, seeing the big picture of how all of the various pieces fit together, and second, starting small with what you know.

Portfolio assessment is authentic assessment that is on-going and multi-dimensional. This type of assessment is based on a collection of the student's work samples in written format as well as observational data that both the student and the teacher have collected in the form of checklists, rating scales, and comments (Tierney, Carter, & Desai, 1991; Harp, 1991; Glazer & Brown, 1993). This chapter focuses on two key questions: What is the rationale for using portfolio assessment in the adult education setting? What are the steps that adult education programs should consider when implementing portfolio assessment? Throughout the discussion of these two questions will be reference to particular items that might be included in an adult learner's portfolio.

A Rationale for Using Portfolio Assessment in Adult Education

The rationale for portfolio assessment in adult education focuses on five areas: dissatisfaction with standardized tests, compatibility of portfolio assessment with tenets of adult education, the relationship of portfolio assessment to current learning theory, student mobility, and a possible effect of portfolio use upon retention.

Dissatisfaction with Standardized Tests

Dissatisfaction with standardized tests has encouraged adult educators to look to other avenues for verifying learner achievement. Standardized tests are limited in what they measure with a variety of factors in addition to learner ability and effort being influencing factors (Neill & Medina, 1989; Shepard, 1989). The score earned does not really tell the teacher what the student can and can't do. Standardized tests are not reflective of classroom instruction. In few classrooms is the mode of instruction focused on having students read short paragraphs and answer multiple choice questions. Although marked gains have been made in reading instruction, assessment approaches have not kept pace (Pearson & Danning, 1985; Valencia & Pearson, 1987).

Adult education students in federally funded Adult Basic Education (ABE) programs test students at fairly frequent intervals although there are no written guidelines regarding specifically when this must be done. One Midwestern state requires testing twice per year, provided the adult has had 37 hours of instruction since the previous test (Adult Education and Literacy Section/Illinois State Board of Education, 1993). Some states require more frequent testing than this; others require less frequent testing. Adult education teachers frequently find themselves in the unpleasant situation of having to explain to students why their scores are lower than they were the time before.

Although teachers may understand such concepts as standard error of measurement and how it affects the student's score, adult learners do not understand this and see lower test scores as indicative that they not only have not made progress but are getting worse. The portfolio can be a way of affirming to the student that progress has indeed been made.

Compatibility with Adult Education Tenets

Portfolio assessment is compatible with the major tenets of adult education. Malcolm Knowles (1970) identified these four tenets more than two decades ago. First, the adult is an independent learner. One of the key concepts behind portfolio assessment is independence. The learner self-evaluates and does much of his own record-keeping, whether it be a list of books read, assignments to be done, or strategies with which he feels comfortable. Portfolio assessment encourages learners to accept more responsibility for their own learning. The portfolio itself gives students a sense of ownership. The portfolios are always available to them. As students organize their portfolios, reflect on their achievement, plan for future growth, and share their portfolios with others, they engage in authentic self-assessment.

Second, the adult possesses a reservoir of rich experiences. The portfolio reflects and documents this student learning.

Third, the adult is a problem-solver who seeks to learn the answers to authentic problems. In portfolio assessment, the problem posed is the following: "How can we best document what you have learned?" The learner has input into the procedure and explores with the teacher various ways that his or her learning might be illustrated.

And finally, adults recognize and need what is practical and useful. Again, portfolio assessment reflects this tenet. Portfolios illustrate that learners have authentic and meaningful responses. They also show what students can do and have done well, as well as what they still have difficulty with and want to learn next. Portfolios chronicle student progress in a way that adult learners can understand.

Compatibility with Current Learning Theory

Portfolio assessment is grounded in current learning theory (Orem, 1993).

(1) Learning theory recognizes the diverse backgrounds and interests of any given classroom of learners. Diversity is also evident in student portfolios (perhaps called Career Portfolios) as students have a degree of choice about what goes into their portfolios to best represent their achievement.

(2) Learning requires the learner's active involvement. Portfolio assessment mirrors this involvement on the part of learners as they self-reflect and evaluate their own learning. One example of an activity that promotes active involvement is "What I've Learned as a Writer" (Atwell, 1987). Students complete a form documenting knowledge gained through writing after conferencing with the teacher about their work.

Another self-evaluation activity requires that students respond to the following questions on a cover sheet attached to a piece of writing: What changes have I made from the rough draft? What do I particularly like about this piece of writing? What was important or difficult about writing this piece? How is this piece of writing different from my other writing? Relatedly, students who are writing essays can self-evaluate their essays, using a checklist to note if the major components of the essay have been included. (See Figure 1).

Other activities are for the learner to fill out a "Reading Strategies Used" checklist (Figure 2) or to reflect on their learning via a learning log (Glaze, 1987) which becomes an artifact in the portfolio.

(3) Learning is most effective when it is a collaborative effort among learners or between learners and the teacher. Accordingly, portfolio assessment has a peer collaborative component. An adult learner may comment on another class member's writing by noting what was particularly enjoyed, questions he or she would like to ask the writer because something wasn't clear, or specific suggestions regarding how the piece might be improved (Lyons, 1981).

In portfolio assessment learners are also constantly collaborating with the teacher rather than simply depending upon the teacher to tell them whether they have learned or not. Although the teacher certainly has evaluation responsibilities, the student should often be the first evaluator of his or her own work. Teacher and learner can use the same checklists or rating scales and discuss their ratings with one another. Self-esteem increases as the students perceive themselves to be members of the assessment team.

(4) Instruction is most effective when a variety of instructional modes is utilized and include both individual and group experiences. Similarly, variety is the mainstay of portfolio assessment. A learner's portfolio might include student designed learning aids, individual work samples, and learning log entries as well as both teacher and learner evaluations in the form of checklists, rating scales, and anecdotal records. For collaborative learning experiences that the adult learner participates in, perhaps an interview project or a theme study, group interaction can be self-assessed by those participating.

Checklist for a Structured Essay in Answer to a Posed Question
(useful for practicing essay writing for the GED exam)

I. Before You Write
  • Remember the five paragraph structure.
  • Remember to underline words you're not sure of so that you can
    go back and think about the spelling later rather than letting spelling
    problems keep you from getting your ideas down.
  • List the three main points that will answer the question.

II. As You Write
  Paragraph 1: Two sentences
    • Answer the question in one sentence. Pretend that your reader doesn't
      know what question you're replying to in your essay.
    • Combine your three main points of support (Part I) into one sentence.
  Paragraph 2: Focus on Point #1
    • Provide general information about point #1 in one or two sentences.
    • Support Point #1 with a specific detail and/or an example.
    • Support Point #1 with a second specific detail and/or a second example.
  Paragraph 3: Focus on Point #2
    • Provide general information about point #2 in one or two sentences.
    • Support Point #2 with a specific detail and/or an example.
    • Support Point #2 with a second specific detail and/or a second example.
  Paragraph 2: Focus on Point #3
    • Provide general information about point #3 in one or two sentences.
    • Support Point #3 with a specific detail and/or an example.
    • Support Point #3 with a second specific detail and/or a second example.
  Paragraph 5: Conclusion
    • Restate the answer to the question in one or two sentences.
    • Give your opinion.

III. Proofread Your Essay
  • Check the length; 200 words is a good rule-of-thumb.
  • Go back to underlined words and consider the spelling.
  • Check for run-on sentences. (Read the essay without pausing until
    you get to a period (or other end punctuation mark).
  • Check for complete sentences. If you read your essay starting with
    the last sentence and moving backwards through the essay, incomplete
    sentences will stand out more clearly.
  • Check to see if your subjects agree with your verbs: e.g., the idea is;
    ideas are.

Figure 1. Essay Evaluation: "Just the Facts, Ma'am...Just the Facts"

Directions: Score two (2) points for a strategy that is frequently used, one (1) point for one that is sometimes used, and zero (0) points for one that is never or very seldom used.

___1.   Looks over the selection before starting to read - checking difficulty, level of interest in reading, important ideas that might be covered.

___2.   Can discuss background knowledge/experiences related to what is to be read; can make predictions.

___3.   Brings up related ideas without "coaching," tying the reading of the selection to what s/he already knows.

___4.   Comments that something was not read correctly or was not understood (even if s/he is not sure what was wrong or what should be done about it), i.e., is aware when something doesn't make sense.

___5.   Re-reads confusing sections, realizing that the text is supposed to make sense.

___6.   Stops to ask a questions while reading, clarifying what didn't make sense.

___7.   After reading can retell/discuss important ideas from the selection.

___8.   After reading initiates discussion (comments and questions) to cement understanding.

___9.   Changes rate and approach based on the purpose for reading and the material itself.

___10. Is willing to take a risk and read materials where difficulty in reading may be encountered.

___11. Tries to pronounce unknown words rather than waiting for the tutor/teacher to supply the word.

___12. Can skip the word and go on; doesn't get hung up on making multiple attempts to sound out the word.

___13. Uses sentence/paragraph/text context to predict what the word might be.

___14. Uses letter cues to narrow down the predictions that fit the context.

___15. Uses context to self-correct when misreading the text doesn't make sense.

___16. Uses phonic skills to figure out unknown words.

___17. Uses structural analysis skills to break the word into manageable parts.

___18. Does not rely on ineffective pronunciation strategies such as spelling the word and trying to memorize phonic rules.

Figure 2. Literacy Strategies

Since not being able to get along with peers in the workplace is one of key reasons for workers losing their jobs (Paulson, 1988), learning in small group settings and being able to self-evaluate one's efforts and the efforts of one's group are very important. A form to evaluate individual effort as well as group effort on a collaborative venture might include rating how equally all participated, how adept the group was at solving its own problems rather than relying on the teacher, and how encouraging group members were of one another, as well as an open-ended question regarding what each individual group member might do to be a more effective member of the group.

(5) Learning is most effective when the learner has goals and understands the "Why?" of instruction. This is mirrored in portfolio assessment through having a goal assessment sheet with a record of short-term, intermediate, and long-term goals, a list of what the student might do to make progress toward each goal, and a list of personal/family/social/economic factors that might interfere goal achievement. It is also evidenced in discussing with the adult the reasons for using portfolio assessment. It is much easier for adult learners to understand why portfolio assessment is an accurate reflection of their learning than it is for them to understand why a test score reflects what they know and don't know.

(6) Learning is an on-going, never-finished process. Similarly, the portfolio also is never finished. Periodically selections are culled to make room for new learning samples. As students move from the ABE to the GED class or from one adult education program to the next, their portfolios follow them.

Student/Teacher Mobility

In addition to dissatisfaction with standardized tests, the compatibility of portfolio assessment with adult education, and the close tie between instructional theory and portfolio assessment, two other reasons to use portfolio assessment in the adult education classroom should be considered. With the mobility of the staff and the mobility of adult students, having readily available, in-depth information about adult learners is important. Teacher mobility, due to the part-time nature of the instructional staff and high staff turnover, results in adult learners frequently having a number of instructors at various times during their participation in an adult education program. Each teacher doesn't have time to rediscover what a previous teacher has already learned about an adult learner. Additionally, many adult learners themselves move from class to class or program to program. As we become better at tracking these students, their having portfolios that follows them should be very helpful.

Student Retention

And finally, portfolio assessment might be a partial answer to the retention problem in adult education. According to a recent evaluation of adult education programs, 36 percent of new adult learners leave the program before completing 12 hours of instruction; of those who remain, 50 percent leave before completing 16 weeks (Young, 1993). It is imperative to find ways to keep the adult in the program. The high drop-out rate after the first several sessions may in part be due to the discomfort that adult learners feel in the alien school situation. They are fearful of testing and fearful of failing.

The introduction of portfolio assessment early in the adult's association with the program may be key to student self-esteem and willingness to remain involved. Although retention research in adult education is not yet available, some adult education programs are experimenting with the portfolio concept. An evaluation of the Literacy Volunteers of New York City Program (Fingeret & Danin, 1991) found that when adults felt the instructional approach was democratic, changes in their perceptions of the program were positive. This program used aspects of portfolio assessment (e.g., writing samples and rubrics) although it did not specifically focus on retention rate.

Implementing Portfolio Assessment

After establishing the rationale for using portfolio assessment, adult educators must consider how to effectively implement portfolio assessment. Portfolio assessment is a new world for both teachers and learners.

Step 1: Decide upon the general uses of the assessment procedures. What do you plan to do with the results? Do you want the portfolio to be accessible to a number of teachers who might be providing assistance to the same adult education student? Do you want to justify keeping the student in the program despite achievement not being demonstrated on standardized tests? Are you using the portfolio to demonstrate student progress and/or to make justification to funding sources? Do you want to use the portfolio to make decisions about which course the adult learner should be placed into? Why you want to use portfolio assessment determines what you do and how you do it.

Step 2: Decide upon the particular instructional goals to which your portfolio assessment procedures will be tied. Do you want to use the portfolio to assess literacy achievement at the lower levels only? Do you want to use the portfolio to assess progress by GED students? Do you want to assess achievement in areas other than reading and writing? Once you've decided on academic areas for portfolio goals, you might find a yours, mine, and ours strategy effective for deciding what should be included. Instructors will want to require that some types of items be included by the learner and may also determine that some specific items should be in the portfolio because they illustrate particularly well the student's abilities and growth. They will also want to include evaluative information that they have completed themselves (checklists, rating scales, etc.). On the other hand, the student may select some pieces that the teacher may not view as important but which are important to the student. Other pieces may be viewed by both the learner and the teacher as important ones to include. It's often beneficial for the teacher to require that pieces in certain categories be included but have the student make decisions about which specific items to include. For example, the teacher may require that the first draft and the final draft for a piece of writing be included but leave selection of the particular piece of writing up to the student.

Step 3: Identify the tasks/procedures that COULD be used to meet the general uses and more specific goals stated above. You might have general information about the student that would include an interest interview, a reading-writing interview, a general goal sheet, a literacy goal sheet, and a learning styles checklist. You might also include specific test score data. Reading items might include a record of materials read as well as a listing of favorite readings (songs, poems, sayings, and interesting thoughts). An audio tape of the student reading, a miscue analysis chart, questions for readers to self-evaluate their own miscues, a checklist of reading strategies and a general reader-evaluation form might also be included. Student-designed reading aids such as compare and contrast charts, knowledge guide charts (Ogle, 1986), graphic organizers (Vacca & Vacca, 1989), story maps (Spiegel & Fitzgerald, 1986), bio-poems for character analysis (Gere, 1985), vocabulary quadrant charts, and time lines would also be appropriate.

Writing items might include learning logs, literature response logs, essay self-evaluation forms, peer evaluation forms for written selections, writing logs, and a checklist of good-writer strategies. Student-designed self-help cards for math and student-designed story problems would also be appropriate. Items demonstrating small group work and self-evaluation of personal and group effort could also be included.

Finally, summary information is necessary. This may include forms upon which students describe their growth, a cover sheet for the Career Portfolio upon which students evaluate their chosen items, and an educator summary sheet. Remember that this is a listing of items that MIGHT legitimately be included, and consider the listing a menu to SELECT FROM. You may select only a few items or a larger number of items.

Step 4: Consider the feasibility of using these various tasks and procedures for YOUR program. Whether you have an open-entry/open-exit program or a traditional program, whether you have small classes or large classes, whether you have a single teacher or aides for the teacher, whether the general nature of the classroom is collaborative and comfortable for risk-taking or more competitive and individualized, whether there are monies available for purchasing folders and space for keeping them or whether monies and storage space are limited will all influence not IF but HOW you implement portfolio assessment. Instructor knowledge of the procedures as well as instructional staff and administrative commitment to the concept of portfolio assessment are also important to consider.

Step 5: Select the "place to begin" with an eye toward "where to go next" while keeping in mind the "big picture." Of great importance to the successful implementation of a portfolio assessment program in adult education is effective staff development. Since most teachers in adult education are part-time teachers, they may panic when they first hear about portfolio assessment. It sounds so overwhelming and so different from what they have been doing. Students may feel equally overwhelmed by portfolio assessment, no matter how closely tied to adult education principles it may be. Self-evaluation and collaboration may not come easily for them.

A Place to Begin. The creative administrator can find several sensible places for both students and teachers to begin. The following five scenarios show how five different adult education programs in a Midwestern state began implementing portfolio assessment.

Program A. The administrator of this program asked the question: "What are teachers already doing that might come under the general umbrella of portfolio assessment?" Since portfolio assessment is so tied to instruction, teachers will probably be doing SOMETHING that fits with portfolio assessment. This administrator found that the teachers in her program were already using a goal assessment sheet and were having their students keep a log of everything that they read. Therefore, she began by making that goal-setting process more uniform, having teachers design a uniform goal sheet that was a modification of the several forms that the teachers were using individually. She encouraged teachers to use the goal sheet not only as an intake measure but for periodic reference from an assessment perspective. The administrator of Program A also encouraged her teachers to evaluate what else they might already be doing that would fit into a portfolio assessment framework.

Program B. The administrator of Program B asked the question: "What is the easiest thing for teachers to do because it takes very little teacher time?" All of the part-time teachers in this program were very concerned about portfolio assessment being too time-consuming. The administrator decided to have teachers begin by having them focus on student self-assessment. With the assistance of several interested teachers, he revised self-assessment forms for writing that he had received in a workshop and provided staff development on how to use them effectively.

Program C. This administrator asked the question: "What is it that teachers perceive as instruction that could equally be effective as assessment?" He selected student-designed learning aids and provided an inservice on them, describing their use. They included (a) compare and contrast charts, e.g., showing how WWI and WWII were alike and different; (b) knowledge guide charts where students list what they already know, what they want to find out, what they learned, and what they still don't understand; and (c) vocabulary columns where students list the word to be learned in column one, a personal key phrase for the new word in column two, a definition/synonym in column three, and an antonym in column four. Once teachers had modeled for their students these aids to learning, students were encouraged to use them independently. Independent use of thse aids documents learning and is appropriate to include in the portfolio.

Program D. This administrator asked the question: "Who should begin to use portfolio assessment and with whom?" After initially requiring all teachers to be involved and meeting resistance, she asked two of the less resistant teachers to use portfolio assessment with one class of ABE students. As they felt successful and shared their success, more teachers became interested.

Program E. This administrator asked the question: "How can I involve my staff in making decisions about how to implement portfolio assessment so that they have ownership of this?" She had several staff members attend a portfolio workshop. Then she invited a consultant to a work session with the teachers to discuss how portfolio assessment might be tailored to meet the specific needs of their students, keeping in mind the background and abilities of the participating teachers and the design of their adult education program.

Although each program began in a different manner, the above do not represent mutually exclusive ways to begin implementing portfolio assessment. In fact, a model approach might combine all five approaches. The administrator might involve staff from the very beginning in making implementation decisions and within that framework begin with several teachers most interested in discovering the benefits of this alternative assessment. These teachers might begin with several measures: one or two closely tied to what they were already doing, one or two new assessment measures which take very little teacher time, and one or two which have a particularly strong instructional tie.

Where to Go Next. After "a place to begin," "where to go next" must be considered. When teachers feel successful implementing several aspects of portfolio assessment, they are often ready for more. As they experiment with different assessment measures for different students, they discover what works for them and their students. At this point, program personnel might decide on a core of assessment measures that everyone will use for the sake of continuity. The following is one possible set of measures: (1) a goal-setting sheet; (2) a literacy strategies rating scale; (3) a form to self-evaluate essays or other writing; and (4) a portfolio summary sheet. These four items represent a core of assessments that could be used equally well with beginning and advanced adult education students.

Seeing the Big Picture. Although starting small must be emphasized over and over, seeing the big picture of what portfolio assessment might be and knowing what you hope your portfolio will eventually look like, is also important. For this reason, it's a good idea to have a "model" portfolio to share with teachers as you first begin to consider portfolio assessment. They need to SEE what you are talking about and what they might eventually have for each of their students.

Step 6: Consider the logistics of using portfolios. Portfolios need to be accessible to students. Some teachers have found that keeping the portfolios for one class in a portable cardboard storage box to be effective. If several teachers have the same students, they may want to have a central portfolio for these students where all the information is kept or each teacher may want to keep a separate working portfolio for each student with the Career Portfolio showcasing work from the working portfolios in several classes. Beyond the information in the student's portfolio, you may want to have a locked file cabinet where you keep private information. Although it's important to think about these logistical issues at the very beginning, answers may be found later as portfolio use is implemented.

Step 7: Consider how you are going to summarize the contents of the portfolio. One of the pitfalls of portfolio assessment is that the portfolio becomes a dumping ground for all the work the student has completed. Paying careful attention to Steps 1 and 2 will help to keep this from happening; however, the portfolio can still become unmanageable even if Steps 1 and 2 are followed. Periodically, learner and instructor need to evaluate the contents of the portfolio and make decisions about what stays and what goes. Documents reflecting important progress at the end of month one may be of little importance at the end of month three.

A student might develop the following: (1) a chart listing what the student has learned well (reading strategies, writing strategies, content topics, etc.) and what the student still needs to work on and (2) a career portfolio which contains three-five exemplary pieces or evaluation forms that seem to most significantly illustrate the learner's progress. For each item chosen for the Career Portfolio, the learner explains why the item was chosen and, if appropriate, specifically what was learned. Even adult students may need some guidelines regarding what to include; without them, they either may want to put in everything or think that nothing is good enough to include.

The teacher should also complete a one-page summary sheet for each student, noting specific evidences of growth in key areas, progress toward student-set and teacher-set goals, and possible directions for continued learning. The more frequently the summary sheet is completed (perhaps every four months), the more useful it is for planning additional learning. A "Student as Learner" summary sheet that looks at the student more globally, both in an out of the classroom and assessing social skills and academic attitudes more than specific learning, may also be helpful. See Figure 3.

Step 8: Report the results. This step brings us full circle. Based upon the noted use (Step 1), results are summarized and distributed to the proper persons, whether other teachers or personnel from funding sources. One reporting concern that is sometimes voiced regarding portfolio assessment is the reliance upon subjective data. Although portfolio advocates generally oppose statistically-oriented measures, numerical data can be derived from the more subjective assessments that might be included in a student's portfolio. For example, a teacher might use a rating scale for eight or more reading strategies that good readers typically use, e.g., a modification of Figure 2. At the beginning of the year, she notes which strategies were used frequently (2 points), sometimes (1 points), or never (0 points). A total strategy score can be derived at four month intervals and compared. Similarly, rubrics for the grading of projects and written assignments can be cooperatively designed by students and teacher and used to evaluate the learning activity. Adult learners might find it interesting to design their own "report card" with descriptive

Directions: Score two (2) points for a activity that is frequently done, one (1) point for one that is sometimes done, and zero (0) points for one that is never or very seldom done.

__1.   Attends regularly
__2.   Doesn't waste time
__3.   Gives input into designing his/her instructional program
__4.   Knows own learning style, i.e., what makes learning easy;
          what makes learning difficult
__5.   Works independently
__6.   Works effectively in small group learning situations
__7.   Relies on SELF to figure out problems
__8.   Keeps records

　　___a.   Assignments given/completed
　　___b.   Goals
　　___c.   Literature logs
　　___d.   Learning logs

___9.   Completes assignments to be done outside of class
___10. Reads outside of class (beyond assignments)
___11. Designs reading/learning aids to increase understanding
___12. Is interested in self-evaluation
___13. Effectively self-evaluates abilities in the following areas:

　　___a.   Reading
　　___b.   Writing
　　___c.   Other learning

___14. Widens horizons

　　___a.   Has increased academic interests
　　___b.   Seeks out learning activities beyond what is
             set by the instructor

___TOTAL (40 possible)

Figure 3. The Student as Learner

terms replacing the traditional letter grades. Although some items within the portfolio may be specifically evaluated, the portfolio itself is not graded per se.

Closing Comment

Effective portfolio assessment relies on carefully considering each of the above steps. And beyond these nuts and bolts steps, an understanding of why portfolio assessment is appropriate in the adult education classroom is important. Administrators, teachers, and students must all buy into its worth, seeing the big picture of what portfolio assessment can be in their program but starting with small, manageable steps.

References

Adult Education and Literacy Section/Illinois State Board of Education (1993). *Adult Education/Administrator's Handbook.* Macomb, IL: Curriculum Publications Clearinghouse.

Atwell, N. (1987). *In the middle: Writing, reading, and learning with adolescents.* Portsmouth, NH: Heinemann.

Fingeret, H., & Danin, S. (1991). *They really put a-hurtin on my brain: Learning in Literacy Volunteers of New York City.* New York: LVNYC.

Gere, A. R. (Ed.) (1985). *Roots in the sawdust: Writing to learn across the disciplines.* Urbana, IL: National Council of Teachers of English.

Glaze, B. (1987). *Learning logs. In Plain talk about learning and writing across the curriculum.* Richmond, VA: Virginia Department of Education.

Glazer, S., & Brown, C. S. (1993). *Portfolios and beyond: Collaborative assessments in reading and writing.* Norwood, MA: Christopher-Gordon.

Harp, W. (1991). *Assessment and evaluation in whole language programs.* Norwood, MA: Christopher-Gordon.

Knowles, M. (1970). *The modern practice of adult education: Andragogy versus pedagogy.* New York: Association Press.

Lyons, B. (1981). The PQP method of responding to writing. *English Journal, 70,* 47-52.

Neill, D. M., & Medina, N. J. (1989). Standardized testing: Harmful to educational health. *Phi Delta Kappan, 70,* 688-697.

Ogle, D. (1986). K-W-L: A teaching model that develops active reading of expository text. *The Reading Teacher, 39,* 564-570.

Orem, S. (1993). *Practical procedures for the internal evaluation of adult education programs.* DeKalb, IL: Northern Illinois University, RE/ACE.

Paulson, T. (1988). *They shoot managers, don't they? Making conflict work in a changing world.* Santa Monica, CA: Lee Canter.

Pearson, P. D., & Danning, D. (1985). The impact of assessment on reading instruction. *Illinois Reading Council Journal, 13,* 19-29.

Shepard, L.A. (1989). Why we need better assessments. *Educational Leadership, 46,* 4-9.

Spiegel, D. L., & Fitzgerald, J. (1986). Improving reading comprehension through instruction about story parts. *The Reading Teacher, 39,* 676-685.

Tierney, R. J., Carter, M. A., & Desai, L. E. (1991). *Portfolio assessment in the reading-writing classroom.* Norwood, MA: Christopher-Gordon.

Vacca, R., & Vacca. J. (1989). *Content area reading.* 3rd. Ed. Glenview, IL: Scott, Foresman.

Valencia, S., & Pearson, P. D. (1987). Reading assessment: Time for a change. *Reading Teacher, 40,* 726-732.

Young, M. (1993). *The national evaluation of adult literacy programs: Second interim report: Profiles of client characteristics.* Arlington, VA: Development Associates.

Assessing Developmental Learners' Perceptions of Reading and Writing and the Literacy Demands in College

Maria Valeri-Gold
Georgia State University

The purpose of this descriptive study was to assess college developmental learners' perceptions of themselves as readers and as writers, and in particular, to examine their expectations of the reading and writing demands placed on them in college. The subjects were 46 college developmental studies students enrolled in a ten-week team-taught reading and writing course in a four year urban university located in the southeastern United States. During the first and tenth week of the course, students were asked to reflect on two open-ended questions: 1) "What are your perceptions (views) of yourself as a reader and as a writer?" and 2) "What are your expectations of the reading and writing demands that will be placed on you in college?" Written comments of each student's two reflection pieces for each question were analyzed. These written comments were grouped into seven research-based response categories determined from past and recent reading and writing researchers: purposes for reading and writing, affective awareness, metacognitive awareness, integrated learning, teacher influence, conative (perseverance and endurance), and academic(discrepancies between the reading and writing demands in high school and in college). Further analysis of the students' initial reflection pieces indicated that they were not aware of who they were as readers and as writers. However, students appeared to be metacognitively aware of who they were as readers and as writers in their final reflection comments. Results also indicated that students were aware of the reading and writing demands that would be placed on them in college, and they were willing to meet these academic challenges through persistence and perseverance.

Research studies have been conducted with students of varying abilities, grade levels, and cultures to assess their perceptions of reading and writing (Gillespie, 1993; Hellwege & Sell, 1990; Jongsma, 1993; Marx; 1991; McCoy, 1991; Nelson, 1983; Sison, 1992). Reading and writing attitudinal scales and assessment instruments, such as inventories, surveys, questionnaires, and checklists, have also been developed to measure learners' views toward reading and writing (Linn, 1990; Nieratka & Epstein, 1981). However, such assessment tools represent traditional methods for assessing students' literacy. Other authentic methods for assessing students' reading and writing perceptions need to be explored. According to Afflerbach (1993), authentic assessment occurs when learners become engaged readers and writers who are involved in evaluating their own reading and writing products and processes. When students are actively engaged in their reading and writing, they become aware of how they perceive themselves as readers and as writers for monitoring their present and future literacy goals.

Rationale for Assessment

Overreliance on traditional methods of assessing students' reading and writing may have produced negative results for learners of varying abilities and grade levels (Hiebert, Valencia, & Afflerbach, 1994). The researchers cited four main problems with traditional testing methods: a) traditional norm-referenced tests are not preparing students for higher level reading and writing skills essential for surviving in today's society; b) standardized tests have a negative impact on the school's curriculum, instruction, and learning because teachers are using questions found in the tests as a method of classroom instruction rather than establishing their own course content; c) overreliance on standardized tests has reduced teachers and their students to passive observers of assessment rather than active collaborators in the process; and d) overdependency on standardized tests has caused administrators, community, government agencies, and leaders to look only at standardized test results and to discredit other authentic methods of assessing students in the classroom.

As a reaction to this overreliance on traditional norm-referenced tests, teachers have begun to experiment with newer, more authentic methods for assessing their students' reading and writing. These alternatives may help to move away from the traditional emphasis on a skill-driven curriculum to the creation of a comprehensive integrated literacy-based program which provides students with classroom experiences asking them to create, produce, and self-evaluate their own reading and writing processes and products. Such classroom experiences must be meaningful and cause students to use higher-order thinking and problem-solving skills. The instructional activities developed for assessing student progress in college reading and writing programs should also reflect current research and theory, be appropriate to the philosophy and goals of the program, and be unique to the characteristics of the students (Simpson & Nist, 1992).

Students need to learn about who they are as readers and writers in order to assess, reflect, and plan for present and future growth in literacy. Helping students to question their beliefs and attitudes about their literacy abilities aids them in understanding how language works, how it can be used, and how it can foster metacognition. More importantly, students' awareness and understanding of their learning processes helps them to monitor their own comprehension. Students need to be able to think about the ways they read and write. Allowing students to assess themselves can also help teachers know much more about their students as readers and as writers, in particular, the students' "interests, choices, strategies, and skills" (Chittendon, 1991, p. 28). According to Harp (1993), students' interests and attitudes toward a subject can affect their comprehension.

Teachers need to develop new and viable assessment alternatives so that they can observe their students' strengths and abilities in a variety of settings. Thus, the teacher's role will change from passive observer to "teacher as inquirer" who discovers the students' needs, attitudes, and interests (Chittenden, 1991). Authentic assessment requires students to change their views of themselves as readers and as writers. Students need to become risk-takers who judge and review their own literacy over time. According to Zessoules and Gardner (1991),

> Theirs is the work of posing questions, making judgments, integrating criticisms, reconsidering problems, and investigating new possibilities. With this work comes the responsibility of assessment. Students must educate themselves to become evaluators of their own efforts. They must come to recognize and build on their strengths in their work and to diagnose and treat their weaknesses. No longer the passive subjects of testing and evaluating, students are key players in the process of assessment (p. 64).

Purpose

The purpose of this descriptive study was to assess college developmental learners' perceptions of themselves as readers and as writers and, in particular, to examine their expectations of the reading and writing demands placed on them in college.

Background Information

In our ten week long team-taught college developmental reading and writing course used, students are provided with meaningful classroom activities and learning assignments to help them assess their own reading and writing processes. Authentic self-assessment instruments such as *Personal Language Preferences, Learning-Awareness Surveys, Portfolio Self-Evaluation Inventories,* and portfolios containing collections of their reading and writing products are used (Valeri-Gold & Deming, 1994). These assessment techniques help gather and organize information about students' literacy needs. Students also assess their reading and writing growth by reflecting in their journals. Students are strongly encouraged to share responses with their instructors and peers regarding their own personal and academic dilemmas and insight concerning their own literacy.

Developmental learners read thematically arranged literary selections on the family, work, media, social concerns, learning, human behavior, and controversial issues. They are required to write essays and summaries on both unassigned and assigned topics related to these themes. By reading a variety of literary genre and experimenting with a multitude of real-life, meaningful reading and writing experiences, students develop their cognitive, social, affective, and metacognitive skills (Herman, Aschbacher, & Winters, 1992). These reading and writing activities and assignments are then placed in portfolios. Through involvement in this assessment process, students become independent learners who continually evaluate their own reading and writing processes and products and plan for personal and academic literacy goals.

Method

Subjects

The subjects were 46 college developmental studies students enrolled in a ten week team-taught reading and writing course in a four year urban university located in the southeastern United States. Placement in this class was based on scores on the *Collegiate Placement Exam* (CPE) (less than or equal to 75). The CPE is a state-mandated test required for students who do not meet regular college admission standards in the areas of reading, composition, or mathematics. Placement was also determined by students' *Scholastic Aptitude Test* verbal scores (less than or equal to 350) and high school grade point averages (less than or equal to 2.0).

Twenty-eight subjects were females and eighteen were males. Ages ranged from seventeen to thirty years of age. The sample consisted of six African-American males and fifteen females, nine Caucasian males and six females, two Hindu males and one female, one Asian-American male and three females, and three Hispanic-American females.

Procedure

During the **first** and **tenth** week of the course, students wrote responses to two open-ended questions in class: 1) "What are your perceptions (views) of yourself as a reader and as a writer?;" and 2) "What are your expectations of the reading and writing demands that will be placed on you in college?" No time constraints were given. The instructors collected, analyzed and compared the two reflective pieces for each question written by each student. These reflective pieces were again analyzed by both instructors to note similarities and/or differences between and among the students' responses at the end of the quarter. At this point student comments were classified according to response. Seven response categories were developed based upon reading and writing research which stressed the importance of integrating learning and motivation with the development of students' affective, social, and metacognitive skills (Chase, Gibson, & Carson, 1993; Gillespie, 1993; Herman, Aschbacher, & Winters, 1992; McCombs, 1991; Nist, 1993; Weinstein & Meyer, 1991). Two developmental reading instructors and a writing instructor from within the developmental studies department were chosen as outside raters to verify the accuracy of the seven response categories.

Results

Question 1

Student responses to the first open-ended question "What are your perceptions (views) of yourself as a reader and as a writer?," fell into five research-based categories: 1)purposes for reading and writing (Gillespie, 1993), 2) affective awareness (Herman, Aschbacher, & Winters, 1992), 3) metacognitive awareness (McCombs, 1991; Weinstein & Meyer, 1991), 4) integrated learning (Harp, 1993), and 5) teacher influence (Nelson, 1983). Each of the five categories are defined and explained below; samples of students' responses in each category are also provided.

Purposes for reading and writing may be defined as students' awareness of the "hows" and "whys" of what they read and wrote (Gillespie, 1993). In this category, students' initial responses revealed what and why they read rather than how they viewed themselves as readers and as writers. Specifically, some students listed the types of materials they read including fiction and nonfiction books, newspapers, and magazines. Two students indicated names of favorite authors such as Terry McMillan, Danielle Steele, Sidney Sheldon, V. C. Andrews, and Jackie Collins.

205

Sample student responses

I always read anything I could get my hands on. I seldom read big books. I read them only if I had to. I used to read a lot of comics.

But lately, I have read some good books, and I am more interested in them. I enjoy reading certain things such as about peoples' lives, fiction and nonfiction books, that are not boring, and successful events that occur from writing poems and how I feel according to how my day went.

I do not mind reading and writing and I usually find enjoyment in it when I take time to read. I like to read stuff that is interesting and keeps me on the edge of my seat to find out what is going to happen next.

Students also explained their purposes for writing by describing what and why they wrote, as well as the forms of writing they enjoyed such as poetry, songs, and short stories.

Sample student responses

I love to write poetry, maybe because it's free-style. I like to express my feelings better on paper than in words.

I hardly ever just pick up and read a book. I always like to write. I love to write poetry, that's mainly how I'm feeling at the moment.

I love to read! When I read, I have "control." Faces, characters, expressions, places, and all that stuff can be determined by me.

Students' final reflections did not indicate their purposes for reading and writing; they focused rather upon students' metacognitive awareness of themselves as readers and writers.

Affective awareness reflects students' knowledge and appreciation of their individual reading and writing preferences and styles and their ability to enjoy and value learning because of their self-confidence and motivation to read and write more effectively (Herman, Aschbacher, & Winters, 1992).

Students' replies in the affective awareness category indicated their attitudes (positive and/or negative), interests (likes and/or dislikes), and motivation (desire to read and write) toward literacy.

Sample student responses

Reading and writing are difficult for me. When I am reading, I tend to wander off into another world. I have to pace myself and read a little at one time. Writing is a spur of the moment situation for me. If I am thinking hard about a specific thing, then I'll jot my thoughts down on paper. I enjoy reading and writing, but it all depends on the material. I love to read books that I'm interested in, and write topics that I feel comfortable about.

My perception as a reader is that if the story is interesting than I am interested. My perception as a writer is that I try to write something interesting or something close to home which will move the reader.

Students' responses ranged from personal frustration with literacy tasks to recognition of marked improvement and definite progress. In the first reflective piece, 11 students stated that they were better readers than writers, 12 students felt that they were better readers than writers, and two students noted that they were competent in both areas. Seven students revealed that they did not like to read or write unless they could choose the topic. When students chose their own topics, they indicated that the topics needed to be fun, exciting, and interesting.

Five students noted that they felt frustrated and anxious when asked to read and write in class. They experienced difficulty in overcoming reading and writing obstacles such as comprehending texts, choosing topics for their essays, developing thesis statements, focusing on the topic, and revising and editing their essays and summaries. Six students stated that their reading and writing would improve if they had more time and opportunities to practice.

In their final reflective pieces, 24 of the 46 students wrote that they definitely showed marked improvement in their ability to read and write by the end of the quarter. However, two students wrote that they showed some progress in reading and writing, eight stated that they had made no progress in reading and writing, five noted progress in reading, but not writing, one student indicated progress in writing but not reading, and six students did not comment on whether they had improved.

Twenty-four of the 46 students who showed improvement in attitudes toward literacy indicated in their final responses that they were motivated to read and write. They had gained confidence in themselves as readers and as writers and improved their comprehension and their grades on essays. In one case, transfer of learning appeared to occur. The student noted that she was now able to apply the writing strategies taught in class to an essay she was required to write for an exam in a study skills course.
The student wrote:

> In my seminar class on our test, I had to write an essay. I received a 10/10 and my teachers pointed out how well written it was.

Metacognitive awareness may be interpreted as the students' ability to reflect, discuss, apply, and evaluate the reading and writing strategies they have been taught (McCombs, 1986; 1991; Weinstein and Meyer, 1991). None of the students' initial responses indicated metacognitive awareness. However, students' responses in their final reflective pieces indicated that they had used the prereading and prewriting (previewing, highlighting, brainstorming), during reading and writing (identifying and formulating the thesis statement with supporting evidence), and after reading and writing (revising and editing) strategies modeled for them in class as they read and wrote essays and summaries.

Sample student responses

> I'm more aware of details and how they support the main idea. I've noticed "fillers" and how they can be a little misleading. Now as a writer, I have learned more about prewriting strategies and how to start and get organized. But I still have problems.

> I know and understand what a thesis is. I understand the different paragraph patterns. By writing reflection pieces, essays, and summaries, they help me understand more.

> My perceptions of reading and writing I believe are still the same. Finding main ideas and rearranging details are even harder.

In their final reflective pieces, eight students' responses revealed that they had employed reading and writing strategies taught in class. Students

208

explicitly described the processes they used to write their essays and summaries. Thus, these students appeared to be actively involved in assessing their own reading and writing processes and products.

Integrated learning refers to as the students' ability to experience the interrelatedness between reading and writing (Harp, 1993). Initial responses did not indicate any knowledge of integrated learning. However, in their final reflective pieces, students wrote that they experienced the connection between reading and writing while they read and wrote their essays and summaries.

Sample student responses

As a reader, I can tell what the main idea is trying to get across to me the reader. As a writer, I can form a better paper that has meaning. Now that I see reading and writing really go hand in hand, I can combine the two in my future classes.

My views on reading and writing in college are reading and writing go hand in hand, without one, you can't do the other.

My views as a reader and writer have changed in the past five weeks. I understand now that reading and writing are connected in many ways.

Teacher influence refers to the teachers' attitudes toward the subject that appeared to influence the students' reading and writing performances (Nelson, 1983). In their initial responses, students did not mention teachers' impact on their reading and writing behaviors. The researchers felt that students did not comment on how we may have an influence on them because they did not know what we expected from them, and the building of trust between students and teacher had not yet occurred. However, students' responses in their final reflective pieces indicated that they had perceived that their reading and writing had improved because of the instructors' role and teachers' attitudes toward the subject.

Sample student responses

I thank you for a superb job. First, by giving me the confidence to know that I am a good reader and writer. Secondly, for telling me when my paper was wrong and showing me the various techniques on how to improve it. Last of all, I just want to thank both of you for being loving and caring people.

I enjoy DS 070/080 and I personally feel that with these classes I am sharpening my sword of knowledge. The teachers are wonderful and are helping me to fulfill my college expectations.

I hope to be a very successful student here at GSU, and graduate in less than five years. I also hope to have more professors like (instructors' names).

Eleven students commented that the teachers' attitude toward the subject was a major factor affecting their improvement in reading and writing.

Results
Question 2
Student responses to the second open-ended question "What are your expectations of the reading and writing demands that will be placed on you in college?," fell into two major categories: 1) conative (Cooter, 1993), and 2) academic (Chase, Gibson, & Carson, 1993; Nist, 1993). Both categories are defined and discussed and include sample student responses.

Conative refers to the students' willingness to endure and pursue their present and future literacy goals (Cooter, 1993). In the conative category, both students' initial and final replies revealed that they do have the persistence and perseverance to accept the reading and writing demands which will be placed on them in college.

Sample student responses

I know that there will be times when I am expected to read a book a week, or even try to write on a subject that I can't possibly relate to. But I am willing, and hopefully to be successful at doing whatever it is I have to do.
My expectations in reading and writing have changed. At first I thought that it would be hard, but I feel that things are not what they are always made out to be! I was told that I would never make it in

college, but yes I can! I feel I'm doing well in all my classes, and I know if I keep trying I'll make it!

Twenty-one students indicated the willingness to improve their reading and writing and to face the challenges their college courses demand from them.

Academic refers to students' perceptions that there were discrepancies between the reading and writing demands in high school and in college, they had clearly defined literacy goals, and they were aware of teacher expectations (Chase, Gibson, & Carson, 1993; Nist, 1993). In the academic category, students revealed clear understanding of the differences between the literacy demands placed upon them in high school and college in both their initial and final reflection pieces. Only two students remarked that the literacy demands were the same in the two places. Eight students said that the literacy tasks in college were more difficult than in high school and two noted that the literacy demands in high school were different than in college.

Sample student responses

College will be different from high school. I know that I must put more time and thought into reading and writing because there will be more of it.

I feel that I have improved my reading and skills and enjoy reading a lot more than I did in high school. As a writer, I feel frustrated than I did in high school because the system has gotten a lot harder and the grading has been very critical.

My high school teachers used to tell all kinds of horror stories about how hard your English classes will be. They also said they expected a lot more out of you than we did. Taking in fact that this is a DS class makes no difference because I've talked to friends who are in English 111 and find no change with what they did in high school. I think my DS classes are easier than my high school classes.

Discussion

In the purposes for reading and writing category, students' initial responses to the first open-ended question, "What are your perceptions (views) of yourself as a reader and as a writer?" were similar to the findings reported by previous researchers (Gillespie, 1993; Gillespie & Powell, 1990). In Gillespie & Powell's study (1990), 191 developmental reading students responded in writing to ten survey questions which assessed their definitions of reading and their perceptions of their ability to read. Even though more than one half of the at-risk students considered themselves readers, they had a false perception of their reading abilities and defined their perceptions based upon what and why they read and wrote. For example, a student wrote that "reading was something that was done for enjoyment and for relaxation." (Gillespie, 1993).

The findings of this study were somewhat similar. Some students found it difficult to describe how they perceived themselves as readers and as writers and instead, they described the types of books they read and their reasons for reading.

In this initial statements collected in this study, students' indicated that they found it difficult to comprehend challenging reading materials. Furthermore, these comprehension problems may have affected their ability to write essays and summaries. It appeared that students were not applying strategies they had been taught in class to other learning situations. As McCombs (1986) noted, students can be taught strategy instruction indefinitely, but they must be motivated for effective transfer of instruction to occur.

In this study, twenty-four students indicated in their final reflective pieces that their attitudes toward reading and writing had improved as a result of the class. Students also stated that they became more interested in reading and writing and they were more motivated to read and to write. These findings confirm previous studies (Marx, 1991; Regan, 1984) wherein student reading and writing attitudes improved after participation in developmental classes.

Students' responses in the affective awareness category also revealed that they perceived that their writing had improved when they were given opportunities to choose and write on topics of their own choice in the present study. Students said when they chose their own personal topics, they were more focused and interested. Students further stated that their essays had improved because they had been given sufficient class time to revise their papers. These findings confirm the work conducted by Perkins (1993) and Linn (1990).

In this study, students' final reflective pieces further revealed that as their attitudes toward reading and writing improved, they were more motivated to achieve academically. As a result of these attitudinal changes, students' grades improved. Results from the students' final reflections in the affective awareness category further revealed that their reading and writing had improved because of classroom instructions and attitudes of the instructors toward the subject. This finding concurs with the work conducted by Nelson (1983) whose findings suggests that the major influence on students' reading ability is the teacher. Regan (1984) likewise noted that the instructor's role and attitudes toward the students and the subject were highly influential on students' composing processes.

In the metacognitive awareness category, students' final responses revealed that they used reading and writing strategies they were taught in class. Students responses revealed that they believed their essays and summary writing had improved because they had employed these literacy strategies. Students perceived that they were able to assess their own reading and writing processes. Students also perceived that they had experienced the connections between reading and writing. In the team-taught class, individual, collaborative, and small group instruction were developed to foster the relationships between reading and writing. In particular, students were asked to write reflective pieces, assess their reading and writing products through the development of a portfolio, do a collaborative group presentation, and react to their peers' essays during group conferences with instructors and lab tutors.

Findings from the second open-ended question, "What are your expectations of the reading and writing demands that will be placed on you in college?" fell into two categories, conative and academic. In the conative category, initial and final reflection pieces revealed students' continual desire to persist and to persevere in meeting the reading and writing demands which will be expected of them in college. Findings from this study concur with those of Cooter (1993) who noted that persistence and perseverance are two important factors which are related and may have an impact on academic achievement.

In the academic category, a majority of students remarked that there were definite discrepancies between the reading and writing demands which were placed on them in college and in high school in their initial and final reflection pieces. Students' responses concur with the findings from a study by Chase, Gibson, & Carson (1993) who found that reading and writing demands across disciplines in high school and college varied, and these differences were based on course content, methodology, and purpose.

Implications

The results of this study have classroom implications for college developmental educators. Developmental learners should be provided with a variety of authentic assessment measures which allow them opportunities to assess

This should be done in PRIMARY school.

themselves in reading and writing. In this study, students experienced difficulty in assessing who they were as readers and as writers. Thus, developmental educators should give their students meaningful reading and writing activities and assignments that help them to become metacognitively aware.

In this study, the students who used the before, during, and after reading and writing strategies taught in class indicated that they believed they had improved as readers and as writers. According to Schunk (1986), strategy instruction may aid learners in developing positive self-concepts about their reading and writing capabilities.

Affective awareness methods should be developed to enhance developmental students' reading and writing performance. Chiseri-Strater (1991) noted that students need comprehensive classroom demonstrations, modeling, and instruction on reading within a discipline. Specifically, developmental educators "need to think more about how motivation and other affective variables influence academic literacy" (Nist, 1993, p. 17).

The two conative factors, persistence and perseverance, also offer classroom implications for developmental educators. Cooter (1993) stated that "even though the dialogue on affective dimensions in particular has been rich and informative, we still cannot reliably calculate the effect of these factors on reading achievement" (p. 515). In this study, students' responses revealed that they will continue to achieve academically in the areas of reading and writing in their future courses, and they will accept this academic challenge.

According to Wolf (1993),

> Effective assessment requires a setting in which teachers can work together to establish a sound and shared vision of the curriculum, to set clear goals for instruction and purposes for assessment, and to develop a coherent schoolwide system for evaluating and reporting on student learning" (p. 522).

Findings from the study conducted by Chase, Gibson, and Carson (1993) concur with Wolf's comment (1993). If differences in the reading and writing demands in high school and college classes exist, then "greater attention should be given to initiating students into the teaching and learning style of the university. The responsibility of this initiation, however, needs to occur in both the high school and university setting" (Chase, Gibson, and Carson, 1993, p. 10).

214

References

Afflerbach, P. (1993, February). Assessing engaged reading. Paper presented at the National Reading Research Center, The University of Georgia, Athens, GA.

Chase, N. D. , Gibson, S. U., & Carson, J. G. (1993). Preparing students for college: Making the transition. *Georgia Journal of Reading, 19*, 4-17.

Chiseri-Strater, E. (1991). *Academic literacies: The public discourse of university students*. Portsmouth, NH: Heinemann.

Chittenden, E (1991). Authentic assessment, evaluation, and documentation of student performance. In V. Perrone (Ed.), *Expanding student assessment* (pp. 22-31). Alexandria, VA: Association for Supervision and Curriculum Development.

Cooper, D. J. (1993). *Literacy: Helping children construct meaning.* Boston, MA: Houghton Mifflin.

Cooter, R. B. (1993). A think aloud on secondary reading assessment. *Journal of Reading, 36*, 584-586.

Gillespie, C. (1993). College students' reflections on reading. *Reading Horizons, 33*, 329-340.

Gillespie, C., & Powell, J. (1990). At-risk college students: Their perceptions of reading. In N. D. Padak & J. L. Logan (Eds.), *Challenges in reading* (pp. 177-183). Provo, UT: College Reading Association.

Harp, B. (1993). Principles of assessment and evaluation in whole language classrooms. In B. Harp (Ed.),*Assessment and evaluation of whole language classrooms* (pp. 32-52). Norwood, MA: Christopher-Gordon.

Hellwege N. C., & Sell, J. L. (1990). *Different strokes for different folks.* Miami, FL: Southeast Florida Training Center for Adult Literacy Educators. (ERIC Document Reproduction Service No. ED 329 655)

Herman, J. L., Aschbacher, P. R., & Winters, L. (1992). *A practical guide to alternative assessment.* Alexandria, VA: Association for Supervision and Curriculum Development.

Hiebert, E. H., Valencia, S. W., & Afflerbach, P. P. (1994). Definitions and perspectives. In S. W. Valencia, E. H. Hiebert, & P. P. Afflerbach (Eds.), *Authentic reading assessment: Practices and possibilities* (pp. 6-21). Newark, DE: International Reading Association.

Jongsma, K. S. (1993). What students' written reflections reveal about literacy. In L. Patterson, C, M. Santa, K. G. Short, & K. Smith (Eds.), *Teachers are researchers: Reflection and action* (pp. 122-129). Newark, DE: International Reading Association.

Linn, J. B. (1990). The development of a reliable and valid scale to measure writing attitudes (Doctoral dissertation, Pennsylvania State University, 1989). *Dissertation Abstracts International, 51*, 771A.

215

Marx, M. S. (1991, March). *Writing abilities, writing attitudes, and the teaching of writing.* Paper presented at the annual meeting of the Conference on College Composition and Communication, Boston, MA.

McCombs, B. L. (1986). The role of self-system in self-regulating learning. *Contemporary Educational Psychology, 11,* 314-332.

McCombs, B. L. (1991). The definition of measurement of primary motivational processes. In M. C. Wittrock, & E. I. Baker (Eds.), *Testing and cognition.* Englewood Cliffs, NJ: Prentice-Hall.

McCoy, D. (1991, October). *Surveys of independent reading pinpointing the problems, seeking the solutions.* Paper presented at the annual meeting of the College Reading Association, Crystal City, VA.

Nelson, R. L. (1983, October). *How college students feel about their reading experiences.* Paper presented at the annual meeting of the Great Lakes Regional International Reading Association Conference, Springfield, IL.

Nieratka, E., & Epstein, J. (1981). *College students' self-perceptions on factors which have influenced their writing ability.* (ERIC Document Reproduction Service ED 213 003)

Nist, S. L. (1993). What the literature says about academic literacy. *Georgia Journal of Reading, 19,* 11-18.

Perkins, N. S. (1993). The echoes project: Five case studies of students writing research papers using primary sources in a collaborative community (Doctoral dissertation), Illinois State University, 1992). *Dissertation Abstracts International, 53,* 4306A.

Regan, S. B. (1984, March). *The effect of combined reading-writing instruction on the composing processes of basic writers: A descriptive study.* Paper presented at the annual meeting of the Conference on College Composition and Communication, New York, NY.

Schunk, D. H. (1986). Verbalization and children's self-regulated learning. *Contemporary Educational Psychology, 11,* 347-369.

Simpson, M. L., & Nist, S. L. (1992). Toward defining a comprehensive assessment model for college reading. *Journal of Reading, 35,* 452-458.

Sison, M. P. A. (1992). The relationship of college student attitudes, motivation, and anxiety to second language achievement: A test of Gardner's model (Doctoral dissertation, University of Southern California, 1991). *Dissertation Abstracts International, 53,* 4239A.

Valeri-Gold, M., & Deming, M. P. (1994). *Making connections through reading and writing.* Belmont, CA: Wadsworth.

Weinstein, C. E., & Meyer, D. K. (1991). Implications of cognitive psychology for testing: Contributions from work in learning strategies. In M. C. Whittrock, & El L. Baker (Eds.), *Testing and cognition.* Englewood Cliffs, NJ: Prentice-Hall.

Wolf, K. P. (1993). From informal to informed assessment: Recognizing the role of the classroom teacher. *Journal of Reading, 36,* 518-523.

Zessoules, R. , & Gardner, H. (1991). Authentic assessment: Beyond the buzzword and into the classroom. In V. Perrone (Ed.), *Expanding student assessment* (pp. 47-71). Alexandria, VA: Association for Supervision and Curriculum Development.

The ALERT: One Answer to Literacy Screening

Rita M. Bean, Meryl K. Lazar, Rhonda S. Johnson,
Dorothy D. Burns, Richard C. Cox, Suzanne Lane,
and Naomi Zigmond
University of Pittsburgh

There is an increasing need for quick and thorough alternative contextual assessment practices which are relevant to the workplace and link learning gains to work outcomes. An alternative method which has proven successful for evaluating reading, mathematics, and writing skills is Curriculum Based Measurement (CBM). Many educational researchers have found Curriculum Based Measurement (CBM) to be a reliable and viable method for screening, monitoring and evaluating reading, mathematics and writing performance. Given these findings, it was hypothesized that curriculum based measures could be developed for workplace settings and used to create a screening device to identify employees needing further testing and possible instruction in reading, math and writing. This article describes such a screening measure, the ALERT (Adult Literacy Employment-Related Tasks), developed at the University of Pittsburgh.

Because of the drastic change in employee expectations created by today's technological workplace, literacy issues related to job proficiency in the workplace have come to the forefront. Technology has changed the nature of existing jobs while creating new jobs for which employees are not qualified. These changes have created new demands which reveal basic skill deficiencies where none appeared to exist before (*The Bottom Line: Basic Skills in the Workplace, 1988*). In addition to basic skill demands, workers are expected to be self-directed, flexible, open to change, skillful at problem solving, active questioners, critical thinkers, and participants in work teams (SCANS Report, 1992, Soifer, et al., 1990).

Demands will only increase. Miller and Imel (1987) state that it was once possible for marginally literate adults to function in the workplace, but advances in technology are making it increasingly necessary for employees to demonstrate higher levels of literacy. The changing nature of work from segmented, routinized duties to coordinated production processes requires higher level literacy skills.

Workplace Assessment

For years, practitioners and policymakers in the field of adult literacy have struggled to develop appropriate assessment. The need for improved test measures has also surfaced in the workplace as more employers are facing a proficiency gap among employees which is threatening the well being of their companies. These proficiency gaps have been well documented at all levels within the workforce (Askov, 1989; Bean, 1988, McCrossan, 1992).

Concern about literacy in the workplace has spawned interest in and concern about the relevance of the assessment tools used in places of employment. Most often, standardized achievement tests are used because of their relative ease of administration. These tests tend to be academic-based skill tests modeled on those developed for students in school. They measure prior knowledge of a general body of knowledge as well as skills developed in school settings using grade level equivalencies as the standard of measurement. However, because they do not measure the kinds of problem-solving skills most relevant for judging ability to perform on the job (*Guidelines for Developing an Educational Program for Worker Literacy*, 1986; McCrossan, 1992), educators criticize their appropriateness in workplace environments. What is measured by items on these tests does not match what the examinee needs to know to perform successfully on the job (Salvia & Ysseldyke, 1981; Jenkins & Pany, 1978; Thurlow & Ysseldyke, 1982).

There is an increasing need for quick and thorough alternative contextual assessment practices which are relevant to the workplace and link learning gains to work outcomes. An alternative method which has proven successful for evaluating reading, mathematics, and writing skills is Curriculum Based Measurement (CBM). Many educational researchers (Bean et al., 1988; Deno et al., 1982; Deno, Mirkin & Chang, 1982; Fuchs, Deno & Marston, 1982; Fuchs, Fuchs & Deno, 1982; Martson & Magnusson, 1985; Tindal, Germann & Deno, 1983) have found Curriculum Based Measurement (CBM) to be a reliable and viable method for screening, monitoring and evaluating reading, mathematics and writing performance. Given these findings, it was hypothesized that curriculum-based measures could be developed for workplace settings and used to create a screening device to identify employees needing further testing and possible instruction in reading, math and writing. This article describes such a screening measure, the ALERT (Adult Literacy Employment-Related Tasks), developed at the University of Pittsburgh.

Description of the ALERT Screening Test

The ALERT is a simple screening instrument which can be administered to individuals or groups of adults for rapid identification of those who might require further diagnosis and/or instructional assistance in the basic skills of reading, math and writing. It is designed to be a quick, efficient and simple means of screening workers to determine whether a more careful diagnosis is needed. It can also be used as a model or prototype for developing more specific measures related to a particular job.

The ALERT is comprised of an expository reading passage with a maze format, a series of math problems requiring basic computation skills, and a work-related writing prompt. Both the reading and math sections have cut-off scores indicating either "a need for assistance," a "possible need for assistance," or "no need for further assistance."

Reading Subtest

Developing appropriate tasks to include in the screening measure was a lengthy process requiring thoughtful, research-based, decision-making. In developing the reading subtest, the decision was made to use general interest expository prose, because workers may be faced with this type of reading and, further, it would be relevant across worksites. Passages at the fourth grade reading level were chosen because of research evidence that "easy" passages can discriminate among readers as well as passages at more difficult levels (Deno, 1988). At this reading level, passages are easy enough to not frustrate a beginning level reader while still yielding information about advanced level readers. Four such passages were field tested and one was chosen for inclusion in the test.

The reading passage is administered using a modified cloze or maze reading task. The maze format was prepared following guidelines suggested by Johnson (1980). The first sentence in the passage was copied intact. Thereafter, every seventh word was deleted and replaced with three alternative words: an incorrect word from another class, an incorrect word from the same word class (eg. a verb for a verb), and the correct word. Administration time for the reading measure is two minutes.

Math Subtest

This subtest is comprised of 80 single and double digit math problems of addition, subtraction, multiplication, and division problems. Some fractions and decimal problems are also included. All problems were taken from a fourth grade math curriculum. Administration time is two minutes.

Writing Prompt

Many researchers have found writing fluency to be an efficient and feasible means of evaluating writing performance (Deno et al., 1982; Marston, Tindal & Deno, 1982a). Further, Haswell (1988) found that essays of poorer writers averaged fewer words than higher rated student essays. Bean (1988) administered several writing prompts to adult literacy students to determine which proved most interesting and generated the highest number of words. The prompt which met these criteria and was selected as the writing subtest asked subjects to describe features of their occupation. Writers are given one minute to organize their thoughts and three minutes to write.

Validating the Measure

The Vocabulary, Language Expression, and Mathematics Computation subtests of the California Achievement Test, Level 18 (grades 7.8-9.2) were administered to the validity group to provide concurrent validation data. This level was chosen because it fell within currently used parameters for entry into JTPA programs (6th grade reading level) and entry into vocational education programs (8th or 9th grade reading level) (Askov, 1989).

The vocabulary subtest was used because it took less time to administer, yet research indicates a high relationship between vocabulary and comprehension (Anderson & Freebody, 1983). The Mathematics subtest offers items testing addition, subtraction, multiplication, and division of whole numbers, fractions and decimals, and was similar to the tasks on the ALERT. The Language Expression subtest asks for identification of grammatical parts of sentences, identification of sentence patterns, topic sentences and sentence sequence within paragraphs. Although demands of this subtest were not similar to the writing fluency task on the ALERT, administration of the subtest did provide some indication of the relationship between performance on the ALERT measure and performance on another measure of written language expression.

The Sample

The validation and normative samples were adults working in local companies, those involved with service organizations, those enrolled in adult education programs, college, and those in JTPA screening and career development programs. Overall, 701 adults participated in testing. Of those, 98 agreed take the *California Achievement Test*. The remaining 603 people served as the normative group. The majority of individuals in the normative group were employed (56%) females (61%) who were in the 22-34 age range.

Forty nine percent were African American and 43% were white. Education levels varied. Thirty three percent had some college experience, 18% had completed high school, 19% had complete a few years of high school, and 19% had some vocational training.

Demographics of the validity group (98 people) were similar. The majority were employed (62%) females (71%) in the 22-34 year age range. Fifty seven percent were African American and 49% were white. Sixteen percent had some college experience, 14% had completed high school, 38% had some high school, and 15% had vocational training.

Validation Procedures

Over a four month period, the ALERT was administered to the 603 adults in the normative group and both the ALERT and the *California Achievement Test* (CAT) were administered to the 98 adults in the validity group. Means and standard deviations were calculated for reading, math, and writing for both the normative and validity groups.

Criterion-related validity was determined by correlating results on the ALERT subtests with performance on the three subtests of the *California Achievement Test,* Level 18. Correlation coefficients were $r = .79$ for reading, $r = .66$ for math, and $r = .49$ for writing. The lower correlation on the Writing Subtest reduced our confidence in the test's ability to discriminate those needing assistance from those needing no further assistance. There was, however, a high correlation between the scores of subjects in the validity group on the ALERT Reading Subtest and on the California Written Expression Subtest ($r = .74$).

Establishing Cut-off Scores

Cut-off scores were established using three methods. First, we used scores from the ALERT from both the validity and normative groups to establish cutoffs for those "in need of assistance" and those needing "no further assistance." Second, we analyzed CAT and ALERT scores from subjects in the validation group (98 people) by calculating a multiple regression. Scaled scores from the CAT reading, math and writing subsets were used (8th grade level). Finally, scores of subjects in the validation group were used to determine whether individuals had been accurately identified using their scores on the *California Achievement Test* subtests as the criterion measure. The range of scores for each ALERT classification was compared with CAT cut-off scores for each subset (above or below the eighth grade equivalency level). Using these three measures we decided that, although the ALERT tended somewhat to over refer, it would be better to identify individuals for additional assessment than to omit someone who might benefit from further assessment and/or instruction. Cut-off scores for the writing subtest were not established; however, if the writing sample is used as a means of holistically evaluating writing, this subtest can provide meaningful information relative to an individual's ability to formulate ideas and communicate them in writing.

Administration, Scoring and Interpretation

Administration

The reading passage is first in the screening battery beginning with two sample paragraphs used to familiarize examinees with the maze procedure. Next is the math assessment followed by the writing task.

The Examiner's Manual provides essential information for administration and recommends a practice session prior to actual testing. Directions are given concerning needed materials, procedures for establishing rapport prior to testing, and procedures for each section. Scripts are provided as well as practice items for the reading and math sections to make certain examinees understand the tasks. Examinees record their responses in individual response booklets. All sections are times by the examiner and examinees are told when to begin and to stop.

For example, the reading test begins with a two-paragraph sample passage. The examiner reads the first paragraph (see below) to the group, saying "blank" when coming to a three-word choice and then asking for the answer.

"No Time for Breakfast"

At some time, you've heard breakfast is the most important meal of the day. If this is true, then why (go, do, so) people skip breakfast so often? Two (noted, reasons, terms) given are "I don't have time" (to, or, so) "I don't feel like eating in (the, a, at) morning." In each case a little planning (yet, and, was) knowing about good health will help."

Examinees are then directed to complete the next paragraph independently. Adults are given two minutes to complete the actual reading passage and are told to stop when the time is up.

The math test follows immediately and examinees are informed that some of the problems are addition or subtraction, some multiplication or division, and some fractions or decimals. Problems are from a fourth grade curriculum and involve single and multiple digit operations. Examinees are given two minutes to complete this section and are told to "stop" at the end of the time limit.

Finally, the writing subtest directs examinees to: "Assume you meet an old friend who asks you about your job. Describe your job and include as many details and examples as you can." They are told to take one minute to think about what they would like to write. Then, they are given an additional three minutes to get their thoughts down on paper and are told to "stop" at the end of the three minutes. Examinees are told that both their ideas and how much they can write are important.

Scoring

Both the reading and math tests are scored by counting the number of correct responses. For the writing sample, the number of words generated are counted (qualifications are given for what constitutes a word).

Using cut-off scores in reading and math enables examiners to quickly place adults who are tested into one of three categories.

- Needs Further Assistance - individuals need further diagnosis or instruction
- Possible Assistance Needed - individuals experience some difficulty; some follow-up diagnosis may be warranted to determine a possible need for instructional intervention
- No Further Help Needed - these individuals need no further diagnosis or instruction

In writing, since there are no cut-off scores, samples may be evaluated by analyzing writing as to mechanics, ideas, and organization. Categories of errors can be obtained by looking at individual words, punctuation, spelling, grammar, usage, sentence construction, quality of ideas, degree of development of ideas, and the ability to clearly address the issue.

Discussion

The ALERT test can serve as a valuable model which can be used by each workplace or adult literacy program to develop customized measures using their own materials and following procedures used in developing the original ALERT instrument. Thus, both reading passages and math problems can be taken from workplace-related tasks. Likewise, the prompt used for assessing writing can also be workplace specific. Our experiences with the ALERT lead us to make the following suggestions. First, at least two reading passages

224

should be administered so that students have more experience with the cloze procedure and opportunity to read different content. Second, the 80-item math test should be administered as two 40-item tests.

In addition to its potential versatility and its success as a screening instrument, the approach described in the ALERT also has the potential to be useful as a means for measuring ongoing progress of adults receiving instruction in reading, math and writing. Using curriculum materials, maze passages can be created and used regularly as timed assessments for measuring progress in reading comprehension. Similarly, math computation measures can be created with math operations most recently taught. These can be administered as timed assessment measures. Writing prompts can be developed using topics discussed or read about during instruction; timed writing samples can be administered regularly to gauge progress in fluency and quality of writing. In this manner, student progress is regularly being assessed using actual instructional materials, and results are being used to regularly inform instruction through assessment-based decisions. Research on curriculum based measures has indicated that they are sensitive to student progress, and thus can be used to document ongoing development and performance in literacy-related tasks.

Copies of the ALERT test can be obtained for a $5.00 fee through the authors at the University of Pittsburgh.

References

Anderson, R.C., & Freebody, P. (1983). Reading comprehension and the assessment and acquisition of word knowledge. In B. Huston (Ed.), *Advances in Reading/Language Research* (pp. 231-256). Greenwich, CT: JAI Press.

Askov, E. N., Aderman, B., & Hemmelstein, N. (1989). *Upgrading basic skills for the workplace*. Pennsylvania: The Institute for the Study of Adult Literacy, The Pennsylvania State University.

Bean, R.M., Burns, D. D., Cox, R.C., Johnson, R., Lane, S., & Zigmond, N. (1989). *Adult literacy employment-related tasks (ALERT)*, Pennsylvania: Institute for Practice and Research in Education, University of Pittsburgh.

Bean, R.M., Byra, A., Johnson, R., & Lane, S. (1988). Using curriculum based measures to identify and monitor progress in an adult basic education program. 310 Grant funded by Pennsylvania Department of Education, Division of Adult and Basic Literacy Education.

Deno, S. (1988). Letter to directors of "educating learning disabled and mildly handicapped students in general education classrooms." *Projects, Federal Grants, and Contracts Weekly,* Virginia: Capitol Publications.

Deno, S., Martson, D., Mirkin, P., Lowery, L., Sindilar, P., & Jenkins, J. (1982). *The use of standard tasks to measure achievement in reading, spelling and written expression: A normative and developmental study.* (Research Report No. 87). Minneapolis, MN: University of Minnesota Institute for Research on Learning Disabilities.

Deno, S., Mirkin, P., & Chang, B. (1982). Identifying valid measures of reading. *Exceptional Children, 49,* 36-45.

Fuchs, L., Deno, S., & Marson, D. (1982). *Use of aggregation to improve the reliability of simple direct measures of academic performance.* (Research Report No. 94), Minneapolis, MN: University of Minnesota Institute for Research on Learning Disabilities.

Fuchs, L., Fuchs, D., & Deno, S. (1982). Reliability and validity of curriculum based informal reading inventories. *Reading Research Quarterly, 18,* 6-25.

Guidelines for developing an educational program for worker literacy. (1986). Boston: Massachusetts State Education Department. (ERIC Document Reproduction Service No. ED 284 071).

Haswell, R.E. (1988). Dark shadows: The fate of writers at the bottom. *College Composition and Communication, 39,* 303-315.

Jenkins, J.R. & Pany, D. (1978). Standard achievement tests: How useful for special education? *Exceptional Children, 44,* 448-453.

Learning a living: A blueprint for high performance. (April, 1992). The Secretary's Commission on Achieving Necessary Skills, U.S. Department of Labor.

Marston, D. & Magnusson, D. (1985). Implementing curriculum based measurement in special and regular education settings. *Exceptional Children, 52,* 266-276.

Martson, D., Tindal, D. & Deno, S. (1982a). *Eligibility for learning disability services: A direct and repeated measurement approach* (Research Report No. 89), Minneapolis, MN: University of Minnesota Institute for Research on Learning Disabilities.

McCrossan, L.V. (1992). *Reading, writing and critical thinking for second level employees in small and mid-sized businesses.* 353 Grant funded by the Pennsylvania Department of Education, Division of Adult and Basic Literacy Education.

Miller, J. & Imel, S. (1987). *Some current issues in adult, career, and vocational education. Office of Educational Research and Improvement.* (ERIC Document Reproduction Service No. ED 281 899).

Salvia, J. & Yesseldyke, J. (1981). *Assessment procedures in special and remedial education.* (2nd ed.) Boston: Houghton Mifflin.

226

Soifer, R., Irwin, M.E., Crumrine, B.M., Honzaki, E., Simmons, B.K. & Young, D.L.(1990). *The complete theory-to-practice handbook of adult literacy: Curriculum design and teaching approaches.* NY: Teachers College Press.

The bottom line: Basic skills in the workplace. (1988). United States Department of Labor.

Thurlow, M.L. & Yesseldyke, J. (1982). Instructional planning: Information collected by school psychologist vs. information considered useful by teachers. *Journal of School Psychology, 20,* 3-10.

Tindal, G., Germann, G., & Deno, S. (1983). *Descriptive research on the Pine County norms: A compilation of findings.* (Research Report No. 132),Minneapolis, MN: University of Minnesota Institute for Research on Learning Disabilities.

Developing and Assessing Emergent Literacy Through Children's Literature

Nancy A. Anderson
University of South Florida

Anderson discusses the importance of using children's literature to develop and assess emergent literacy with young children. Specific examples of strategies that can be used in daily classroom activities are given.

For decades first-grade teachers bore the awesome burden of getting their students ready to learn to read. The first six weeks were devoted to reading readiness; a teacher-centered curriculum in which children were led through activities (requiring numerous worksheets) that included learning the names and configurations of the letters of the alphabet as well as the sounds that each "made." Other activities included instruction in visual and auditory discrimination using a variety of stimuli such as pictures of toys and sounds of birds chirping. After successfully demonstrating mastery of these and other skills on a standardized test of reading readiness, children were deemed ready to learn to read and were given their first book: a preprimer from a basal reading series.

I remember how proud I was that October day in 1953 when I took the certificate home to my parents. It boldly declared that I had successfully completed the reading readiness program, and that I could now have formal reading instruction. Though I did not notice at the time, I am sure some of the children in my class went home without a certificate. Perhaps those children did not have a father who told them bedtime stories or a mother who read to them or a big sister who had already taught them the alphabet. For them, six weeks of readiness instruction was inadequate and inappropriate.

About a decade ago, our new understanding of how children become literate led to a shift away from the concept of traditional reading readiness to the view that children's literacy emerges naturally. We have learned that emergent literacy is a continuous process that begins in infancy with exposure to oral language, written language, books, and stories in the home. This process continues in kindergarten with real books and genuine writing experiences, and it gradually culminates sometime in the primary grades as children become independent readers. (See Madison, 1993, for a concise history on this paradigm shift.)

As a result of this shift, experts have begun to emphasize the important role of using children's stories and picture books to further children's literacy development. In fact, Wells (1982) described experiences with literature as probably the best way of encouraging the development of literacy skills. Moreover, Peters' (1993) review of studies that examined the effects of story reading on literacy development led her to contend that story reading ought to be considered "as a teaching and learning vehicle by which literacy knowledge is acquired, practiced and applied" (p. 5).

Though experts urge parents and other caregivers to share books with children daily, not all children receive this benefit. However, with early intervention programs and mandatory kindergarten attendance in nearly every state, most children can have numerous experiences with children's literature before participating in formal reading instruction in first grade.

The values of sharing literature with young children are fourfold (Morrow, 1989):

1. Children's interest in reading increases.
2. They become familiar with written language and its function.
3. Their vocabulary development increases.
4. They learn a sense of story structure.

In addition, access to lots of literature can lead to rich engagement in emergent reading activities and active, high-level discussion (Sulzby, Branz, & Buhle, 1993).

Literature is a natural medium, not only for fostering emergent literacy, but also for assessing a child's progress. Otto's (1993) research led her to conclude that teachers can become aware of children's current and developing literacy-related knowledge by encouraging them to interact with storybooks. In this article, I describe ways to use literature to both develop and assess four components of emergent literacy: (a) letter-sound and letter-name correspondence, (b) concepts of print, (c) concepts of word and speech-to-print match, and (d) sense of story structure.

Letter-Sound and Letter-Name Correspondence

Though many parents and teachers tell children a particular letter makes a sound (for example, "**b** says buh"), children must internalize the principle that letters and letter groups **represent** sounds of our language and that letters have unique names and configurations. If carefully selected, alphabet books are an excellent vehicle for teaching these concepts. Among the most useful books are those depicting the letters in both upper- and lowercase, such as *Dr. Seuss's ABC* (Geisel, 1963). Even though uppercase letters are frequently taught first, about 90% of the text that children will encounter in print consists of lowercase letters.

For each letter, books should have illustrations of several items that children can label with words from their speaking or listening vocabulary. A book that depicts an anvil for the letter a, for example, would be of limited benefit on subsequent independent viewings by children who do not have this word in their listening or speaking vocabularies. Also, the names of the items should **begin** with a phoneme that is commonly represented by the particular letter. In using only words that are related to a selected theme, some books require children to match a letter with a phoneme at the end or even middle of a word, for example, "**g** is for pig." Because beginning readers acquire the ability to segment initial phonemes before ending and medial phonemes, this example would at best be meaningless.

Repeated exposure to alphabet books allows children to learn not only the name and configurations for each letter, but also the sound(s) the letter commonly represents. Once a book has become familiar to a child, adults can use the book to informally assess a youngster's understanding of these concepts. For example, before turning a page in a book we can ask children to supply another word (not depicted in the illustrations) that begins with the sound. Consonant sounds are difficult to form in isolation, so a complete word should be elicited. This will also give the child critical practice in mentally segmenting initial phonemes of familiar words.

Later, the adult can cover the illustrations with the hand or a sheet of paper, and ask the child to name the letter and a word that begins with the sound the letter represents. To determine if the child truly recognizes each letter—rather than the order of the letters—this can be done from back to front and then in random order.

A final assessment can be completed with a Letter Recognition Inventory such as the one published by Gillet and Temple (1990). It requires the child to name the letters, both upper- and lowercase, out of order, including the alternate manuscript forms of the letters a and g. This instrument was developed to assess letter-name correspondence, but it can also be used to assess letter-sound correspondence if children are asked to name a word that begins with the **sound** represented by the letter. Any word beginning with the appropriate sound (but not necessarily spelled with that letter) would be considered a correct answer. For example, a response of "city" for the letter s would be correct.

Concepts of Print

Initially, young children believe that the story in a picture book is told to them, much like a favorite bedtime story, but with the addition of visual prompts. This is evident when a child, ready to view the next illustration, turns the page before the reader has finished. Children must learn that the print, rather than the pictures, carries the meaning of the text, and that unlike a bedtime story, it is fixed and does not vary from one telling to the next. Other concepts of print in the English language that children need to acquire include the knowledge that (a) books are read front to back, (b) a page is read top to bottom, and (c) a line is read left to right. In addition to recognizing these directional arrangements visually, children also need to comprehend the terms *beginning, end, front, back, top, bottom, letter, word*, and *page.*

Young children who have frequently experienced viewing a book while the reader is voice pointing (simultaneously tracking the print with a finger while it is being read) readily acquire these concepts. Thus, the first time a book is shared, the reader should not point in order to allow the child to thoroughly examine the illustrations. Instead, the adult should ask prediction questions (This will be described in the last section). During subsequent readings, the reader should point to the bottom of each word as it is read at a normal rate with good intonation. Also, it is important for the adult to discuss the book with the children and ask questions about the illustrations and text using reading terminology such as *word, letter, end,* and *top.*

When reading with one or two children, the adult can position the child or children next to her on either side. However, when working with a group, adults will need to use big books so that all children can see the text. The adult should point to the print with a pointing stick, being careful to position the stick below the word rather than on it.

It is necessary to select big books with print large enough to be easily viewed by all members of the group. Many trade books that are enlarged to big book size do not have this quality. In addition, big books that contain illustrations on one page and text on the facing page, for example *The Wheels on the Bus* (Kovalski, 1987), lend themselves well to this activity, as children can be annoyed by a hand or arm that obstructs illustrations. Also useful are big books such as *Mouse Paint* (Walsh, 1989) that contain print beneath the illustrations.

When children are familiar with the story and illustrations, the reader can occasionally pause to let them supply a word. This will encourage the children to track the words with their eyes. In this way, an understanding of the directional arrangement of print can be acquired naturally. In Otto's (1993) study of storybook reading with inner-city kindergartners, 32% of the children were attempting to track print at post-assessment, whereas no children focused on print during the pre-assessment.

Concepts of print can be assessed by the *Concepts About Print Test* (Clay, 1979). Gillet and Temple (1990) summarize the relevant procedures of the test. They suggest using a picture book unfamiliar to the child. The examiner begins by handing the book to the child with the spine facing the child, and saying, "Show me the front of the book."

Next, the examiner opens the book to a place with text on one page and an illustration on the facing page and says, "Show me where I begin reading." The examiner notes whether the child points to the print, rather than the picture. If so, it is important to note whether the child pointed to the upper left-hand corner of the page.

Then the examiner says, "Show me with your finger where I go next," and "Where do I go from there?" A child who understands the directional orientation of print will sweep a finger from left to right across the line then drop to the beginning of the next line and repeat the motion.

Handing the child two small squares of blank paper, the examiner directs the child to "Put these on the page so that just **one word** shows between them," and then, "Now move them so that **two words** show between them." This should be repeated substituting **letter** for **word**. An incorrect response to any of these directions will indicate concepts of print that need to be developed in future book sharing sessions.

Concept of Word and Speech-to-Print Match

It is not unusual for children to confuse the concepts of *letter, word*, and *line*. For example, in the above assessment, a child might show the examiner two **letters** instead of two words or one **line** instead of one word. Children must have a well developed concept of word before formal reading and writing instruction can be effective. First, they must be able to mentally segment individual words in spoken language. Next, they must understand that each spoken word has a written counterpart which is a string of letters bounded by blank space on each side.

Children will acquire this concept when the voice-pointing procedure is used. This works best with picture books with simple, predictable text, such as *Brown Bear, Brown Bear, What Do You See?* (Martin, 1983). Most children can recite the text of this book, prompted by the illustrations, after listening to it once or twice. The reader can move the child's pointing finger as the child recites the text, being careful to make a speech-to-print match. (If the child is reciting too rapidly, it may be necessary to choral read the text at an appropriate pace.) Next, the child should practice this voice-pointing procedure independently.

The ability to identify words as written units in print can be assessed using the Voice-Pointing Procedure (Morris, 1983). It is best to use a book that is new to the child but with a familiar text. *Mary Had a Little Lamb* (Hale & de Paola, 1984) is a good example. Before introducing the book, the examiner ensures that the child can recite the first four lines. Next, the child can examine the illustrations in the book while sitting adjacent to the examiner. Then, the examiner reads the first four lines, pointing under each word as it is read at a normal pace, while the child observes. The book is then passed to the child who is asked to do the same.

The examiner observes whether the child is able to achieve a speech-to-print match, self-correcting any errors. A child who points to letters for words or words for syllables needs more experience with the read and point activity.

Sense of Story Structure

In order to comprehend stories, first by listening and later by reading, children must develop a schema for the way stories are structured. All stories have a beginning where the author introduces the characters, setting, and problem; a middle that consists of several attempts to overcome the problem; and an ending where the problem is resolved. Children need numerous opportunities to listen to literature for their sense of story to develop.

When a child listens to a book for the first time, the Directed Listening-Thinking Activity (DLTA)(Stauffer, 1980) can be used to assess a child's sense of story structure, as long as the book has a strong plot. The reader should first read the title and allow the child to study the cover or first illustration. The next step is to ask the child, "What might happen in this story?" After the child makes the first prediction, the reader reads the story stopping two or three times (just before something important happens) to ask, "What do you think might happen next?" The adult may ask a child to back up a prediction with the question, "Why do you think so?" A child with a well-developed sense of story structure will be able to make logical predictions based on prior events in the story and his or her background of experience. *Frog and Toad Together* (Lobel, 1972) and other books in this series lend themselves especially well to this activity.

The DLTA can be used only the first time a child listens to a particular story. After subsequent readings, the adult may wish to use the Oral Retelling of Stories Assessment (Anderson, 1993) to assess the child's developing sense of story structure. After listening to a story, the child is asked to tell in his or her own words what the story was about. The examiner checks off each of the components of story grammar that the child mentions:

1. **Characters** (note the name of each mentioned)
2. **Setting** (where and when the story occurred)
3. **Problem** or conflict encountered by the main character
4. **Goal** that the main character sets to overcome the problem
5. **Attempts** to reach the goal, or **events** leading to the resolution (note each different attempt/event mentioned)
6. **Resolution** (how the problem is solved)

The adult may probe children's responses by asking, "What else do you remember?" With any given story, children's retellings should become increasingly complex over time. Both the DLTA and the oral retelling strategies develop, as well as assess, a child's sense of story structure, and they should be used frequently as a part of the book sharing experience.

Summary

Emergent literacy is a process that is nurtured from birth by all caregivers: parents, grandparents, baby-sitters, day-care workers, teachers, librarians, aides, and older siblings. Children's books are likely the first type of print that children will want to read independently, so they provide a natural choice for developing children's understanding of the reading process. They can also be used to assess a child's progress in the development of some of the components of emergent literacy, thus helping us understand the nature and extent of children's progress on the road to becoming a reader.

References

Anderson, N. A. (1993). *Emergent literacy assessment battery*. Unpublished manuscript. University of   South Florida, Tampa.

Clay, M. M. (1979). *Stones: The concepts about print test*. Exeter, NH: Heinemann.

Geisel, T. S. (1963). *Dr. Seuss's ABC*. New York: Random House.

Gillet, J. W., & Temple, C. (1990). *Understanding reading problems: Assessment and instruction* (3rd ed.). New York: Harper Collins.

Hale, S. J., & de Paola, T. (1984). *Mary had a little lamb*. New York: Holiday House.

Kovalski, M. (1987). *The wheels on the bus*. Boston: Joy Street/Little Brown.

Lobel, A. (1972). *Frog and Toad together*. New York: Harper & Row.

Madison, S. G. (1993). *Public preschool teachers' construction of classroom literacy environments*. Unpublished doctoral dissertation. The University of New Orleans.

Martin, B., Jr. (1983). *Brown bear, brown bear, what do you see?* New York: Holt, Rinehart, & Winston.

Morris. D. (1983). Concept of word and phoneme awareness in the beginning reader. *Research in the Teaching of English, 17*, 359-373.

Morrow, L. M. (1989). *Literacy development in the early years: Helping children read and write*. Englewood Cliffs, NJ: Prentice Hall.

Otto, B. W. (1993). Signs of emergent literacy among inner-city kindergartners in a storybook reading program. *Reading & Writing Quarterly: Overcoming Learning Difficulties, 9*, 151-162.

Peters, S. J. (1993). Where have the children gone? Storyreading in kindergarten and prekindergarten classes. *Early Child Development and Care, 88*, 1-15.

Stauffer, R. G. (1980). *The language-experience approach to the teaching of reading* (2nd ed.). New York: Harper & Row.

Sulzby, E., Branz, C. M., & Buhle, R. (1993). Repeated readings of literature and low socioeconomic status black kindergartners and first graders. *Reading & Writing Quarterly: Overcoming Learning Difficulties, 9*, 183-196.